FRACTAL PROGRAMMING
AND RAY TRACING WITH C++

FRACTAL PROGRAMMING AND RAY TRACING WITH C++

Roger T. Stevens

M&T BOOKS

M&T Books
A Division of M&T Publishing, Inc.
501 Galveston Drive
Redwood City, CA 94063

© 1990 by M&T Publishing, Inc.

Printed in the United States of America

Limits of Liability and Disclaimer of Warranty
The Author and Publisher of this book have used their best efforts in preparing the book and the programs contained in it. These efforts include the development, research, and testing of the theories and programs to determine their effectiveness.

The Author and Publisher make no warranty of any kind, expressed or implied, with regard to these programs or the documentation contained in this book. The Author and Publisher shall not be liable in any event for incidental or consequential damages in connection with, or arising out of, the furnishing, performance, or use of these programs.

Library of Congress Cataloging-in-Publication Data

Stevens, Roger T., 1927-
    Fractal Programming and Ray Tracing in C^{++} / Roger T. Stevens.
    p.   cm.
    Includes index.
    ISBN 1-55851-134-2
    1. C^{++} (Computer program language)   2. Fractals--Data Processing.
        I. Title
QA76.73.C153S74   1990
005.265--dc20

                                        90-13388
                                        CIP

Trademarks:

All products, names, and services are trademarks or registered trademarks of their respective companies.

Cover Design: Lauren Smith Design

Dedication

For Barbara - again

Barbara says that I already have too many computer
books dedicated to her, but who else should I dedicate it to?
When I come up for air out of my computer room, she's always there,
and although I spend a lot of my time alone writing,
I wouldn't feel like doing it if it weren't for her love
and encouragement. She's just as responsible for
this book as I am, and I think she deserves
all the recognition I can give her.

Contents

Acknowledgements

All of the software in this book was written using Zortech C++ furnished by Zortech, Inc., 4-C Gill St., Woburn, MA 01801. It was also checked with Turbo C++ furnished by Borland International, 4835 Scotts Valley Drive, Scotts Valley, CA 95066.

Valuable technical information on the format of the .PCX files and a copy of PC Paintbrush were supplied by Shannon of Z-Soft Corporation, 1950 Spectrum Circle, Marietta, GA 30067.

Software was developed and tested on computers using a Vega VGA card and a Vega VGA 1024i card both furnished by Headland Technology Inc., 46221 Landing Parkway, Fremont, CA 94538. Color pictures were viewed on a NEC Multisync Plus Color Monitor furnished by NEC Home Electronics (U.S.A.) Inc.

I am also indebted to Peter Watterberg and John Mareda of Sandia National Laboratories for letting me look at their ray-tracing software.

I am further indebted to Christopher D. Watkins for his contributions to the quaternion concepts and software used in this book.

Why this Book is for You

It is assumed that the reader of this book will have some knowledge of programming in the C language and some basic knowledge of computer graphics on the IBM PC or equivalent. In order to view most of the displays, you will need a VGA card and monitor. You will also need the Zortech C++ compiler, version 2.0 or later. Unless you have a lot of time to spare, you will find that a system with a math coprocessor will be the fastest and best way to work.

This book includes some instruction in how to use C++ that should get you started with this language and help you to use and/or modify the programs. The programs have not been fully tested with Turbo C++, but you should be able to run them with this language with a little ingenuity. Some clues are given as to differences between Turbo C++ and Zortech C++.

Exccutable files for rendering ray-traced scenes and julia sets and dragons in the quarternions are supplied on the disk that accompanies this book in two forms: one for use with the math coprocessor, and one for use in systems without a math coprocessor. If you only want to run these programs without delving any deeper into the programs, you can do so. All information for setting up data files for your own pictures is given in the book.

If you don't have a VGA display system, you can still use the program to render pictures and store them on disk files, but you will not be able to view the results except on a VGA-equipped computer. However, since rendering can take hours and viewing requires only a few minutes, you may want to render on one machine and view on another.

CHAPTER 1

Introduction

C++ is the programming language of the future. Every major software house that now has a C compiler is coming out with a C++ compiler. Within a few years everyone will be using C++ because it not only has all of the capabilities of C, but has object-oriented and operator overloading capabilities that let you write elegant programs. If you want to get started learning about C++, here's your chance. First, forget everything you've heard about object-oriented programming being a unique way of thinking that programmers don't understand. We're going to use C++ as a natural extension that is required when objects are important parts of our program. And we'll explore a ray-tracing program, which is at the forefront of PC graphics, and demands that we try some object-oriented techniques. The result may not be optimum code for the purist, but will make you familiar with the capabilities of C++ and help you make a natural transition from a C programming background.

Ray Tracing

Ray tracing is a technique for creating a two dimensional picture of a three dimensional world. There are many methods of doing this, some involving very simple constructive geometry. Ray tracing is different in that it attempts to cause the computer to duplicate an actual photographic process. This enables us to specify a scene of simple primitive objects (spheres, parallelograms, triangles, etc.), together with patterns to be projected on surfaces, light sources, and position of the observer. The ray tracer will trace every beam of light, creating complex shadows and reflections with breath-taking realism.

Let's begin by postulating a scene made of various primitive objects and light sources. At some point, an observer is looking at this scene through a translucent screen. Each tiny point on the screen (corresponding to a pixel on a color monitor) appears to have some color associated with it; the color is of the ray of light that intersects the screen and strikes the observer's eye. Now, let's project the light ray backwards from observer to screen and then to the nearest object. The color of the ray at the intersection with this object is what appears on the screen; we shall build a file of color data in which we assign that pixel on the screen to the light ray color.

The color of the ray at the object intersection is not something that can be determined casually. It depends upon what happens to the light ray before it gets to this point. If the light is totally emitted by the object, and is of a specified color, our problem is solved. But if the surface is transmitting a color from within a partially transparent object, reflecting a color, or changing a color that is originally projected by a light source, we have to follow the path of the light ray back toward the light sources and sum the various color contributions to determine the actual ray color at the object intersection.

Obviously this is no trivial task. Figure 1-1 shows the geometry of the situation. This is very simple geometry, to give you the idea of how things are done. Take a look at Figure 1-2, where a few additional objects and light sources have been added, together with shadows and some reflections. You begin to see how complicated things may be. Remember, however, that in specifying the scene, we only have to enumerate the very primitive objects of which it is composed. All of the complicated interactions of light and shadow are performed by the computer program.

Assuming we can perform all of these ray-tracing tasks within the constraints of an IBM PC or compatible, we are then in the picture-generating business. Bear in mind that we are going to define a scene in terms of primitive geometric objects. Many of the characteristics that we need to know in the course of performing ray-tracing computations are unique to particular types of objects. For example, the normal for a sphere is different from the normal for a triangle. The point of intersection of the light ray and a sphere requires a particular set of calculations. The calculations of the intersection of the light ray with a parallelogram are the same for all parallelograms but different from those for a sphere. We begin to note a couple of important facts. First, the computer

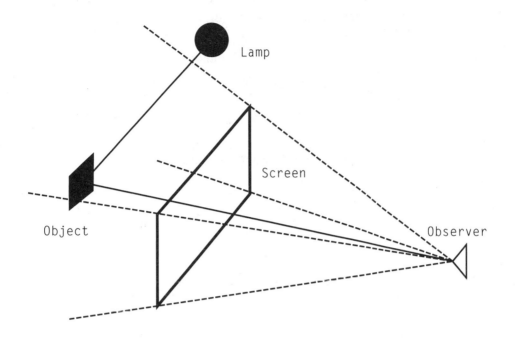

Figure 1-1. Ray Tracing Geometry

operations are computation intensive. Second, the methodology is highly suggestive of object-oriented programming. In other words, our orientation in creating the program is to specify what is to be done to various objects letting the programming language handle the mechanics (it sorts out which object is being referred to for each operation) appropriately for that object. There are a number of object-oriented software packages available, but many of them are very poor at performing extensive mathematical computations. Since C++ is not only object oriented, but has all the mathematical capabilities of C, it turns out to be a natural for programming a ray tracer. In addition, C++ is capable of overloading the definitions of the mathematical operators, permitting addition, subtraction, multiplication, etc. of complex numbers.

Object-Oriented Programming - Myth and Fact

Chapter 2 starts by exposing the myth of object-oriented programming. The myth is that while object-oriented programming somehow follows the natural processes of human thought, it is unnatural to experienced computer programmers and mathematicians. This is simply not true. Many computer languages already include some object-oriented capabilities, and full object-oriented programming languages are simply a natural extension of existing capabilities. If some object-oriented languages appear strange to experts, it could be they lack the tools to do some things we naturally want to do, and thus require strange and unnatural work-arounds to do what should be simple to accomplish.

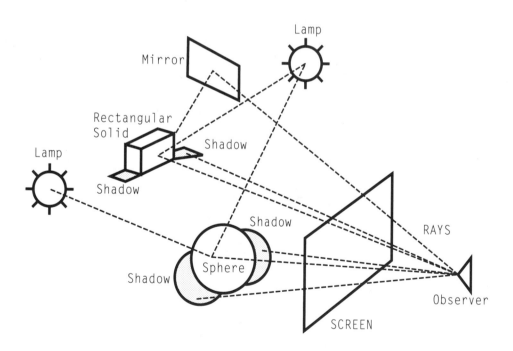

Figure 1-2. A More Complex Ray Tracing Diagram

Newton's Method - An Example of the Power of C++

Chapter 3 begins by providing the methodology for solving a simple problem in generating a fractal using Newton's method. It then shows how, if the equation being operated upon is made more complex and includes more higher-powered terms, it becomes almost impossible to decompose it. If the C language is the only tool available, a series of complicated and "unnatural" functions need to be created to handle the problem and, even then, they don't do a very good job. Next, we show how C++, particularly using the overloading of operators, can set up the class of complex numbers so that they can be treated in the same way as other number types (floating point and integer, for example). We then present a generalized program for Newton's method fractals, and show a typical result.

Three-Dimensional Vectors

Three-dimensional vectors are an important tool of ray-tracing. Rays of light and object positions are defined in terms of three-dimensional cartesian coordinates. Vectors between the origin and various pairs of points are manipulated using conventional vector mathematics to perform the operations required in ray-tracing. Using ordinary languages, a number of complicated functions must be developed to perform these ray-tracing tasks. In Chapter 4, we show how C++ can define the class of three-dimensional vectors and overload mathematical operators to perform vector mathematics as simply as the mathematics of more traditional types of numbers. In addition, several specialized functions for handling vectors are provided that simplify the processes used in the ray-tracing program.

Classes for Ray Tracing

The start of the ray-tracing program is a header that includes, among other things, the definition of the various classes that are used in the process. One of these is the class of color data, which describes the color characteristics of any object, such as the ambient lighting, the light diffused by the object, the mirror-like reflection characteristics, the specular reflection characteristics, and the transmission and density characteristics if the object is partially or totally transparent. Another is the line class which defines the location and direction of a light ray and includes a flag to indicate whether the ray is within or outside of a transparent object. Lamp and pattern classes are also defined. Finally, there is a generic definition of the characteristics of an object, and then derived classes for each particular primitive object that the program can handle. Figure 1-3 is a diagram showing the relationship of these classes. All of these are described in detail in Chapter 5. It is important to note that adding another object class in this header and defining its associated functions in the "objects" part of the program is all that is necessary to accommodate a new class of object.

Rendering the Screen

Chapter 6 describes the main rendering program, which makes use of a number of functions to perform the ray-tracing tasks. This program first initializes the default color data and the world, then defines overloading of the equals operator for color data and object data, opens and closes the output data file, and prints out some interesting statistics about the ray-tracing process. It then loads the world, makes bounding boxes, and traces the scene.

Ray Tracing Rendering Interfaces

One of the most critical aspects of a ray-tracing program is determining an easy and familar way of generating data files and passing them to the program. Chapter 7 discusses this problem and describes several interfaces that have been used for describing objects and techniques to a ray tracer, including the proposed

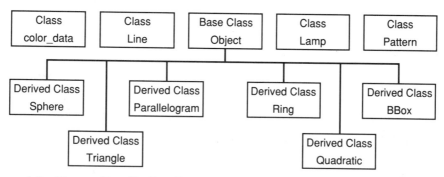

Figure 1-3. Classes Used in Ray-Tracing Program

RenderMan interface standard. The QRT language is also described.

Communicating with the Ray Tracer

In Chapter 8, we describe a parser which provides maximum flexibility in reading the input data file. Next, we describe how the data is handled within the program, including the use of linked lists to tie the object list together. This section also includes description and uses of bounding boxes.

Using the Language

Chapter 9 gives instructions in how to use the language that was created in order to specify the objects, lamps, observer, and more which make up the scene to be rendered.

Functions that Match an Object

We have already mentioned that there are a number of functions that we want to be specific to a particular type of object. These functions include: ray intersection, determine position, find normal-to-object surface at point of intersection, find a bounding box around an object, and change-scale of an object. These functions are described briefly in Table 1-1. Bear in mind that there is a separate version of the function for each type of object and that C++ automatically keeps track of which version of function to call for a particular object. Chapter 10 shows how using the C++ capability for defining virtual functions makes it possible to use a single function and have it do the right thing for whatever object is being treated.

Determining Ray-Object Intersections

The set of intersection functions which are listed in Chapter 8 combined with the overall function for controlling intersection computations found in Chapter 11, make up the capability to determine whether a ray intersects with any of the objects that are listed in the scene. This is a critical kind of determination that tells us what the color of light for each pixel will be. Chapter 11 covers this separately from the two files in which it is intermingled.

Function	Description
Constructor (has the same name as the object)	Creates an object and initializes it.
FindNorm	Generates a vector that is normal to the surface of the object at the specified position.
FindBBox	Computes the coordinates of the top left corner and bottom right corner of a bounding box which encloses the object.
Scale_Instance	Scales the size of an object which is part of an instance as defined by x and y multipliers.
Position	Computes two position variables needed for the intersection computation.
CollisionTest	Computes the time of intersection of a ray line with the surface of the object.

Table 1-1. Functions that Match an Object

Tracing the Ray

Chapter 12 describes the functions used to trace the path of each light ray in the scene. We discuss in detail how shadows, mirror reflections, specular reflections, and transmission through a transparent medium are treated. We also discuss treatment of the sky and how patterns are projected onto a primitive surface. Finally a number of example scenes are given and pictures shown to illustrate the characteristics of different scenes.

Putting it All Together

Chapter 13 shows how the *make* capability of C++ operates and gives a listing of the make file used to compile and link the various sections of the ray tracing program. This eliminates the repeated recompiling of portions of the program that have not been modified since the previous pass. The output of the *make* capability is the completed ray-tracing program, ready to be run.

Displaying the Created Scene

The output of the ray-tracing program is a file containing red, green, and blue data for each pixel that makes up the scene. The color is defined in up to 262,144 different shades, but the VGA in its maximum color mode can display only 256 colors. They make a good-looking picture once we figure out the best 256 colors to use. Chapter 14 describes a program that counts the occurrence of each color in the scene, assigns the 256 most frequently used colors to the 256 VGA palettes, and then assigns the remaining colors in the scene to the nearest of the 256 selected colors. The chapter also includes a program to convert the scene to a .PCX file for storage in compressed form.

Rendering Fractal Scenes

Fractal scenes represent the same kind of problem for ray-tracing that was described in the section above. In my book, *Fractal Programming in C*, we got around the problem by using the midpoint-displacement method in two dimensions and then randomly applying one of two colors to each generated triangle. By rights, however, we should use the midpoint-displacement method in three dimensions and then apply ray-tracing to the resulting surface to determine the appropriate colors. If we try to do this directly, the number of computations becomes impossibly large. We can minimize the computations by using bounding boxes in the same way that we did for reducing the intersection computations with groups of objects. We first compute all of the triangle patches that make up a fractal mountain. Then we put a bounding box around each group of four adjacent patches, and a bounding box around each group of four bounding boxes, until we end up with one bounding box surrounding the whole fractal. In tracing the ray to see if it intersects with the fractal, we first check it against the largest bounding box. If it doesn't intersect, we are through. If it does intersect, we check too for intersection with the four bounding boxes at the next level down. We only need to proceed further with those boxes it intersects, if any. We proceed with this process until we work our way down to the triangle patches, reporting back any of those that were intersections. This eliminates a very large amount of intersect computation —which is the most time-consuming operation in the process—and brings the time for generating a scene within reasonable limits. The resulting techniques for generating realistic scenes are shown in Chapter 15.

Quaternions

Chapter 16 gives a description of quaternions, four-dimensional vectors first discovered by Lord Hamilton. We describe in detail the uses of quaternions and the derivation of their mathematics. In Chapter 17, we show how the class and operator overloading features of C++ can be used to permit handling of quaternions as if they were just another type of number.

Chapter 18 describes the generation of Julia sets and dragons in the quaternions. A Julia or dragon quaternion needs to be described by a set of coordinates (quaternions) at a sufficient number of points on its surface so that there is no ambiguity in transferring a slice of it to two dimensions. If we attempted the task of checking the intersection of every ray in our ray-tracing program with every one of these points, millions of operations would be required and we wouldn't have enough computer time to do the job on our small computer. Using a Z buffer technique, we set up a matrix of screen pixels, giving the height of each point, and compute the color and shading of each pixel from this data.

Hardware and Software Requirements

What does it take to do all of this? First of all, you need Zortech C++ version 2.06 or greater. That is the software in which all of these programs were developed. It is excellent, both as a C compiler and as a C++ compiler. It has a provision for optimizing the code for fastest and most efficient operation, but you'll have to be a little careful if you're going to use that feature. I found several bugs, where the compiler refused to accept perfectly good expressions when it was in the optimizing mode. These bugs will no doubt be corrected in future revisions. In the meantime, compile everything in the normal mode and try optimizing one file at a time to see what happens. Turbo C++ has just been released by Borland and the ray-tracing program has been tested against it. It is possible to run the programs with Turbo C++ with some modifications. If you have come up with another version of C++, you're on your own. Walter Bright, who developed Zortech C++ maintained frequent communication with Bjarne Stroustrup, the original developer of the C++ language, so this version is quite close to the originator's intent. This may not be true of every version of C++.

Since the ray-tracing routines are computation intensive, it pays to have a fast computer. You really need a math coprocessor; you can use the ray-tracing program without it but it may take days to create a single picture file. Also a 286 or 386 machine is desirable; the faster the clock speed, the better. Since the ray tracer creates a file of picture data, rather than an actual picture, you can generate files regardless of the kind of display that you have. However, you probably want to look at them as well as generate them. This requires a VGA display and VGA color monitor. The 256 color mode is minimal and hopefully there will be another generation of color displays with more colors. If there are, any scene files that you have generated with the ray tracer will contain all the color data you need to take advantage of more color capability.

These programs have been tried on several different computers and have worked without difficulty. However, there are many different computer configurations available at present, and all of them have their own particular quirks and eccentricities. To help you in case of difficulty, Appendix C gives some details of the machines on which these programs were tested.

Expanding Your Horizons

A tremendous amount of literature has been written about ray-tracing and many exciting pictures have been published. Unfortunately none of it has described software which will permit you to do it on your home computer. In this book, you have the source code to do your own ray-tracing. If you buy the disk, you'll be ready to run the program without typing in or debugging. The ray tracer is a simple one, which doesn't include a lot of esoteric features such as advanced shading models and extensive anti-aliasing. Once you get a basic ray tracer running, you may decide that you want to read up on such features and add them to your own. Or you may want to add some additional kinds of primitive objects. The possibilities are limitless, once you have a basic program to serve as a platform.

CHAPTER 2

Object-Oriented Programming: Myth and Fact

In the Beginning

In August 1981, *Byte* Magazine devoted its entire issue to articles on Smalltalk, one of the first object-oriented languages. Smalltalk had been under development at the Xerox Palo Alto Research Center since 1971. *Byte* was slightly apologetic because there was no version of the language available for use with personal computers, but was so impressed with the potential of the language that it thought a special issue was worthwhile and necessary.

Smalltalk was presented as a whole new approach to programming. Instead of using computer procedures to operate upon data, Smalltalk centered computer operations upon objects. The information on an object consisted of a description of the object, together with descriptions of how the object was to accept messages sent to it and messages it was to provide in response. David Robeson's article in that *Byte* issue, entitled *Object-Oriented Software Systems*, began by saying, "Many people who have no idea how a computer works find the idea of object-oriented systems quite natural. In contrast, many people who have experience with computers initially think there is something strange about object-oriented systems." Thus, according to Smalltalk's developers the object-oriented approach corresponds much more closely to the way in which humans normally think and consequently seems natural and easy to use by computer neophytes. The only ones who were likely to have trouble with Smalltalk were experienced computer programmers, who found this method of operation exceedingly strange.

Nine Years Later

One might think, then, that the growth of object-oriented languages would have been inevitable; upon finding a way of programming that appears more understandable, everyone should gravitate to it. Interestingly enough, however, I don't know of a single commercially successful piece of software written with object-oriented language up to this point. Over the nine years since Smalltalk first appeared on the scene, there have been tremendous improvements in word processors, spreadsheets, and data base programs, and almost unanimously, these programs have been written in C rather than in an object-oriented language. This is not a very good track record. Does this mean that object-oriented languages are at a dead end? Not at all. But I do think it means that although the newest versions of object-oriented languages (Turbo Pascal 5.5 and Zortech and Turbo C++) are being proclaimed as requiring a whole new way of looking at the world, this approach has not been good for object-oriented programming and has actually impeded its development.

Object-Oriented or Conventional - What's the difference?

Before proceeding further, we need to understand the difference between object-oriented and conventional computer languages. According to the proponents of object-oriented languages, most conventional programming languages are concerned with data. This data is introduced into a computer program, processed by various procedures and ultimately yields a result. On the other hand, an object-oriented language is concerned with objects. Each object has a number of different, associated responses, so that when you send a particular message to an object, it provides a unique response. Ultimately, you do all your programming by defining classes and responses up to the point where you can send a message to one class and get back the answer to your problem, whatever it may be.

Let's expand on this a little further. In the first place, an essential quality of objects is that they hide many of their characteristics. From the outside, you send a message to the object and it responds. However, you have no idea what is going on that translates the message to the correct response. In fact, from the

16

inside; things begin to look a lot more like conventional computer programming, with the necessary code to translate an incoming message into an outgoing response. But all of this is hidden from the user of the object; it can't be tampered with.

Another characteristic of object-oriented languages is the concept of classes. A class is a description which applies to one or more similar objects. For example, *Lassie* is an object which belongs to the sub-class of *collies* which in turn belongs to the class of *dogs*. If you send the message Speak to Lassie, the object will be appropriately manipulated and *Lassie* will respond with the message *Arf, arf*. Thus, you can define a class, together with many common messages and responses, and have most of your programming done. All you need to complete the project is to identify the objects which are specific to the classes which you have previously defined.

Suppose, however, that one object has all the characteristics of a particular class, and is unique in that it has additional characteristics or responds differently to a particular message. (Sandy may respond *Arf, arf*, but Lassie may respond *Bow, wow*, for example.) To cope with this situation, the object-oriented language has the characteristic of inheritance. In this situation, a base class is modified to create another derived class. A derived class inherits all of the characteristics of its base class, but then may be modified to be different in content or behavior.

The Word is Paradigm

The word most in vogue to promote object-oriented languages is *paradigm*. A paradigm is a model. As used in the object-oriented language discussions, you have a paradigm of the world (which is not the real world, but your model of it). It is claimed that object-oriented programming is a paradigm of the world very close to the paradigm we carry around in our heads, and thus we can more easily program with it. This is patently nonsense. To be sure, you know of an object *Joe* and want to send him a message *Come*. However, it is pretty artificial to say that we have as an object a set of numbers and that we are going to send them the

17

message *Sum* whereupon they will respond with the answer. Moreover, there is plenty of reason to believe that rather than selecting a language that corresponds to our view of the world, our view of the world is largely determined by our habitual language.

Some Philosophical Background

Alfred Korzybski, founder of General Semantics, says in his book *Science and Sanity:*

> "We do not realize what tremendous power the structure of an habitual language has. It is not an exaggeration to say that it enslaves us through the mechanism of semantic reactions and that the structure which a language exhibits, and impresses upon us subconsciously, is 'automatically projected' upon the world around us."

What Korzybski is saying is that our thought processes are dominated by the language that we are used to, rather than the language being a reflection of a way of thinking. If this is true, how do we apply it to the implication that object-oriented languages are "more natural" to computer neophytes, but strange to computer professionals. (There is something very strange about a philosophy that says that a product is to be commended because it is liked by those with no experience in the field but is disliked by the experts.) I think one of the obvious implications is that the thought patterns most natural to us using English and other European languages correspond to object-oriented computer languages, and the thought patterns of those versed in mathematics correspond to traditional computer languages.

Is there a relation between certain types of language and contributions to the growth of civilization in general? There's plenty of room for argument on this issue. However, it seems clear that the expansion of civilization to its current level is primarily due to the contributions of mathematicians, scientists, and engineers. We may not be too happy about what these contributions have done to the environment. But without the contributions of science, although the environment might be less spoiled, world food production could never meet the global population demands, and many of us would not be here.

The case is much less clear for the contributions of those whose favorite language is English or a European language. Communication of critical data appears fuzzy, to say the least. The languages have not lent themselves to fostering understanding and friendly relations. Korzybski claims that this is because all of our languages have heavy Aristotelian philosophical roots, which tend to make us look for solutions to all problems as black or white (yes or no) instead of perceiving shades of gray important in achieving peaceful compromises. We know that both computers and brain cells work in a binary (Aristotelian) mode, so perhaps we are incapable of anything but Aristotelian thinking. At any rate, there doesn't appear to be any good reason for embracing a language that has many features in common with languages that have failed to handle the world's problems to date.

The Non-Aristotelian World

Korzybski claimed that our languages imposed upon us a strong tendency to seek "Yes" or "No" solutions to all problems. This seems to be just what has happened in promoting object-oriented languages. We are expected to force all our problems into one mold or the other, when in reality they can benefit from the advantages of both approaches. To begin with, let's note some evident similarities between the characteristics of an object-oriented language and some of the conventional computer languages. The C language, for example, has the *class* of *integers* and the *class* of real numbers (called *float*). When you use a plus or minus sign with these different classes of numbers, the internal (hidden) operations are different so that integer or floating point arithmetic is performed. Extending this to the realm of mathematics, the same operators (+, -, etc.) are used to denote operations on such classes as complex numbers and vectors. Some computer languages can handle these two classes, but not all of them. Similarly, C has *structures,* which look a lot like objects, except that you can't do many things with them that you would like to do with objects. If you are interested in making the best use of object-oriented programming techniques,

19

you should forget all of this hype about learning a new way of thinking and let the object-oriented approaches flow when they are needed. This demands a language that supports both conventional and object-oriented programming techniques. The best example is C++.

Some Good Words about C++

Now that we've thoroughly mixed up the concepts of conventional and object-oriented programming, let's attempt to use a little common sense to bring the whole subject into perspective. Suppose we forget about this idea of object-oriented programming being welcomed by the inexperienced and instead look at what the object-oriented approach can do for us in the way of solving problems. The most important characteristics are:

1. The language should make it possible to create classes like complex numbers, vectors, quaternions, etc. and operate upon them in the way we operate on ordinary numbers.

2. The language should make it possible to have sets of functions, each set using a single calling statement that identifies the type of object being called and executes the proper function for that type of object.

Other object-oriented features such as inheritance and hiding private data are useful, but not essential. Note that the only object-oriented language that provides for overloading of a mathematical operator (essential to achieving the first goal presented above) is C++. When you also consider that C++ has all the detailed mathematical and data manipulation capabilities included in C, then it becomes a natural choice for those who want to use object-oriented capabilities in complicated mathematical programming. The rest of this book assumes that C++ is the wave of the future, and naturally fits into the problem of creating ray tracing programs to generate advanced graphics and fractal pictures.

CHAPTER 3

Beyond C with C++: A Newton's Method Example

We begin our examination of the advantages of using C++ for advanced graphics using Newton's method. It is an iterated numerical approximation technique developed by Sir Isaac Newton to obtain solutions of equations that do not have a closed form. The method works as follows:

1. Suppose we want the root of the generalized equation which cannot be solved by ordinary methods:

   ```
   f(z) = 0            (Equation 3-1)
   ```

   where z is a complex number.

2. To begin Newton's method, we make a guess as to a root of this equation. The guess is z_0.

3. Next, we compute the expression:

   ```
   z_n+1 = z_n - (f(z_n)/(f'(z_n)))    (Equation 3-2)
   ```

   where f' is the derivative of f. For the first pass, we have z^0 on the right side of the equation and obtain z^1 on the left.

4. This process is repeated as many times as you desire. Each new value for z will be a closer approximation to the actual root of the equation.

This iteration process is similar to that used to obtain Julia sets and dragon curves. In fact, the graph of the process for a number of starting values throughout the complex plane looks like a fractal display, but in this case, there is an additional mathematical meaning attached to the results.

Graphics Functions

Before showing the first Newton's method program, we need to address three simple graphics functions which are used with either C or C++ in all of the Newton's method programs that follow. These functions are shown in Figure 3-1. They are *setMode, cls,* and *plot.* If you want to get into the nuts and bolts of these functions, which make use of the ROM BIOS video services and direct calls to the video registers, you'll need to look at my book *Graphics Programming in C.* However, the functions are simple and the details of how they work are not important to the application described here. The first function, *setMode,* simply sets the mode of the display screen. In the Newton's method programs, we shall always set to mode 16, which is 640 pixel by 350 line graphics using 16 colors. This mode will work equally well with EGA or VGA adapter boards. The second function, *cls,* works only when the system is in display mode 16. It clears the existing information from the screen and fills the screen with whatever color (0 to 15) is passed to the function as a parameter. The third function, *plot,* also works only with mode 16. It plots a point on the screen. The parameters passed to this function are *x* (display column), *y* (display row), and *color* (pixel color). The function designates location and color to the pixel.

Program for Plotting a Simple Equation Using Newton's Method

The program given in the listing of Figure 3-2 is repeated from my book *Fractal Programming in C.* It plots the solutions for the equation:

$$z^3 - 1 = 0 \qquad \text{(Equation 3-3)}$$

```
/*
        ┌──────────────────────────────────────────────┐
        │                                                │
        │           setMode() = Sets Video Mode          │
        │                                                │
        └──────────────────────────────────────────────┘
                                                            */

void setMode(int mode)
{
        union REGS reg;

        reg.h.ah = 0;
        reg.h.al = mode;
        int86 (0x10,&reg,&reg);
}


/*
        ┌──────────────────────────────────────────────┐
        │                                                │
        │           cls() = Clears the Screen            │
        │                                                │
        └──────────────────────────────────────────────┘
                                                            */


void cls(int color)
{
        union REGS reg;

        reg.x.ax = 0x0600;
        reg.x.cx = 0;
        reg.x.dx = 0x184F;
        reg.h.bh = color;
        int86(0x10,&reg,&reg);
}


/*
        ┌──────────────────────────────────────────────┐
        │                                                │
        │       plot() = Plots a point at (x,y) in color │
        │                for Enhanced Graphics Adapter, using │
        │                Turbo C port output functions   │
        │                                                │
        └──────────────────────────────────────────────┘
                                                            */

void plot(int x, int y, int color)
{
        #define seq_out(index,val)  {outp(0x3C4,index);\
                                            outp(0x3C5,val);}
        #define graph_out(index,val)  {outp(0x3CE,index);\
```

```
                                        outp(0x3CF,val);}
    unsigned int offset;
    int mask, dummy;
    char far *mem_address;

    offset = (long)y * 80L + ((long)x / 8L);
    mem_address = (char far *) 0xA0000000L + offset;
    mask = 0x80 >> (x % 8);
    graph_out(8,mask);
    graph_out(3,0x00);
    seq_out(2,0x0F);
    dummy = *mem_address;
    *mem_address = 0;
    seq_out(2,color);
    *mem_address = 0xFF;
    seq_out(2,0x0F);
    graph_out(3,0);
    graph_out(8,0xFF);
}
```

Figure 3-1. Graphics Functions for Newton's Method Programs

The program is written in C. It is fairly simple, because we can decompose the real and imaginary parts of the underlying equation and compute them with ordinary mathematics. It begins by determining the distances on the real and imaginary axes which correspond to the distance between adjacent pixels on the display. It then goes through a pair of nested loops. At each iteration, the starting value for the Newton's method estimate is determined for a particular pixel location. The Newton's method computations are repeated until an additional iteration provides no change in the resulting root. (Note that in the real world, we often cannot converge to the exact value of a root, but using the computer, the limitation on the precision of computer numbers causes an apparent convergence in every case.) Once we get a root, we can plot in 16 possible colors. For this equation, we have three possible roots. We allow five colors each for two of the roots and six for the third. We then cycle through the colors allowed for each root, using the number of iterations required to obtain the root as the parameter for determining which color in the group will be used. The pixel is then plotted on the screen in the appropriate color. Hence, the group of colors to which the color belongs indicates which root was ultimately targeted, whereas the color within the group is a measure of the number of iterations required to get there. Normally, we set up the display palette so that one root has all shades of a single color (the first root might have shades of green, the second shades of red, and the third shades of blue, for example).

```
/*
        cnewton3 = MAP OF NEWTON'S METHOD FOR SOLVING Z³ = 1
                                                                */
```

```c
#include <stdio.h>
#include <math.h>
#include <dos.h>
#include <process.h>
#include "tools.h"

void cls(int color);
void setMode(int mode)
void plot(int x, int y, int color)

const int maxcol = 639;
const int maxrow = 349;
const int max_colors = 16;

char strings[80];
int col,row,i;
int max_iterations = 64;
int max_size = 4;
int LINEWIDTH=1, OPERATOR=0, ANGLE, XCENTER, YCENTER;
int CURSOR_X=0,CURSOR_Y=0;
unsigned long int PATTERN=0xFFFFFFFF;
float  Xmax = 3.5, Xmin=-3.5, Ymax=2.50, Ymin=-2.50;

main()
{
    double deltaX, deltaY, X, Y, Xsquare,Xold,Yold,
```

```
        Ysquare,Ytemp,temp1,temp2,denom,theta;

int color, row, col;

setMode(16);
cls(7);
deltaX = (Xmax - Xmin)/(maxcol);
deltaY = (Ymax - Ymin)/(maxrow);
for (col=0; col<=maxcol; col++)
{
    if (kbhit() != 0)
        break;
    for (row=0; row<=maxrow; row++)
    {
        X = Xmin + col * deltaX;
        Y = Ymax - row * deltaY;
        Xsquare = 0;
        Ysquare = 0;
        Xold = 42;
        Yold = 42;
        for (i=0; i<max_iterations; i++)
        {
            Xsquare = X*X;
            Ysquare = Y*Y;
            denom = 3*((Xsquare - Ysquare)*(Xsquare -
                Ysquare) + 4*Xsquare*Ysquare);
            if (denom == 0)
                denom = .00000001;
            temp1 = .6666667*X + (Xsquare - Ysquare)/denom;
            Y = .6666667*Y - 2*X*Y/denom;
            X = temp1;
                if ((Xold == X) && (Yold == Y))
                break;
            Xold = X;
            Yold = Y;
        }
        if (X>0)
            color = i%5;
        else
        {
            if ((X<-.3) && (Y>0))
                color = (i%5) + 5;
```

```
        else
            color = (i%6) + 10;
        }
        plot(col, row, color);
    }
  }
  getch();
}
```

Figure 3-2. Program to Solve z^3 - 1 = 0

If you look at the part of the program which computes the Newton's method iterations, note that the mathematics is fairly simple for this equation. Consider what happens, however, when we use a more complex equation having higher powers of *z* and more terms. Decomposition is no longer possible. Of course, we can create a lot of special purpose functions to attempt to address the problem, but, using C++, there is a simpler and more elegant way.

The Concept of Classes in C++

In order to be able to create a simple program for generalized plotting of Newton's method solutions to equations, we create a class of complex numbers. If you are familiar with the concept of structures in the C language, the concept of classes will not seem strange to you; the class is an extended type of structure that is unique to C++. A structure, you will remember, is a collection of variables which may contain any of the variable types that exist in C, as well as arrays and other structures. The grouping of these into a structure permits them to be treated collectively as a single unit as well as being accessed as individual entities. A class differs from a structure in that all data in a structure is available to the outside world, whereas it is possible to specify for a class which data is accessible or not. Also there are some interesting ways of relating similar classes to each other, which will be described later. The class definition begins with the word *class,* followed by the name of the class. The second part of the class definition is the body, which contains the definition of the variables and functions that make up the class. This body is enclosed in curly brackets and terminated by a semicolon, or by a list of objects of the class type.

It is conventional to include the class definition in a file having the extension *.hpp* and the listing of the class's functions in a file having the same name but with the extension *.cpp*. These files are then linked to the main program. However, for the simple example given here, you may include all of the *Complex* class information at the beginning of the program. Figure 3-3 is a listing of the code for the class *Complex*. The class contains two double precision floating-point numbers, *real* and *imaginary,* which make up the complex number. Note that for all of the C++ programs in this chapter, the listings are for use with Zortech C++. The programs will run with Turbo C++, but you will have to change every instance of *#include <stream.hpp>* to *#include <iostream.h>*.

```
/*
        ┌─────────────────────────────────────────────────┐
        │                                                 │
        │         Complex = class of complex numbers      │
        │                                                 │
        └─────────────────────────────────────────────────┘
*/


#include <stdio.h>
#include <math.h>
#include <dos.h>
#include <process.h>
#include <stream.hpp>   iostream.h
#include <conio.h>;

void cls(int color);
void plot(int x, int y, int color);
void setMode(int mode);

class Complex {
     double real,imaginary;
public:
     Complex();
     Complex(double r, double i);
     Complex(Complex &);
```

```
        Complex operator+(Complex &);
        Complex operator-(Complex &);
        Complex operator=(Complex &);
        Complex operator*(Complex &);
        Complex operator*(float & );
        Complex operator/(Complex &);
        Complex operator~();
        int operator!=(Complex &);
        int operator==(Complex &);
        void print(char * name = "");
        double r();
        double i();
        friend ostream &operator<<(ostream&,Complex&);
};
```

*] * dully aerloaded*

Declares that this overloaded defn can be used by ostream.

```
Complex::Complex()
{
        real = 0;
        imaginary = 0;
}

Complex::Complex(double r, double i)
{
        real = r;
        imaginary = i;
}

Complex::Complex(Complex & othercomplex){
        real = othercomplex.real;
        imaginary = othercomplex.imaginary;
}

Complex Complex::operator+(Complex & arg){
        Complex result;
        result.real = real + arg.real;
        result.imaginary = imaginary + arg.imaginary;
        return result;
}

Complex Complex::operator-(Complex & arg){
        Complex result;
        result.real = real - arg.real;
```

```
        result.imaginary = imaginary - arg.imaginary;
        return result;
}
Complex Complex::operator*(Complex & arg){
        Complex result;
        result.real = real * arg.real - imaginary * arg.imaginary;
        result.imaginary = real * arg.imaginary + imaginary *
         arg.real;
        return result;
}
Complex Complex::operator*(float & arg){
        Complex result;
        result.real = real * arg;
        result.imaginary = imaginary * arg;
        return result;
}
Complex Complex::operator/(Complex & arg){
        double temp;
        Complex result;
        temp = arg.real*arg.real + arg.imaginary*arg.imaginary;
        result.real = (real * arg.real + imaginary *
         arg.imaginary)/temp;
        result.imaginary = (imaginary * arg.real - real *
         arg.imaginary)/temp;
        return result;
}
Complex Complex::operator~(void){
        double temp;
        Complex result;
        temp = real*real + imaginary*imaginary;
        result.real = real/temp;
        result.imaginary = -imaginary/temp;
        return result;
}

Complex Complex::operator=(Complex & rvalue){
        real = rvalue.real;
        imaginary = rvalue.imaginary;
        return *this;
}

int Complex::operator==(Complex &rvalue)
```

```
{
      if ((fabs(rvalue.real - real) < 0.01) &&
             (fabs(rvalue.imaginary - imaginary) < 0.01))
                     return 1;
      else
                     return 0;
}

int Complex::operator!=(Complex &rvalue)
{
      if (float(rvalue.real - real) == float(rvalue.imaginary -
                 imaginary))
                     return 0;
      else
                     return 1;
}

ostream &operator<<(ostream& s,Complex& arg)
{
      if (arg.imaginary > 0)
                     s << "(" << arg.real << " + " << arg.imaginary
                            << "i)";
      else
                     s << "(" << arg.real << " " << arg.imaginary
                            << "i)";
      return s;
}

double Complex::r()
{
      double temp;
      temp = real;
      return temp;
}

double Complex::i()
{
      double temp;
      temp = imaginary;
      return temp;
}
```

Figure 3-3. Class *Complex* for Complex Numbers

Public, Private, and Protected

The C++ language has the capability of hiding data within a class. By tradition, the keywords are *public, private,* and *protected.* However, everything not specified in a class definition is *private* by default, so it is seldom necessary to use the *private* keyword. If you look at the definition of the *Complex* class in Figure 3-3, you'll see that the variables making up a complex number (*real* and *imaginary*) are private by default. This means that these variables can only be accessed by members of the *Complex* class (namely those functions that form the rest of the class definition) or by *friends* of the *Complex* class. (We'll discuss *friends* later.) They cannot be accessed by any external function or even by functions of a class derived from the specified class. You can see that it is possible to have everything about a class private, but that would be useless, since there would be no way of accessing class results.

The *protected* keyword identifies members of a class that are hidden from external functions but appear as *public* to classes that are derived from the specified class. There are no derived functions for the complex number class (we'll speak more about derived functions in later chapters) so there is no need for any members to be *protected.*

The *public* keyword indicates that designated members of the class are accessible from anywhere within the C++ program where a class object is within scope. If you are trying to achieve maximum data protection, all of your class variables will be *private* and the only access to them from the outside world will be through various functions that are *public.* On the other hand, it is perfectly acceptable to have the entire contents of a class be *public.* (We'll see some examples of this in later chapters.) You gain in flexibility but pay the price of losing data protection from the outside world. Note that all of the functions used by the *Complex* class are *public.* In order to permit needed access to the individual hidden variables the functions *r* and *i* were created. They wouldn't have been needed if the two variables had been public. Things were left in this form to demonstrate an alternate method of access.

Ordinary Functions within a Class

Look at the last two functions within the *complex* class definition. These are ordinary functions called in a manner similar to that used for structures.

In other words, if we have a variable *temp* of the class *Complex,* and a variable *real* of type *float,* we can write

```
real = temp.r();
```

which will cause the function to return the real part of the complex number to real. The two ordinary functions used with the *Complex* class are quite simple. The function *r* returns the value of the real part of the complex number and the function i returns the value of the imaginary part. Instead of making the real and imaginary parts public, this technique enables us to get the values of the real and/or imaginary parts for external use but does not permit us to modify them by direct external action.

Assigning Memory for a Class

In the C language, variables and structures that are defined globally (not within a function) are automatically assigned the proper amount of memory and continue to own that memory for the duration of the program. Variables and structures defined within a function are automatically assigned the proper amount of memory each time they come within scope (when the function is called) and the assigned memory is automatically returned to free memory when they pass out of scope (the function terminates). When the address of a structure or variable is defined, only the memory space for the address is allocated; one of the family of *malloc* functions must be used to allocate the memory for the variable or structure itself. The same is true for C++ as far as variables are concerned. For structures or classes, the situation is somewhat different. When a member of a structure or class is defined, memory is automatically assigned to it, and this memory remains allocated to it until explicitly freed. There is a special C++ function called a *destructor,* which, if defined by the programmer for a class, will automatically be called whenever the class member goes out of scope. This can be used to delete the memory assigned to a member as well as any other housekeeping that is necessary. In the case where only the structure or class address is defined, as in C, only the memory for the address is allocated. However, C++ has the function *new* which can be called to allocate the memory for a class or structure. Fortunately, C++ knows just how much memory to allocate for a particular structure or class. There is also a companion function *delete,* which is used to deallocate the memory assigned by *new.* If memory is assigned by *new,* it will not be deallocated by the *destructor;* the *delete* function must be used. The C++ language also has a function called a *constructor.* This function is used to initialize a newly created object in any desired way.

Constructors

The constructor is a special function which is identified by the fact that it has the same name as the class itself. This function provides for the initialization of a class object. It is invoked by the compiler whenever a new object of the class is created. The C++ language supports the concept of function overloading, which means that you can have more than one definition of a function, providing the parameters passed to the function are different for each instance. As you can see in the listing of Figure 3-3, right after the *public:* statement, we have made use of this capability to define three constructors. The first constructor is used when we create a new instance of *Complex* without passing any parameters. In the second case, we pass two numbers of type *double* to the new instance. In the third case, we pass another complex number to the constructor. Looking down a little further, you will come to the place where these constructors are defined. Prototypes of all associated functions must be included within the class definition, but the actual body of code may be developed separately. The format for creating a constructor is to begin with the type of data that is to be returned (in this case *Complex,* followed by a double colon, followed by the class name, which for a constructor is identical to the function name). The body of the function for the first constructor simply sets the real and imaginary parts of the complex number to zero. This is the default case when no parameters are specified. The second constructor sets the real and imaginary parts of the complex number to the two numbers that are passed as parameters.

Overloading Operators

One of the most important capabilities of C++ is the capability to overload operators. We have found it quite easy to define the class of complex numbers, but what makes all of this worthwhile is the fact that we will be able to handle operations of complex numbers arithmetic just as easily as arithmetic for integers or floating point numbers. For the complex class, we have overloaded the +, -, =, *, /, ~, ==, and != operators. Now let's see how this is done. Look at the definition for overloading the + operator in Figure 3-3. The format for the function definition begins like any class function with the type of variable to be returned, followed by the class name and two colons. Next comes the keyword *operator* followed by the function to be overloaded (in this case +). Next, in parentheses, are the arguments to be passed to the function. Note that you can't pass just any variables. The number of variables that can be passed is determined by the operator that you select. More about that later. We see then that in the case of the + operator, we are passing one complex number's pointer to the function, and the function already has access to its own native complex number. The body of the function definition sets up a complex number to contain the result, adds the real and imaginary parts of the two complex numbers separately, and returns the result. Thus when you write

```
c = a + b;
```

where *a*, *b*, and *c* are all complex numbers, the new definition of the + function for complex numbers applies. Its native complex number is *a* and the complex number *b* is passed to it. The addition is performed, returned, and *c* is set equal to it. This implies something, however; that the = operator is capable of performing its function for complex numbers. The definitions of C++ state that the = operator is automatically overloaded for each class created.

The Zortech C++ compiler is sometimes unable to handle this and returns a compiler error. We have defined our own overload for this operator that sets real and imaginary parts of the native complex number equal to their counterparts in the complex number passed to the function. Similarly, the operators for subtraction, multiplication, and division are overloaded to properly perform these operations on complex numbers. The operator ~ takes only one argument; we have used it to represent the reciprocal of a complex number.

The == and != operators are needed in performing comparisons of complex numbers in the Newton's method programs. The way we have overloaded them shows both the flexibility and the dangers inherent in C++. For the != test, we do not want to check for exact equality, since this is either not achieved, or the whole solution blows up as we try to zero in too closely, due to the limited precision of computers. Consequently we have chosen to convert the double precision numbers to floating-point numbers before performing the test. The result in this test returns false when the double precision numbers are not exactly equal to each other, but fall within a tolerance range that makes their truncated floating point equivalents equal. This is very useful for us. But if we used this method to define an operator overload for a totally generalized complex number class, programmers that used the class would have an unexpected result. This is even truer for the == class, where the tolerance for equality has been made even larger. We are using this operator to determine which of several roots we have approached most closely. It is very appropriate for this use, but in other cases, serious problems might occur.

Output, Input, and Friends in C++

Most implementations of the C++ language include an excellent example of overloading of operators as part of the standard library supplied. These are the functions used for handling input and output. Here, we will just concern ourselves with output to the screen. Bear in mind that there are much wider applications.

This application makes use of *cout*, a streamlined replacement for the *printf* function using overloading of the shift left (<<) operator. The function begins with *cout* << followed by a string or by any type of variable. The overloading automatically functions out what type of variable is used and displays it appropriately. Also, the function returns itself, so you may concatenate the left shift operators into as long a series as you like. For example:

```
cout << "This is a test of" << variable <<"items.\n";
```

is perfectly legal. Note that a semicolon must appear at the end of the series.

Now we are almost ready to consider overloading so that *cout* can be used with our *Complex* class. But first, we need to know about *friends*. A *friend* of a class is a nonmember of a class, either a function, a member of another, previously defined class, or a complete class, which is allowed access to the nonpublic members of a class. This relationship must be declared within the class, using the keyword *friend*.

Now let's see what would happen if we were to overload the double shift operator within the Complex class in the normal manner. We would have the prototype:

```
ostream& operator<<(ostream&);
```

and some code to define what would be output when the operator was invoked. However, this invocation (for a complex number *temp,* for example) would be of the form:

```
temp<<cout;
```

which is very unlike the normal way of using *cout* for other types of data. What we need to do is have a prototype of the form:

```
ostream& operator<<(ostream&,Complex&);
```

Since *ostream* is independent of our class, we cannot include this prototype in our class. However, it requires access to the private data within the *Complex* class. We achieve this by defining it as a *friend*. Looking at the listing of Figure 3-2, you can see how this is done and the code for performing the operator overloading. The *cout* function can now be used with complex numbers in the same way as with other data types and the *Complex* class of data can indeed be concatenated with other data types in the output statement.

Some Complications with Newton's Method

Before proceeding further, we need to point out some complications with Newton's method. First, it is important to note that Newton used intelligent guessing of the initial roots. We have chosen to create plots where each pixel represents the result of starting with a particular number and performing the Newton's method iterations. Unfortunately, some numbers are bad places to start. For example, in Figure 3-2, if we begin with a guess of zero, the derivative will be zero and when we try to divide by zero, the solution will fail instead of converging on a real solution. We were lucky that the program worked because we didn't hit zero exactly as one of our initial guesses. As we describe the more generalized programs below, note that if there is a coefficient of z, the program can always be run safely, since there will always be a derivative other than zero. But if the first power of the variable is missing, singularities can occur. Therefore, we have used tests involving the inequality operator and also limited the number of iterations to attempt to prevent such disasters (which are usually recognized by the program quitting with a floating-point overflow message). If you look at Plate 3, you'll see that for this solution of Newton's method, there is a white circle right in the center of the picture. This represents an area where these singularities prevent the method from zeroing in on one of the roots.

Generalized Newton's Method Display Program

Now that we have complex numbers under control, we are ready to look at the program for generating generalized Newton's method displays. This program is listed in Figure 3-4. First this program gives the user the opportunity to enter ten coefficients, corresponding to the coefficients of the powers of z

from 0 to 9. The next few lines of code are very much like the Newton's method program of Figure 3-2, setting up the values associated with each pixel location and going into a double loop to compute for each pixel. When we get to the arithmetic, it is all done with complex numbers and can be simply written for these possibly complex equations as the arithmetic for the simple equation used in Figure 3- 2. Note how we initially define z as a complex number. We first enter a loop which puts together the values of f and f', power-by-power from the zeroeth to the next-to-last. We then add in the last power for f (there isn't one for f'). The expression to compute the new Newton estimate is a single line. We then compare the old and new values of the complex root and quit if they are the same, or continue if they are not. (Note that it would be a little more convenient to use the equality test here, but because of the way we have overloaded the operators, we have to use the inequality test to obtain the tolerance that we want.) As for determining the colors to plot, in this case we haven't tried to assign groups to different roots, since determining all of the roots would be too complicated. Instead, we cycle through the available colors based upon the number of iterations it took to find a root. This program is an example of C++ at its best and at its worst. It is at its best because you can see how simple it is to write the software; the most difficult part is writing the functions and definitions for the complex number class. Once you have done this, the actual program is simple, and since this same complex class can be used again whenever you encounter a complex number problem, the next program will be even simpler. (Watch out if you use our peculiar inequality and equality overload functions in a different application, however.) This is C++ at its worst because the few simple and elegant lines of code that make up the program conceal a whole lot of mathematical operations. The result is that this program will require days to generate a display even with a fast computer and a math coprocessor, so don't use it unless you have a lot of patience. If you do, you will be rewarded by interesting displays like that shown in Plate 3, which is the plot of the equation:

$$z^6 - 2z^5 + 4z^4 - z - 1 = 0 \qquad \text{(Equation 3-4)}$$

```
/*

   ┌─────────────────────────────────────────────────────────────┐
   │                                                               │
   │   newtgen = Program to map the generalized Newton's method    │
   │                                                               │
   └─────────────────────────────────────────────────────────────┘
                                                                  */


#include <stdio.h>
#include <dos.h>
#include <iostream.h>
#include <math.h>
#include <conio.h>

void cls(int color);
void plot(int x, int y, int color);
void setMode(int mode);

int col,row,i,j;
int max_iterations = 64;
int max_size = 4;
float Xmax= 2.0, Xmin= -2.0, Ymax=1.20, Ymin=-1.20,deltaX,deltaY;
Complex z,old_z;
Complex f,f_prime,z_power;
float arguments[10];
float temp;
const int maxcol = 639;
const int maxrow = 349;
const int max_colors = 16;

main()
{
    int color, row, col, degree;

    for (i=0; i<10; i++)
    {
        arguments[i] = 0;
        cout << "\nEnter " << i << "th coefficient: ";
        cin >> arguments[i];
    }
    setMode(16);
    for (i=9; i>=0; i--)
```

```
    {
        if (arguments[i] != 0)
        {
            degree = i;
            break;
        }
    }
cls(7);
deltaX = (Xmax - Xmin)/(maxcol + 1);
deltaY = (Ymax - Ymin)/(maxrow + 1);
old_z = Complex(42,42);
   for (col=0; col<=maxcol; col++)
   {
     if (kbhit() != 0) break;
     for (row=0; row<=maxrow; row++)
     {
         z = Complex(Xmin + col * deltaX,Ymax - row * deltaY);
         i = 0;
         while (i<max_iterations)
         {
             f = 0;
             f_prime = 0;
             z_power = 1;
             for(j=0; j<degree; j++)
             {
               f = f + z_power * arguments[j];
               f_prime = f_prime + (z_power * arguments[j+1]) *
                         (float)(j+1);
               z_power = z*z_power;
             }
             f = f + z_power * arguments[degree];
             z = z - f/f_prime;
             if (z != old_z)
             {
                 old_z = z;
                 i++;
             }
             else
             break;
         }
         color = i%16;
         plot(col, row, color);
```

```
        }
    }
    getch();
}
```

Figure 3-4. Generalized Newton's Method Program

Another Newton's Method Program

In Figure 3-5, we list a Newton's method program which handles equations from degree three to ten, but only for the simple equation:

$$z^n - 1 = 0 \qquad \text{(Equation 3-5)}$$

We are able to simplify the mathematics somewhat and create a switch statement to optimize the iterated multiplications needed for solving equations of a higher degree. This provides a considerable speed-up of the program. In addition, for this equation, the roots are known to be spaced equally around a unit circle in the complex plane, so that we can offer two color options; either the cyclical colors used in the previous program, or pairs of colors associated with each root, which are determined by comparing the root obtained by the Newton's method solution with the actual roots to see which one is most closely approached. The results of using this program are shown in Plate 1 for a fifth degree equation and Plate 2 for a seventh degree equation.

New Directions

Now that we've been exposed to creating classes and using them to simplify programming, we'll go on to the next chapter, where we'll look at the functions and definitions needed to treat three-dimensional vectors. This will eventually lead us into using these vector operations in the ray tracing program.

BEYOND C WITH C++: A NEWTON'S METHOD EXAMPLE

```
/*
        ┌─────────────────────────────────────────────────┐
        │                          .                      │
        │        newton = Program to solve Z^n - 1 = 0     │
        │                                                 │
        └─────────────────────────────────────────────────┘
                                                              */

const int maxcol = 639;
const int maxrow = 349;
const int max_colors = 16;

int max_iterations = 64;
double Xmax= 2.0, Xmin= -2.0, Ymax=1.20, Ymin=-1.20,deltaX,deltaY;
Complex z,old_z,z_power,z_power2,z_sq;
Complex roots[10];
int degree;

main()
{
        int i,j,color, row, col,flag;
        double a,b,twopi=6.2831853;

        setMode(16);
        cout << "Enter degree of equation (3 - 10): ";
        cin >> degree;
        cout << "\nEnter '0' for cyclical colors;\n"
                    << "'1' for colors associated with root: ";
        cin >> flag;
        if (degree < 3)
                    degree = 3;
        if (degree > 10)
                    degree = 10;
        if (flag < 0)
                    flag = 0;
        if (flag > 1)
                    flag = 1;
        a = 1.0/(float)degree;
        b = 1 - a;
        for (i=0; i<degree; i++)
        {
                    roots[i] = Complex(cos(i*twopi/(float)degree),
                                    sin(i*twopi/(float)degree));
```

```
      }
   cls(7);
   deltaX = (Xmax - Xmin)/(maxcol + 1);
   deltaY = (Ymax - Ymin)/(maxrow + 1);
for (col=0; col<=maxcol; col++)
{
   if (kbhit() != 0) break;
   for (row=0; row<=maxrow; row++)
   {
       z = Complex(Xmin + col * deltaX,Ymax - row * deltaY);
       old_z = Complex(10000,10000);
       i = 0;
       while ((z != old_z) && (i<64))
       {
                  old_z = z;
                  z_sq = z*z;
                  switch(degree)
                  {

                     case 3:
                         z_power = z_sq;
                     case 4:
                         z_power = z*z_sq;
                         break;
                     case 5:
                         z_power = z_sq*z_sq;
                         break;
                     case 6:
                         z_power = z*z_sq*z_sq;
                         break;
                     case 7:
                         z_power = z_sq*z_sq*z_sq;
                         break;
                     case 8:
                         z_power =
                            z_sq*z_sq*z_sq*z;
                         break;
                     case 9:
                         z_power = z_sq*z_sq;
                         z_power = z_power*z_power;
                         break;
                     case 10:
```

```
                                  z_power = z_sq*z_sq;
                         z_power = z_power*z;
                         break;
            }
         z_power = ~z_power;
         if (z_power != Complex())
            z = z*b + (z_power)*a;
         else
            z = old_z;
         i++;
      }
   if (flag == 1)
   {
               color = 15;

               for (j=0; j<degree; j++)
               {
                     if (z == roots[j])
                          color = 1 + j%8 + 8*(i%2);
               }
         }
         else
               color = i%16;
               plot(col, row, color);
      }
   }
   getch();
}
```

Figure 3-5. Another Newton's Method Program

CHAPTER 4

Three Dimensional Vector Mathematics with C++

In this chapter, we are going to look in some detail at using C++ to define the class *Vector* of three dimensional vectors. All of the information needed to define these vectors for use in the ray tracing program is included in two files. The first of these, *vmath.hpp*, is a header file which contains the definition of the class. It is listed in Figure 4-1. The second file, *vmath.cpp*, contains the detailed definitions of all of the functions that are contained within the class. It is listed in Figure 4-2.

First, look at Figure 4-1. The class of three dimensional vectors is defined as containing three floating-point variables, one for each of the three coordinates of a Cartesian coordinate system. Two things should be observed about how this definition is structured. First, the keyword *public* appears at the very beginning of the class definition, so all members of the class are completely available to external functions. Second, there are three constructors; one for use when no parameters are passed at initialization, another for use when three floating-point variables are passed, and a third for use when another vector is passed. Thus we can have the statement:

```
c = Vector(6,7,8)
```

where *c* as a vector takes on the *x,y,z* values of 6, 7, and 8 respectively, and we can also have:

```
c = Vector()
```

where *c* as a vector takes on the *x*, *y*, *z* values of 0, 0, and 0.

```
/*
```

```
    vmath.hpp=Header File for Three Dimensional Vector Mathematics
```

```
*/

#include <stream.hpp>
#include <math.h>

class Vector {
  public:
  float x, y, z;

  Vector();
  Vector(float x1, float y1, float z1);
  Vector(Vector &);
  Vector operator+(Vector &);
  Vector operator-(Vector &);
  Vector operator-();
  Vector operator=(Vector &);
  Vector operator*(Vector &);
  Vector operator*(float );
  Vector operator/(float );
  float operator%(Vector &);      // Dot product
  Vector operator^(Vector &);     // Cross product
  Vector operator~();                   // Normalize vector
  Vector min(Vector &);
  Vector max(Vector &);
  Vector Rotate(float cos1, float sin1, float cos2, float sin2);
  Vector Rev_Rotate(float cos1, float sin1, float cos2, float
        sin2);
  friend ostream &operator<<(ostream&,Vector&);
  void get_vector();
};
```

Figure 4-1. Vector Mathematics Header File

Overloading of Vector Operators

First, we are going to look at the details of the operator overloading for the *Vector* class. Refer to Figure 4-2 for the listings. The first two, addition (+) and subtraction (-) of two vectors, are very simple. For the first, the values of each pair of like coordinates are added together. For the second, the value of each coordinate for the second vector is subtracted from the value of the like coordinate for the first vector. Now, look at the next function, which is overloading of - for a single vector only. This occurs in expressions like:

```
c = -a;
```

where both *c* and *a* are vectors. This will only work because the - operator is already defined in C++ as being applicable to a single variable as well as the difference between two variables. Note that if, for some reason, we decided to use the operator / as the operator for subtraction, we could only use it to define subtraction between two vectors, since there is no single variable variation of /.

Now, let's look at multiplication (*). We have two overloading definitions of multiplication. The first is multiplication of two vectors. Each of the three new vector coordinates is the product of the like coordinates of the two vectors being operated upon. The second type of multiplication occurs when a vector is multiplied by a floating-point number. In this case, the new vector coordinates are the products of the floating-point number with each of the respective coordinates of the original vector. Note that you can only use expressions like:

```
a = b * c;
```

where *b* is the vector and *c* is the floating-point number. This won't work if *b* is the floating-point number and *c* is the vector, since we haven't provided for overloading in this way. To do so, we would have to overload the multiplication operator for the class *float*. Unfortunately, C++ won't recognize standard number types as classes, even though they have a lot in common. Next, look at the operator for defining the dot product of two vectors. The dot product is a scalar (floating-point number) obtained by multiplying corresponding pairs of coordinates for two vectors and taking the sum of these products. In regular C language mathematics, there is no operator for the dot product, so we have to select an existing operator that is suitable which we won't use for something else. We choose the % operator, ordinarily used for modulus arithmetic. We won't use any modulus arithmetic with vectors, so it is available for overloading. It also operates upon two inputs, so it is satisfactory for this operation. Similarly, we need an operator that we can overload to produce the vector cross-product, which has no corresponding operation in ordinary arithmetic. We choose the ^ operator, which is ordinarily used as a *bitwise exclusive or* operator by C. We won't be doing any exclusive *or*'s on vectors, so it is available, and since it handles two variables, it is suitable for the vector cross product. Look at the listing of the overload of the ^ function to see how the vector cross product is calculated, or refer back to your old book on vector analysis.

```
/*
      vmath.cpp = Classes for Three Dimensional Vector Mathematics
*/

#include "render.hpp"

extern char string_buf[32];


/*
                        Vector Constructors
*/

Vector::Vector()
{
   x = 0;
   y = 0;
   z = 0;
}
```

```
Vector::Vector(float x1, float y1, float z1)
{
  x = x1;
  y = y1;
  z = z1;
}

Vector::Vector(Vector & otherVector)
{
  x = otherVector.x;
  y = otherVector.y;
  z = otherVector.z;
}

/*
        Vector Overload of + Operator
*/

Vector Vector::operator+(Vector & arg)
{
  Vector result;
  resulL.x = x + arg.x;
  result.y = y + arg.y;
  result.z = z + arg.z;
  return result;
}

/*
        Vector Overload of - Operator (a - b)
*/

Vector Vector::operator-(Vector & arg)
{
  Vector result;
  result.x = x - arg.x;
  result.y = y - arg.y;
  result.z = z - arg.z;
  return result;
}
```

```
/*
    ┌─────────────────────────────────────────────────────┐
    │          Vector Overload of - Operator (-a)          │
    └─────────────────────────────────────────────────────┘
*/

Vector Vector::operator-()
{
  Vector result;
  result.x = - x;
  result.y = - y;
  result.z = - z;
  return result;
}

/*
    ┌─────────────────────────────────────────────────────┐
    │     Vector Overload of * Operator (Vector Times a Vector) │
    └─────────────────────────────────────────────────────┘
*/

Vector Vector::operator*(Vector & arg)
{
  Vector result;
  result.x = x * arg.x;
  result.y = y * arg.y;
  result.z = z * arg.z;
  return result;
}

/*
    ┌─────────────────────────────────────────────────────┐
    │     Vector Overload of * Operator (Vector Times a Float) │
    └─────────────────────────────────────────────────────┘
*/

Vector Vector::operator*(float arg)
{
  Vector result;
  result.x = x * arg;
  result.y = y * arg;
  result.z = z * arg;
  return result;
```

```
}

/*
    +------------------------------------------------------------+
    |   Vector Overload of / Operator (Vector Divided by a Float) |
    +------------------------------------------------------------+
*/

Vector Vector::operator/(float arg)
{
  Vector result;
  result.x = x / arg;
  result.y = y / arg;
  result.z = z / arg;
  return result;
}

/*
    +------------------------------------------------------------+
    |              Vector Overload of = Operator                 |
    +------------------------------------------------------------+
*/

Vector Vector::operator-(Vector & rvalue)
{
  x = rvalue.x;
  y = rvalue.y;
  z = rvalue.z;
  return *this;
}
```

we want to set current (LHS) object's x, y, z — *this* *gives address of same,* **this is the Vector object*

```
/*
    +------------------------------------------------------------+
    |  Vector Overload of % Operator (Dot Product of Two Vectors)|
    +------------------------------------------------------------+
*/

float Vector::operator%(Vector & arg)
{
  float result;
  result = x*arg.x + y*arg.y + z*arg.z;
  return result;
}

/*
    +------------------------------------------------------------+
    |Vector Overload of ^ Operator (Cross Product of Two Vectors)|
    +------------------------------------------------------------+
```

```
*/

Vector Vector::operator^(Vector & arg)
{
  Vector result;
  result.x = y*arg.z - z*arg.y;
  result.y = z*arg.x - x*arg.z;
  result.z = x*arg.y - y*arg.x;
  return result;
}

/*
        Vector Overload of ~ Operator (Normalize a Vector)
*/

Vector Vector::operator~()
{
  Vector result;
  float l;

  l = *this % *this;
  l = sqrt(l);
  result.x = x/l;
  result.y = y/l;
  result.z = z/l;
  return result;
}

/*
            max = Return the maximum of two vectors
*/

Vector Vector::max(Vector & arg)
{
  Vector result;

  result.x = MAX(x,arg.x);
  result.y = MAX(y,arg.y);
  result.z = MAX(z,arg.z);
  return result;
```

```
}

/*
┌─────────────────────────────────────────────────────┐
│         min = Return the minimum of two vectors       │
└─────────────────────────────────────────────────────┘
*/

Vector Vector::min(Vector & arg)
{
  Vector result;

  result.x = MIN(x,arg.x);
  result.y = MIN(y,arg.y);
  result.z = MIN(z,arg.z);
  return result;
}

/*
┌─────────────────────────────────────────────────────┐
│                    Rotate a Vector                    │
└─────────────────────────────────────────────────────┘
*/

Vector Vector::Rotate(float cos1, float sin1, float cos2, float
      sin2)
{
  Vector temp, result;

  result.x = x * cos1 + z * -sin1;
  temp.y = y;
  temp.z = x * sin1 + z * cos1;
  result.y = temp.y * -cos2 + temp.z * sin2;
  result.z = temp.y * -sin2 + temp.z * -cos2;
  return(result);
}

/*
┌─────────────────────────────────────────────────────┐
│                 Reverse Rotate a Vector               │
└─────────────────────────────────────────────────────┘
*/

Vector Vector::Rev_Rotate(float cos1, float sin1, float cos2,
float sin2)
```

```
{
  Vector temp, result;

  temp.x = x;
  result.y = y * cos2 + z * -sin2;
  temp.z = y * sin2 + z * cos2;
  result.x = temp.x * -cos1 + temp.z * sin1;
  result.z = temp.x * -sin1 + temp.z * -cos1;
  return(result);
}
```

```
/*
 ┌─────────────────────────────────────────────┐
 │                                             │
 │            Print Out Vector Contents        │
 │                                             │
 └─────────────────────────────────────────────┘
*/
```

```
ostream &operator<<(ostream& s,Vector& arg)
{
  s << "(" << arg.x << "," << arg.y <<"," << arg.z << ")";
  return s;
}
```

```
/*
 ┌─────────────────────────────────────────────┐
 │                                             │
 │            Get Vector from input file       │
 │                                             │
 └─────────────────────────────────────────────┘
*/
```

```
void Vector::get_vector()
{
  get_string(string_buf);
  x = atof(string_buf);
  get_string(string_buf);
  y = atof(string_buf);
  get_string(string_buf);
  z = atof(string_buf);
}
```

Figure 4-2. Vector Mathematics Function File

Next look at the operator used to normalize a vector. In this case, we want an operator that accepts only one input parameter. The ~ normally gives the user the complement of an integer, but is also overloaded to be the destructor for an object. Using it for the normalize operation means that we won't have a destructor for vectors, but this doesn't really present a problem, since we aren't going to be creating a lot of vectors that have to be removed from memory at some later point. Normalization simply divides all components of the vector by its magnitude so that the resulting vector has a magnitude of one.

Other Vector Functions

We now come to some functions that are a part of the *Vector* class, but don't make use of operators. The first two are the *max* and *min* functions. If you are thinking in strictly mathematical terms, you may be wondering exactly what is meant by the maximum of two vectors or the minimum of two vectors. However, the use to which we put these two functions in the ray tracing program is such that what we want for the *max* function is a vector each of whose coordinates is the maximum of that coordinate in the two vectors being tested — and similarly for the *min* function, a vector each of whose coordinates is the minimum of that coordinate for the two vectors being tested. That is what these functions provide.

Next we have two rotation functions. The first rotates the vector a specified angle around the y axis and then another specified angle around the x axis. The second rotates in the reverse direction, first by a specified angle around the x axis and then by a specified angle around the z axis.

The print function is an overload of the << operator of the *ostream* class to make it possible to use *cout,* for example, with vectors as well as other types of data.

The form in which the vector is output is a starting parenthesis, followed by the three floating-point coordinates (separated by commas), followed by a close parenthesis. How this type of overloading is done was explained in the previous chapter.

Finally, there is a special function called *get_vector*. This function reads three strings from the incoming data stream. How these strings are read will be discussed in Chapter 8. Each string is converted to a floating-point number and is then assigned to a vector coordinate in order. Thus this function concludes with having set the designated vector to the three values read from the file.

CHAPTER 5

Ray Tracing Object Structures

At this point, we have learned enough about C++ so that we are ready to begin creating a ray tracing program. We first need to decide how we are going to handle object information and then set up some mechanisms for doing this handling. Traditionally, such information is kept in a header file. The header file, which is called *render.hpp,* will be a part of every ray tracing file. This header file is listed in Figure 5-1.

The header begins with a number of *#define* statements. These are strictly for convenience in understanding the software. When we get into the subject of communicating with the ray tracer (Chapter 8) we'll see that the heart of communication is reading a string from a data file and comparing it with all acceptable strings and assigning a type. The type is simply a number corresponding to the position of the matching string in the array. As we proceed further with the input process, we often set up *switch* statements that take different actions depending upon which type a string is. If the *switch* statement simply provided different actions for different type numbers, it would be obscure. We would have to go back to the string array each time to determine which type of object we were dealing with. To clarify this whole process, for each type we have defined a title that essentially matches the original kind of string to be equal to the type number (the position in the array). Thus in a *switch* statement, we can give this title instead of the number, and the user can identify what type of string is being processed.

Next, we define some constants that will be used throughout the program. Most of them are self-evident. A few need to be set up in the main program; we list them here as *extern* so that they will be passed as global variables.

```
/*
        ┌──────────────────────────────────────────────┐
        │                                                │
        │        Header File for Ray Tracing Program     │
        │           By Roger T. Stevens - 3/1/90          │
        │                                                │
        └──────────────────────────────────────────────┘
*/
#include <stdlib.h>
#include <stdio.h>
#include <math.h>
#include "vmath.hpp"


/*
        ┌──────────────────────────────────────────────┐
        │                                                │
        │                Object Definitions              │
        │                                                │
        └──────────────────────────────────────────────┘
*/

#define PATT_HEADER          0
#define LINE                 1
#define SPHERE               2
#define PARALLELOGRAM        3
#define TRIANGLE             4
#define LAMP                 5
#define OBSERVER             6
#define GROUND               7
#define SKY                  8
#define BBOX                 9
#define RING                 10
#define QUADRATIC            11
#define BEGIN_BBOX           12
#define END_BBOX             13
#define BEGIN_INSTANCES      14
#define END_INSTANCES        15
#define AMB                  16
#define DIFF                 17
#define MIRROR               18
#define TRANS                19
#define DENSITY              20
#define INDEX                21
#define DITHER               22
#define SREFLECT             23
#define REFLECT              24
#define LOC                  25
#define RADIUS               26
```

```
#define PAttern          27
#define REMOVE           28
#define XMULT            29
#define YMULT            30
#define NAME             31
#define DIST             32
#define LOOKAT           33
#define V1               34
#define V2               35
#define ZENITH           36
#define HORIZ            37
#define RAD_1            38
#define RAD_2            39
#define A                40
#define B                41
#define C                42
#define D                43
#define E                44
#define XMAX             45
#define YMAX             46
#define ZMAX             47
#define XMIN             48
#define YMIN             49
#define ZMIN             50
#define DIR              51
#define FOC_LENGTH       52
#define FIRST_SCAN       53
#define DEFAULT          54
#define FILE_NAME        55
#define LAST_SCAN        56
#define XRES             57
#define YRES             58
#define X_SIZE           59
#define Y_SIZE           60
#define START_X          61
#define START_Y          62
#define END_X            63
#define END_Y            64
#define PAREN            65
#define NO_SHADOW        66
#define NO_LAMP          67
#define THRESHOLD        68
```

```
#define UP                      69
#define INSTANCE_OF             70
#define SCALE                   71
#define RECTANGLE               72
#define CIRCLE                  73
#define POLYGON                 74
#define COLOR                   75
#define POINT                   76
#define CONE                    77
#define HEIGHT                  78
#define FRACTAL                 79
#define DIMENSION               80
#define SCALAR                  81
#define NUll                    82
#define last_no                 83
```

```
/*
┌─────────────────────────────────────────────────────┐
│                                                       │
│                  Useful Constants                     │
│                                                       │
└─────────────────────────────────────────────────────┘
*/
```

```
#define TRUE   1
#define FALSE 0
#define SMALL           0.001
#define ASPECT          1.0   // aspect ratio
#define CNUM            63     // number of shades of color minus one
#define MAX_IX          4      // maximum x interpolation
#define MAX_IY          4      // maximum y interpolation
#define max_pixel       800    // max of RGB array size (dots per row)
extern int XSIZE;
extern int YSIZE;
extern int CENTERX;
extern int CENTERY;
extern int XSIZE4;
```

```
/*
┌─────────────────────────────────────────────────────┐
│                                                       │
│                Color Data Definitions                 │
│                                                       │
└─────────────────────────────────────────────────────┘
*/
```

```
class color_data
{
      public:
      Vector      amb,          // ambient lighting
                  diff,         // diffuse lighting
                  mirror,       // % light reflected
                  trans,        // % light transmitted
                  density;      // density
      float       reflect,      // percent specularly reflected
                  index;        // index if refraction
      short       sreflect,     // specular refl coefficient
                  dither;       // color dithering
      color_data operator=(color_data&);
};
```

assignmt of color data object

```
/*
┌─────────────────────────────────────────────────┐
│              Class definition for Line            │
└─────────────────────────────────────────────────┘
*/

class Line
{
      public:
      Vector loc,dir;
      int flag;
};

/*
┌─────────────────────────────────────────────────┐
│              Class definition for Lamp            │
└─────────────────────────────────────────────────┘
*/

class Lamp
{
      public:
      Vector loc;
      float radius, distance;
      Lamp * next_lamp;
};

/*
```

```
┌─────────────────────────────────────────────────┐
│              Class definition for a Pattern       │
└─────────────────────────────────────────────────┘
*/

class Pattern
{
        public:
        short       type;       // type of pattern
        float       xsize,      // pattern size in x direction
                    ysize,      // pattern size in y direction
                    startx,     // x coordinate starting position
                    starty,     // y coordinate starting position
                    endx,       // x coordinate ending position
                    endy,       // y coordinate ending position
                    radius;     // radius of circle pattern
        color_data  col_data;   // color information
        char        name[32];   // name of pattern
        Pattern     *child,
                    *sibling,
                    *link;
};

/*
┌─────────────────────────────────────────────────┐
│              Class Definitions for Object         │
└─────────────────────────────────────────────────┘
*/

class Object
{
        public:
        unsigned char       type,       // object type
                            flag;
        char                name[16];   // object name
        Vector              loc,        // object location
                            vect1,      // three vectors
                            vect2,
                            vect3,
                            lower,      // lower bound
                            upper,      // upper bound
                            norm;
        float               cterm,      // used for quadratic
```

```
                                    // surfaces only
                        xmult,      // x  multiplier for
                                    // patterns
                        ymult,      // y multiplier for
                                    // pattern
                        n1,         // precomputed values
                        len1,
                        len2,
                        cos1,
                        sin1,
                        cos2,
                        sin2;
        color_data      *col_data;  // color information
        Object          *nextobj,   // addr of next object in list
                        *child;     // address of child for
                                    // bounding boxes
        Pattern         *pattern,   // addr of pattern structure
        *remove;        // address of struct to remove
                        // obj section
        Object operator-(Object &);
        virtual void FindNorm(Vector * normal, Vector * position);
        virtual void Position (float * pos1, float *pos2, Vector
                *location);
        virtual int CollisionTest(Line * line, float *t);
        virtual void FindBbox(Vector * v1, Vector * v2);
        virtual void Scale_Instance(Vector *mult, int fflag);
};

class Sphere: public Object
{
        public:
        Sphere();
        void FindNorm(Vector * normal, Vector * position);
        void Position (float * pos1, float *pos2, Vector *location);
        int CollisionTest(Line * line, float *t);
        void FindBbox(Vector * v1, Vector * v2);
        void Scale_Instance(Vector *mult, int fflag);
};

class Triangle: public Object
{
        public:
```

(handwritten note in margin:) Many Better to stao i tree with BBoxes, and avoid repeat. but we sh'd need to find trin really

```
        Triangle();
        void FindNorm(Vector * normal, Vector * position);
        void Position (float * pos1, float *pos2, Vector *location);
        int CollisionTest(Line * line, float *t);
        void FindBbox(Vector * v1, Vector * v2);
        void Scale_Instance(Vector *mult, int fflag);
};

class Parallelogram: public Object
{
        public:
        Parallelogram();
        void FindNorm(Vector * normal, Vector * position);
        void Position (float * pos1, float *pos2, Vector *location);
        int CollisionTest(Line * line, float *t);
        void FindBbox(Vector * v1, Vector * v2);
        void Scale_Instance(Vector *mult, int fflag);
};

class Ring: public Object
{
        public:
        Ring();
        void FindNorm(Vector * normal, Vector * position);
        void Position (float * pos1, float *pos2, Vector *location);
        int CollisionTest(Line * line, float *t);
        void FindBbox(Vector * v1, Vector * v2);
        void Scale_Instance(Vector *mult, int fflag);
};

class Quadratic: public Object
{
        public:
        Quadratic();
        void FindNorm(Vector * normal, Vector * position);
        void Position (float * pos1, float *pos2, Vector *location);
        int CollisionTest(Line * line, float *t);
        void FindBbox(Vector * v1, Vector * v2);
        void Scale_Instance(Vector *mult, int fflag);
};

class BBox: public Object
```

```
{
        int CollisionTest(Line * line, float *t);
        void FindBbox(Vector * v1, Vector * v2);
};


/*
┌──────────────────────────────────────────────┐
│                                                │
│            Structure for the World             │
│                                                │
└──────────────────────────────────────────────┘
*/


typedef struct world
{
        Object      * stack,          // list of objects in
                                      // picture
                    * instances;      // list of user defined
                                      // primitives
        Lamp        * lamps;          // list of lamps
        Line        * line;
        int         objcount,         // number of objects
                    lampcount,        // number of lamps
                    first_scan,       // first scan line
                    last_scan;        // last scan line
        long        ray_intersects,   // statistics
                    primary_traced,
                    to_lamp,
                    refl_trans,
                    bbox_intersects,
                    intersect_tests,
                    pixels_hit,
                    pattern_matches;
        Vector      obsright,         // observer right direction
                    obsup,            // observer up direction
                    obsloc,           // location of observer
                    obsdir,           // direction in which observer
                                      // looks
                    skycolor_horiz,   // sky color at horizon
                    skycolor_zenith;  // sky color at zenith
        float       sky_dither;
        Pattern *   patlist;          // list of pattern addresses
        float       flength,          // focal length
                    globindex;        // global index of
                                      // refraction
```

```
        char        outfile[32];      // output file name
        FILE        *filept;          // output file pointer
        float       threshold;
        float       int_threshold,
                    fractal_dim,
                    fractal_scalar;
        int         level;

}
World;
```

```
/*
    ┌─────────────────────────────────────────────┐
    │                                             │
    │              Math Definitions               │
    │                                             │
    └─────────────────────────────────────────────┘

*/
```

```
#define MIN(x,y) ((x)<(y) ? (x) : (y))
#define MAX(x,y) ((x)>(y) ? (x) : (y))
#define Max(x,y,z)  (x>y && x>z ? x : (y>z ? y : z))
#define Min(x,y,z)  (x<y && x<z ? x : (y<z ? y : z))
```

```
/*
    ┌─────────────────────────────────────────────┐
    │                                             │
    │          Structure of Default Values         │
    │                                             │
    └─────────────────────────────────────────────┘

*/
```

```
typedef struct def_struct
{
        color_data   col_data;    // default colorinfo
        short        shadow;      // compute shadows ?
        float        threshold;   // cutoff point for min refl,
                                  // refl rays
        short        ithreshold;  // integer version of above
}
DEF;
```

```
/*
    ┌─────────────────────────────────────────────┐
    │                                             │
    │              Setup of Variables              │
    │                                             │
    └─────────────────────────────────────────────┘
```

```
*/

extern World WORLD;         // the world of objects in the scene
extern DEF     def;         // default values for some parameters
extern int     linenumber;  // line counter


/*
    ┌─────────────────────────────────────────────────────┐
    │                                                       │
    │          Function Prototypes for RENDER.C             │
    │                                                       │
    └─────────────────────────────────────────────────────┘

*/

void init_world(void);
void init_color(void);
void World_Stats(void);
void Open_File();
void Close_File();
void scanner(Object * test);

/*
    ┌─────────────────────────────────────────────────────┐
    │                                                       │
    │          Function Prototypes for INPUT.C              │
    │                                                       │
    └─────────────────────────────────────────────────────┘

*/

Pattern *Attach_Pattern();
int GetAttrib(int type,char string_buf[]);
Pattern *Get_Circle_Pattern();
int get_color_data(int type, color_data *col_data);
Object * get_data();
int GetLamp();
int LoadWorld();
Object * Get_Object(int type,Object *queue);
Object * GetParallelogram();
int GetPattern();
Pattern *Get_Poly_Pattern();
Pattern *Get_Rect_Pattern();
Object * GetRing();
Object * GetSphere();
int get_string(char string_buf[]);
Pattern *Get_SubPattern(int type);
```

```
Object * GetTriangle();
Object * GetQuadratic();
void Make_Bbox(Object *node);
Object * Name_Find(Object * obj,char *name);
Object * Move_Instance(Object * obj, int fflag);
void Offset_Instance(Object * obj,Vector * offset,int fflag);
Object * Get_Instance_Of();
void Fractal_comp(Triangle * newobj);
Object * Make_fractal_triangles(Vector loc, Vector vect1, Vector
    vect2, Vector vect3, Object * queue, int level);


/*
+------------------------------------------------------------+
|                                                            |
|              Function Prototypes for RAY.C                 |
|                                                            |
+------------------------------------------------------------+
*/
void Trace_Scene();
void DiffuseColor(Vector * color,color_data * col_data,Vector *
norm,Vector * loc,
      Line * oline);
void Dump_Line(int lineno,char r[],char g[],char b[]);
void AmbientColor(Vector * color, color_data * col_data, Vector * norm,
Vector * loc);
void TransparentColor(Vector * color, color_data * col_data,
      Vector *
norm,Vector * loc,
      Line * line,float inmult);
void ReflectColor(Vector * color,color_data * col_data,Vector *
norm,Vector * loc,
      Line * line,float inmult);
void SkyColor(Line * line,Vector * color);
void Dither(Vector * color,float dither);
void Dither(Vector * color,color_data * col_data);
Object * Intersect(Object * CurrObj,Line * line,float *shortest_time,
      short shadow_flag, short init_flag,Vector * atten);
int Trace_Ray(Line * line,Vector * color,float multiplier);
int Find_Color(Object * obj,Pattern *pattern, Vector * location,
      color_data *c_data, float x_mult, float y_mult);
```

Figure 5-1. The render.hpp Header File

We're now ready to think about handling data within the ray tracing program. The first C++ class we are going to set up is *color_data*. This is not a very interesting class, since it contains only one embedded function. It represents all color characteristics that are likely to be associated with an object. A number of these are defined as vectors, which permits them to be treated with vector mathematics, although in this case, the three vector components refer to values of *red, green,* and *blue* that make up the color rather than to position data. All of these values are assumed to vary between zero and the maximum color value (63).

This info is recorded for each object -

The first color to be defined is that for ambient light that falls upon the object. The second color is the diffused color, i.e., the inherent color of the object (the color that it is painted, if you will). If you look around at various objects, you can recognize that you do not actually see the diffuse color of an object at any point on the object, but rather one that depends upon how the object is lighted. The next defined color is the mirror color, which is the proportion of each color reflected by the object. If this is (63, 63, 63), you have a perfectly reflecting mirror; if it is (0,0,0), which is the default value, the object has no mirror-like quality. Other values can cause partial or colored mirror reflection. The next color is the transparency value. It defines the percentage of each color transmitted through a transparent object. Next comes the density factor, which determines how light of each color is attenuated as it passes through a semi-transparent object. These are all of the color vectors associated with an object.

In addition, the *color-data* class contains a floating-point number which is the percentage of light specularly reflected from an object, and a floating-point number which is the index of refraction. There are also short integers which give the specular reflection coefficient and the dithering value. These will be discussed in Chapter 9.

The Concept of Linked Lists

Before we continue, we need to discuss the concept of linked lists, which is essential to an understanding of how to handle lines, objects, light sources, etc. Let's look at linked lists in the context of how we are going to list objects, so that later on the ray tracing program can scan them and determine what to do about intersecting a ray with each object.

We begin by having a list containing no objects, indicated by a variable called *WORLD.stack* containing a NULL. We now create an object by setting up the data space for it and filling in some data values. Then we take the content of *WORLD.stack* and put it into a variable in the object containing the address of the next object. After that, we put the address of the beginning of the data area for our first object into *WORLD.stack*. We repeat this process until we generate all the objects we need.

Now let's see what happens when we want to retrieve data from this list of objects. We first go to the address specified by *WORLD.stack*. There, we find the data for the last object we generated and process that. Then, we go to the address specified by the *next_object* variable in this object. There we find the data for the next-to-last object we created and process it. We continue this process until, after we have processed data for the first object generated, we find that the next object variable contains a NULL, which is a signal for us to quit since we have come to the end of the list. This is basically how a linked list works.

However, sometimes things are a little more complicated. Suppose there are several objects we only want to process if a certain criterion is met. For example, in attempting to intersect arrays with objects, we often draw a box around several objects. The data for the box are in our main list. If a light ray intersects this box, we want to go ahead and process the list of objects that are within the box; otherwise, we want to ignore them and continue down the main list. We get around this by having a variable for each object called *child*.

Now, when we get to the point where we generate the box object, we put the address of the next main object in the *next_object* variable as usual, but we put a NULL in the *child* address variable. Then we process each of the objects that are enclosed in the box, each time taking the address from the *child* address variable and putting it into the *next_object* address of the current object. We take the address of the current object and put it into the *child* address variable of the box. Now when we process data, each time we meet some preestablished criterion, we take the address from the associate *child* address variable and process the data from that object. We then proceed normally through the list of objects in the box. But when we come to a NULL, which indicates that we are through with them, we don't quit, but go back to the box that had the original *child* address and pick up the address in the *next_object* variable. We then continue processing.

This procedure adds a nice technique for branching in the list scanning process. How this all works out for the ray tracing program is shown in Figure 5-2. We pick up the address of the first object in the variable *WORLD.stack*. After processing it, we get the next object address from *next_object*. This process continues until we come to a bounding box. This has an address in *child*. We then branch off and continue the usual process until we hit a NULL address. We then go back up to the bounding box and pick up its *next_object*. When we come to a NULL address in the main stream, the entire process terminates.

Lines, Lamps, and Patterns

The next class defined in the header is the *Line* class. It is one of the simpler classes, simply containing vectors representing the location and direction of a light ray, a flag to indicate whether it is inside or outside of a transparent object, and variables to contain the *next_line* and *child* addresses.

Following this, the *Lamp* class is defined. This is used for all of the light sources that are illuminating the scene. It consists simply of vectors defining the location of the light source, the radius of the light source, and an address for the next lamp, to permit this to be a linked list. The radius is actually an overkill, since we won't be concerned about the radius of the light source in this version of the ray tracing program. For one thing, in all of the demonstration pictures we are careful to define all of the light sources so that they are located outside of the picture. In the future, we might want to include lamps within the picture itself, in which case more details of the lamp characteristics would have to be included and treated by the program.

Next is the class definition of a *Pattern*. The pattern can be a rectangle, a circle, or a polygon. Its parameters include type, size, starting/ending points in the x and y directions, radius (if a circle), complete color data, name, and *child, sibling* and *link* address variables to permit linked lists. The pattern is a definition of a surface which is projected onto one of the objects described in the next paragraph.

Objects and Derived Classes

The next class, the *Object* class, is the most complex and most important class of all. First, if you are familiar with other object-oriented languages, note that this is a class of geometric objects, and is not to be confused with standard root *Object* found in Smalltalk and some other object-oriented languages. We start with the base class, all of whose members are public. It begins with the type of object, then a miscellaneous flag, then a name (which is used infrequently), then the vector defining the location of the object, then three vectors which are used differently for different kinds of objects to define the object extent and shape, then upper and lower bounds of the object, and finally an object normal vector. Following this are four floating-point numbers, *cterm* and *yterm* used only by quadratic objects, and the x and y multipliers which are applied to a pattern before it is mapped to the surface of the object. Following this are a series of floating-point variables that are used in rotating the object or intersecting it with a ray of light. All of these variables have a fixed value for a particular object which doesn't vary for different light rays. Consequently, they are calculated as soon as the object is entered into the data base and stored in the object structure. Next comes the address of the color data for the object and then address variables for the *next object* and *child* to complete the linked list. Finally are addresses for the pattern to be applied to this object and for any part of the object that is to be removed.

The next line is a prototype for the overloading of the = operator to apply to objects. As previously mentioned, it should not be necessary to overload the = operator; this should be done automatically for each class that is created. However, a current bug in the Zortech C++ compiler makes it necessary to do this overloading. Then comes a list of prototype virtual functions.

A virtual function is defined for the base class, but it can be redefined for each class that is derived from the base class. The function can be called as if we were calling the base class function, and yet the compiler automatically selects whichever redefined version of the function is appropriate to the derived class that we are concerned with.

Now, you're wondering what a derived class is. A derived class is a new class which inherits all of the data members and member functions from one or more classes that have been previously defined. It is set up in C++ in this manner;

```
class Sphere: public Object
{
...additional contents of class
};
```

In this case, *Sphere* is the new class. It has all the member variables and member functions of the class *Object,* which has already been defined. If you look at Figure 5-1, you'll see that we have defined six new derived classes, one for each of five types of primitive objects and one for bounding boxes. Each derived class has all of the characteristics of the base class. In addition, within each class description you will see prototypes for each redefinition of each virtual function that is redefined for this class. In Chapter 8, we will list these redefinitions and describe how these functions are used in further detail.

The World According to Ray Tracing

The next section of the header file contains a definition of the *World* structure. The world, as far as ray tracing is concerned, contains the addresses

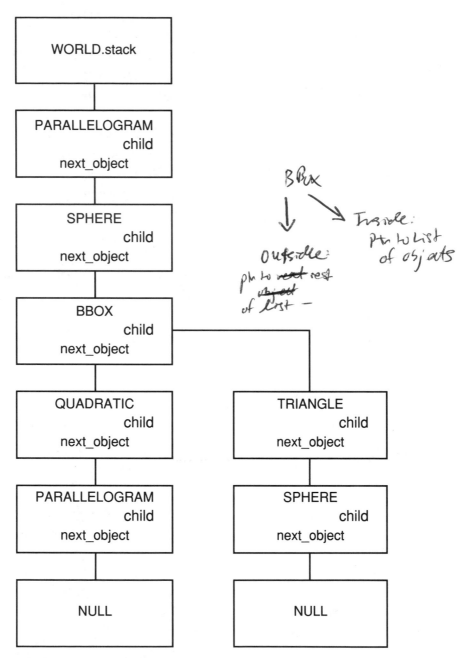

Figure 5-2. Linked List for Ray Tracing Program

for the beginning of the stack (which is the list of objects), the address for the beginning of instances (which will be described in Chapter 6), the beginning of the list of lamps and the beginning of the list of lines. A count of the number of objects and lamps is also kept. Next are variables to store a number of statistics that are collected during the course of rendering a particular scene and data on the observer and the sky. This is followed by a list of the addresses of all patterns. Finally comes the focal length, a global index of refraction, the output file name and pointer, and two threshold parameters. The focal length is supposed to be set up to be similar to a 35 millimeter camera, so that if you enter 50 (a 50 mm lens is a normal lens) you will get a normal perspective of the scene.

Additional Parameters

Continuing with the header file, we have a couple of definitions for obtaining the maximum and minimum of two numbers, then a structure of some default values. This is followed by the actual world and default structures and the definition of *linenumber,* which counts the number of lines of input data read into the program. Finally, the header includes prototypes of all of the functions that are created in each section of the ray tracing program. C++ is more picky about prototype definition than C, and this is all for the good, since intermixing methods of declaring a function prototype can yield some weird results. Anyway, it's good programming practice to put all the prototypes in the header, which supplies a place to look when you know a function name but not its location.

CHAPTER 6

Rendering the Scene—An Overview

In this chapter, the contents of the file *render.cpp* are described. The file principally contains the main program for rendering scenes using the ray tracing technique. This file is listed in Figure 6-1. It gives an overview of the ray tracing program. Once we have the overview we will look in more detail at the functions that do the detailed processing. This takes place in later chapters. At the very beginning of the *render.cpp* file, a few parameters are initialized. These include the parameters *XSIZE* and *YSIZE* which define the size of the display screen in pixels. These are default values; you can override them by putting in new parameters for *XRES* and *YRES* in your scene data file. You will want to do this if you are using a standard VGA card, since the VGA resolution is 320 by 200 pixels, whereas the default values in the program are for a high resolution super VGA mode of 640 by 480 pixels.

Next we define the function *init_world*. This function simply provides default values for the parameters of the *WORLD* structure. Following this is *init_color*, which provides default values for the color data parameters. Remember from the previous chapter that these default values are used for any color parameters not specified in a particular object definition. Remember also that using the *COLOR* string in your data file can change any of the default color parameters.

The code for overloading the = operator for the class *Object.next* appears next in this file. You've already encountered the format for overloading of operators in Chapters 3 and 4. To overload the = operator we simply set each parameter of one object equal to the corresponding parameter in the other. This permits us to have a statement like:

```
a = b
```

where *a* and *b* are both objects and have the contents of one automatically transferred to the other. Since this is a generic overload for the base class object, it is inherited by all of the classes derived from this base class. If you use it with a derived class, however, you should be careful to make sure that both *a* and *b* are of the same derived class. In other words, if *a* is of class *Sphere* then *b* must be of class *Sphere* also. If this isn't the case, (if *a* is of class *Sphere* and *b* is of class *Parallelogram*) you will get a diagnostic telling you that the classes are not the same and the program won't run. This overloading function is followed by a similar overloading function for the class of *color_data*. This overload function makes it possible to transfer all the color data information from one class member to another with a simple = statement. It doesn't do any harm to overload the = operator, but it shouldn't be necessary since this is supposed to be done automatically. With my copy of Zortech C++ the function had to be specifically overloaded for proper compilation.

```
/*
```

```
        Raytrace = Simplified Ray Tracing Program
                By Roger T. Stevens - 1/6/90
```

```
*/
```

```
unsigned _stack = 30000;      ←——— LoTS room needed
#include "render.hpp"
#include <dos.h>
#include <string.h>

extern char string_types[128][32];

#define MAXX    800
int XSIZE = 640;
int YSIZE = 480;                          } Screen dimensions
int CENTERX = XSIZE/2;
int CENTERY = YSIZE/2;
int XSIZE4  = XSIZE/4;
int i;
```

```
World WORLD;        // All of the data to be processed
DEF    def;         // color defaults
int    linenumber;

/*  ┌─────────────────────────────────────────────────────┐
    │                                                       │
    │           init_world() = Initialize the WORLD         │
    │                                                       │
    └─────────────────────────────────────────────────────┘
*/
void init_world(void)
{
  WORLD.stack      = NULL;
  WORLD.instances  = NULL;
  WORLD.patlist    = NULL;
  WORLD.outfile[0] = NULL;
  WORLD.lamps      = NULL;
  WORLD.line       = NULL;
  WORLD.objcount   = 0;
  WORLD.lampcount  = 0;
  WORLD.flength    = 250;
  WORLD.first_scan = 0;
  WORLD.last_scan  = YSIZE-1;
  WORLD.obsup = Vector(0,1,0);
  WORLD.obsloc = Vector(50,70,115);
  WORLD.skycolor_zenith = Vector();
  WORLD.skycolor_horiz  =Vector();
  WORLD.sky_dither = 0;
  WORLD.ray_intersects   =
  WORLD.pixels_hit       =
  WORLD.primary_traced   =
  WORLD.to_lamp          =
  WORLD.refl_trans       =
  WORLD.bbox_intersects  =
  WORLD.pattern_matches  =
  WORLD.intersect_tests  = 0;
  WORLD.globindex = 1.00;
  WORLD.threshold = .1;
  WORLD.int_threshold = WORLD.threshold * CNUM;
  WORLD.fractal_dim = 0.9;
  WORLD.level = 4;
  WORLD.fractal_scalar = 0.002;
}
```

(handwritten annotation: no lights, objects, etc. yet)

(handwritten annotation: statistics counters)

```
/*

            init_color() = Sets up default color data

*/

void init_color(void)
{
  def.col_data.trans   = Vector();
  def.col_data.mirror  = Vector();
  def.col_data.amb     = Vector(25,25,25);
  def.col_data.diff    = Vector(48,27,9);
  def.col_data.density = Vector(.01, .01, .01);
  def.col_data.index   = CNUM;
  def.col_data.dither  = 3;
  def.col_data.reflect = 0;
  def.col_data.sreflect = 10;
  def.shadow        = TRUE;
}


/*

            Overload of '=' operator for Object class


*/

Object Object::operator=(Object & rvalue)
{
  type = rvalue.type;
  strcpy(name,rvalue.name);
  loc = rvalue.loc;
  vect1 = rvalue.vect1;
  vect2 = rvalue.vect2;
  vect3 = rvalue.vect3;
  lower = rvalue.lower;
  upper = rvalue.upper;
  norm = rvalue.norm;
  cterm = rvalue.cterm;
  yterm = rvalue.yterm;
  xmult = rvalue.xmult;
  ymult = rvalue.ymult;
  n1 = rvalue.n1;
```

```
    len1 = rvalue.len1;
    len2 = rvalue.len2;
    cos1 = rvalue.cos1;
    sin1 = rvalue.sin1;
    cos2 = rvalue.cos2;
    sin2 = rvalue.sin2;
    col_data = rvalue.col_data;
    nextobj = rvalue.nextobj;
    child = rvalue.child;
    pattern = rvalue.pattern;
    remove = rvalue.remove;
    return *this;
}


/*
        Overload of '=' operator for color_data class

*/

color_data color_data::operator=(color_data & rvalue)
{
    amb = rvalue.amb;
    diff = rvalue.diff;
    mirror = rvalue.mirror;
    trans = rvalue.trans;
    density = rvalue.density;
    reflect = rvalue.reflect;
    index = rvalue.index;
    sreflect = rvalue.sreflect;
    dither = rvalue.dither;
    return *this;
}
/*
        Function to display ray tracing statistics

*/

void World_Stats()
{
        printf(
"                                                    \n");
        printf(
"||                                                ||\n");
```

```
        printf(
" ||                     World Statistics                    ||\n");
        printf(
" ||                                                         ||\n");
        printf(
" ||   Objects:                    %4d                       ||\n",
          WORLD.objcount);
        printf(
" ||   Lamps:                       %4d                      ||\n",
          WORLD.lampcount);
        printf(
" ||   Intersect tests:            %8ld                      ||\n",
          WORLD.intersect_tests);
        printf(
" ||   Total intersections:        %8ld                      ||\n",
          WORLD.ray_intersects + WORLD.bbox_intersects);
        printf(
" ||   Object intersections:       %8ld                      ||\n",
          WORLD.ray_intersects);
        printf(
" ||   Bounding Box intersections:      %8ld                 ||\n",
          WORLD.bbox_intersects);
        printf(
" ||   Rays traced:                %8ld                      ||\n",
          WORLD.primary_traced + WORLD.to_lamp +WORLD.refl_trans);
        printf(
" ||       Primary:                %8ld                      ||\n",
          WORLD.primary_traced);
        printf(
" ||       To lamps:               %8ld                      ||\n",
          WORLD.to_lamp);
        printf(
" ||     Reflected or Transmitted:  %8ld                     ||\n",
            WORLD.refl_trans);
        printf(
" ||   Pattern matches:            %8ld                      ||\n",
            WORLD.pattern_matches);
        printf(
" ||   Data set to file:           %12s                      ||\n",
```

```
        WORLD.outfile);
        printf(
```

" || ||\n");

" | p   r   i   n   t   f   (|\n");

```
}

/*
```

```
┌─────────────────────────────────────────────┐
│      Function to open file and enter image size      │
└─────────────────────────────────────────────┘
```

```
*/

void Open_File()
{
  if ((WORLD.filept=fopen(WORLD.outfile,"wb"))==NULL)
  {
        cout << "Unable to open output file";
        exit(1);
  }
  fputc((unsigned char)(XSIZE &  0xff),WORLD.filept);
  fputc((unsigned char)(XSIZE >> 8),   WORLD.filept);
  fputc((unsigned char)(YSIZE &  0xff),WORLD.filept);
  fputc((unsigned char)(YSIZE >> 8),   WORLD.filept);
}

/*
```

```
┌─────────────────────────────────────────────┐
│         Function to close output file         │
└─────────────────────────────────────────────┘
```

```
*/

void Close_File()
{
  if (fclose(WORLD.filept))
  {
        cout << "Unable to close output file";
        exit(1);
```

```
    }
  }


  /*
```

```
┌─────────────────────────────────────────────────────────────┐
│                    Main Program for Ray Tracer                │
└─────────────────────────────────────────────────────────────┘
```

```
  */

main()
{
  Object *test, *test2;

  cout <<
"
```

```
  ╔═══════════════════════════════════════════════════╗        ||
                                                              ||\n";
  cout <<
" ||                                                   ||\n";
  cout <<
" ||          Simplified Ray Tracing Program           ||\n";
  cout <<
" ||                                                   ||\n";
  cout <<
" ||        By Roger T. Stevens - January 6, 1990      ||\n";
  cout <<
" ||                                                   ||\n";
  cout <<
" ||          Command Line: render < filename          ||\n";
  cout <<
" ||                                                   ||\n";
  cout <<
 ||                                                    ||\n";
  ╚═══════════════════════════════════════════════════╝
```

```
  init_world();
  init_color();
```

```
if (!LoadWorld())
{
   cout << "Syntax error in loading world\n";
   exit(1);
}
Make_Bbox(WORLD.stack);      /* make bboxes */   makes boxes for
fclose(stdin);                                    each indiv. at shot B —
cout << "\nImage size:  " << XSIZE <<" pixels horizontal by "
        << YSIZE << " pixels vertical.\n";
cout << "\nFile name is: "<< WORLD.outfile << "\n";
Open_File();
Trace_Scene();
Close_File();
World_Stats();
fclose(stdout);
return(NULL);
}
```

Figure 6-1. Listing of render.cpp

Following this, we have the function *World_Stats,* used to print out some statistics about the ray tracing process. These statistics are gathered during the rendering process and are printed out at the completion of the rendering program.

The function *Open_File* opens the data file for the output data. The file name is that which was read in from the input data. If the file cannot be opened an error message is displayed and the program terminates. Otherwise, we immediately write to the file the information on the pixel size of the display in the x and y directions.

Next comes the function *Close_File,* which simply closes the data file. If it cannot be closed, an error message is displayed and the program terminates.

Main Rendering Program

Finally, we come to the main rendering program, which controls the calling of all other functions to render the scene. It begins by displaying a header that shows how the program should be called up. Next, the functions *init_world* and *init_color* are called to provide initialization. The *LoadWorld* function is then called to load in all of the information about the scene from the data file.

Following this, we call the function *Make_Bbox*. This function creates the bounding boxes, wherever one was called for by the input data. After making the boxes, the input data file is closed. The program displays pixel size and the name of the file used to store the output data. The size information is the latest received from the input data file, if such information existed; otherwise the default values will be displayed. Next *Open_File* is called to open the output data file. The function *Trace_Scene* is then called. This function supervises all of the ray tracing activity, including storing the final data to the output file. When the ray tracing has been completed, *Close_File* is called to close the output data file. We then call *World_Stats* to display the statistics that were collected during the ray tracing process. After this, the program terminates.

CHAPTER 7

Ray Tracing Rendering Interfaces

The first major problem that is encountered in designing a ray tracer is determining the proper method of communicating the data describing the scene to the program. This includes descriptions of primitive objects (spheres, parallelograms and quadratics), information on patterns applied to surfaces, a description of background or sky, a definition of light sources which illuminate the picture, and the position of the camera or observer. It would certainly be ideal if there was a standard adopted for every interface with a ray tracing program. Unfortunately, this is not the case. There seem to be about as many ways of defining the data for a scene as there are ray tracing programs. We will discuss a few of the different interface methods used and then go on to develop our own interface software.

Standard Procedural Database

A good place to start is with the Standard Procedural Database. This was proposed by Eric Haines in an article "A Proposal for Standard Graphics Environments" in the November 1987 issue of *IEEE Computer Graphics and Applications*. Haines suggests that various rendering programs can be compared for quality and efficiency through testing on a number of standard scenes. He has prepared software to generate data files for each of the standard scenes. An MS-DOS format disk containing this software is available for $5.00 from:

MicroDoc
c/o F. W. Pospeschil
3108 Jackson Street
Bellevue, Nebraska 68005

Some of these standard displays are beyond the capabilities of the simple ray tracer described in this book. (They were designed for use with ray tracers associated with work stations, minicomputers, or mainframes.) However, many of the standard displays can be simplified enough to produce workable data files for our ray tracing program. One good aspect of Haines software is that source code is provided in C and can be easily modified to create a data file in whatever format you decide is necessary for interfacing. I wrote a program to transform one of these data files to the format used in the ray tracer described in this book. The resultant data listing required some message to produce Plate 8. Right now, we are interested in the format that Haines creates with his software. A partial listing of one of his data files is given in Figure 7-1. This format is fairly obscure. You can guess that the first few lines define the observer's position and that each line beginning with an s defines a sphere. However, if you are attempting to look at the data file and determine something about the scene, you may find it rough sledding.

The RenderMan Interface

Pixar of San Rafael, California has developed the RenderMan interface, which is a comprehensive interface for use between data files and ray tracing programs. They propose this as an industry standard, and already the standard has had considerable acceptance among designers of graphics programs for work station use. A copy of the interface documentation is available for $15.00 from:

Pixar
3240 Kerner Blvd.
San Rafael, California 94901

The current implementation of the RenderMan interface is a set of C language functions which cover just about anything you might want to transfer to a ray tracing program. Figure 7-2 is a list of the RenderMan functions. Each function passes some set of parameters to the ray tracing program. These parameters are defined in detail in the RenderMan interface documentation.

```
v
from 2.1 1.3 1.7
at 0 0 0
up 0 0 1
angle 45
hither 1
resolution 512 512
b 0.078 0.361 0.753
1 4 3 2
1 1 -4 4
1 -3 1 5
f 1 0.75 0.33 1 0 0 0 0
p4
12 12 -0.5
-12 12 -0.5
-12 -12 -0.5
12 -12 -0.5
f 1 0.9 0.7 0.5 3 0 0
s 0 0 0 0.5
s 0.272166 0.272166 0.544331 0.166667
s 0.420314 0.420314 0.618405 0.0555556
s 0.461844 0.304709 0.43322 0.0555556
s 0.304079 0.461844 0.43322 0.0555556
s 0.230635 0.38777 0.729516 0.0555556
s 0.115031 0.4293 0.544331 0.0555556
s 0.082487 0.239622 0.655442 0.0555556
s 0.38777 0.230635 0.729516 0.0555556
. . . . . .
```

Figure 7-1. Partial Listing of a Ray Tracing Data File

It turns out that the RenderMan interface has found a solid niche in the realm of work stations, particularly in interfacing between programs like AutoCad and ray tracing programs designed to convert the graphics outputs into realistic three-dimensional scenes. When one closely examines the RenderMan interface, it does a fine job in this particular area. However, it doesn't claim to provide all the three-dimensional functions which might be appropriate to a large mainframe with higher speeds and more memory than in a work station. On the other hand, Pixar insists that a RenderMan program incorporate all aspects of the

RenderMan interface, which is pushing the limits of a PC. Pixar believes that rendering programs using their interface should be able to handle complicated scenes with 10,000 to 1,000,000 primitives. Your ordinary PC is just not going to be able to do this.

RiAtmosphere(name, parameterlist)	sets the atmosphere shader.
RiAreaLightSource(name, parameterlist)	creates an area light.
RiAttributeBegin()	pushes current set of attributes.
RiAttributeEnd()	pops current set of attributes.
RiBasis(ubasis, vbasis)	sets the basis matrices that define patches.
RiBegin(name)	begins the graphics state.
RiBound(bound)	sets the bound for a bounding box.
RiClipping(near, far)	sets near and far clipping planes.
RiColorSamples(n, nRGB, RGBn)	sets number of color components used in specifying colors.
RiColor(color)	sets an object color.
RiConcatTransform(transform)	concatenate transform onto the current transformation.
RiCone(height,radius,thetamax, parameterlist)	sets parameters for a cone.
RiCoordinateSystem(space)	establishes a special coordinate system.
RiCropWindow(xmin,xmax,ymin,ymax)	renders only a subrectangle of the image.
RiCylinder(radius,zmin,zmax,thetamax, parameterlist)	sets parameters for a cylinder.

RiDeclare(name,declaration)	declares name and type of a variable.
RiDeformation(name,parameterlist)	concatenate the named deformation shader onto the current transformation.
RiDepthOfField(fstop,focallength, focaldistance)	sets the camera lens parameters.
RiDetailRange(minvisible, lowertransition, uppertransition,maxvisible)	sets the current detail range.
RiDetail(bound)	sets the current detail to the area of the bounding box.
RiDisk(height,radius,thetamax, parameterlist)	sets the parameters for a disk.
RiDisplacement(name,parameterlist)	sets the current displacement shader.
RiDisplay(name,type,mode)	sets display name, type and mode.
RiEnd()	end of graphics state.
RiErrorMode(mode,handler)	sets the error handling mode.
RiExposure(gain,gamma)	controls sensitivity and non-linearity of exposure process.
RiExterior(name,parameterlist)	sets current exterior volume shader.
RiFormat(xresolution,yresolution, pixelaspectratio)	sets resolution and aspect ratio.
RiFrameAspectRatio(frameaspectratio)	sets frame aspect ratio.
RiFrameBegin(frame)	start of frame.
RiFrameEnd()	end of frame.
RiGeneralPolygon(nloops,nverts, parameterlist)	define general concave polygon.

RiGeometricApproximation(type,value)   method of approximating a small surface element.

RiGeometry(type,parameterlist)   defines an implementation-specific geometric primitive.

RiHider(type,parameterlist)   controls hidden surface algorithm.

RiHyperboloid(point1,point2,thetamax, parameterlist)   defines a hyperboloid.

RiIdentity()   set current transformation to identity.

RiIlluminate(light,onoff)   add or remove an area light source to the list.

RiImager(name,parameterlist)   select an imager function.

RiInterior(name,parameterlist)   sets the current interior volume shader.

RiLightSource(name,parameterlist)   add a non-area light source to the list.

RiMakeBump(picturename,texturename, swrap,twrap,filterfunc,swidth, twidth,parameterlist)   convert a height field image into a bump map file.

RiMakeCubeFaceEnvironment(px,nx,py, ny,pz,nz,texturefile,fov, filterfunc,swidth,twidth, parameterlist)   project environment onto six cube faces.

RiMakeLattLongEnvironment(picturefile, texturefile,filterfunc,swidth, twidth,parameterlist)   convert an image into a latitude-longitude map.

RiMakeShadow(picturefile,texturefile, parameterlist)   convert a depth image file

	into a shadow map.
RiMakeTexture(picturename,texturename, swrap, twrap, filterfunc, swidth, twidth,parameterlist)	convert an image into a texture file.
RiMatte()	indicates that subsequent objects are matte objects.
RiMotionBegin(n,t0,t1,...,tn)	start the definition of a moving primitive.
RiMotionEnd()	end the definition of a moving primitive.
RiNuPatch(nu,uorder,uknot,umin, umax,nv,vorder,vknot,vmin,vmax, parameterlist.	create a B-spline surface patch.
RiObjectBegin()	start object definition.
RiObjectEnd()	end object definition.
RiOpacity(color)	set the current color.
RiOption(name,parameterlist)	set implementation-specific option.
RiOrientation(orientation)	sets orientation to right-handed or left-handed.
RiParaboloid(rmax,zmin,zmax,thetamax, parameterlist)	defines a paraboloid.
RiPatchMesh(type,nu,uwrap,nustep,nv, vwrap,nvstep,parameterlist)	specifies a quadralateral mesh of patches.
RiPatch(type, parameterlist)	defines a single patch.
RiPerspective(fov)	concatenates a perspective transformation onto the current transformation.
RiPixelFidelity(variation)	sets the amount image values can deviate from true values.

RiPixelFilter(filterfunc,xwidth, ywidth)	sets antialiasing filter.
RiPixelSamples(xsamples,ysamples)	sets sampling rate.
RiPointsGeneralPolygons(npolys,nloops, nverts,verts,parameterlist)	defines general polygons.
RiPointsPolygons(npolys,nverts,verts, parameterlist)	defines polygons.
RiPolygon(nverts,parameterlist)	sets no. of vertices for polygon
RiProcedural(data,bound,subdividefunc, freefunc)	defines a procedural function.
RiProjection(name,parameterlist)	sets type of projection.
RiQuantize(type,one,min,max, dditheramplitude)	sets the quantization parameters.
RiRelativeDetail(relativedetail)	sets relative level of detail.
RiReverseOrientation()	causes current orientation to be toggled.
RiRotate(angle,dx,dy,dz)	concatenates a rotation onto the current transformation.
RiScale(sx, sy, sz)	concatenates a scaling onto the current transformation.
RiScreenWindow(left,right,top,bottom)	defines a window.
RiShadingInterpolation(type)	controls shading.
RiShadingRate(size)	sets current shading rate.
RiShutter(min,max)	sets times that shutter opens and closes.
RiSides(sides)	determines whether surfaces are one or two-sided.
RiSkew(angle,dx1,dy1,dz1,dx2,dy2,dz2)	concatenates a skew

	onto the current transformation.
RiSolidBegin(operation)	defines beginning of a solid.
RiSolidEnd()	defines end of a solid.
RiSphere(radius,zmin,zmax,thetamax, parameterlist)	defines a sphere.
RiSurface(name,parameterlist)	sets the surface shader.
RiTextureCoordinates(s1,t1,s2,t2,s3,t3, s4,t4)	sets the current set of texture coordinates.
RiTorus(majorradius,minorradius,phimin, phimax,thetamax,parameterlist)	defines a torus.
RiTransformBegin()	saves the current transformation.
RiTransformEnd()	restores the last transformation that was saved.
RiTransformPoints(space,points,n)	transforms an array of points from the coordinate system space to the current coordinate system.
RiTransform(transform)	sets the current transformation.
RiTranslate(dx,dy,dz)	concatenates a translation onto the current transformation.
RiTrimCurve(order,knot,min,max,n,u,v,w)	sets the current trim curve.
RiWorldBegin()	begins the rendering process.
RiWorldEnd()	ends the rendering process.

Figure 7-2. The RenderMan Interface Procedures

When setting up a standard, it is not a good idea to try to make the standard be all things to all people. Pixar is wise in not trying to make the RenderMan interface equally applicable to PC's and mainframes. Pixar does have a piece of software called PhotoRealistic RenderMan, which works on a PC, but it requires a 386 machine having a 387 math coprocessor and at least two megabytes of memory. Not everyone has such a high-powered computer readily available. In any case, the RenderMan interface seems to be overkill for the simple ray tracer described in this book. Furthermore, casting everything in the C language fails to take advantage of the natural improvements available for this type of operation using C++. So we need to look further.

The QRT Input Language

Steve Koren has developed a Quick Ray Tracing (hence QRT) program for the IBM and compatible PC, which is available on many bulletin boards. This program includes an input language which is simple and highly descriptive. Figure 9-1 is a sample data file using the QRT input language. It is fairly easy to understand without studying the details. Since Koren has several good demonstrations available with his package, it seemed like a good idea to develop an interface program capable of reading his data files. However, there are some problems with the way the QRT program reads the data. In particular, the parser is so designed that it goes bananas if it encounters a non-displayable character. One example of this is that all spacings in the QRT data, while completely flexible, must be defined by space characters. If you attempt to use a tab, the parser will reject it as an illegal character. Also, in order to use C++, we need to treat the data in an entirely different way when we get it into the program. However, our goal is to retain enough compatibility to be able to read QRT data files.

Striking Out on Our Own

Having looked at a few interface techniques, it is time to design our own. In the main, we shall attempt reading the QRT language, but will make the format requirements of our parser less stringent than those used by QRT. And we won't hesitate to add additional commands to make things easier. Finally, since the number of primitive objects that are defined is small, the techniques used together with the characteristics of the C++ language make it easy for you to add additional objects and include them as part of the new descriptive language. In the following chapter, we will describe our technique for reading in scene data.

CHAPTER 8

Communicating with the Ray Tracer

Having looked at the advantages and disadvantages of various techniques for transferring data to a ray-tracing program, we can create our own techniques for handling this data to provide maximum flexibility without getting into overkill for the simple ray tracer developed in future chapters. Most of the programs for this job are found in the file called *input.cpp*.

The *input.cpp* File

The *input.cpp* file contains functions used to read and pre-process data from a data file for use in ray-tracing operations. The functions are set up so all data is read from a data file specified when the program is called. The technique is to simply run the program with a command like this:

```
render filename
```

where *render* is the name of our ray-tracing program and *filename* is the name of the file containing the data for the scene you want to render. For convenience, we have assigned the extension *ray* to all files containing scene data, but this is not essential. The *input.cpp* file is listed in Figure 8-1.

Creating the Parser

When one analyzes the content of the QRT input language, it becomes evident that only a few basic parts of each expression are necessary. All of the commas, equals signs, and some of the parentheses, while they contribute to readability, are not needed to properly extract the file content. We distill what has to be checked and produce the parser which forms the function *get_string*, which is listed as part of *input.cpp* in Figure 8-1. The function begins by getting

101

a character from the input data file. It converts this character to upper case lettering. If the comment flag is zero, it checks to see if the character is a letter, a number, a decimal point, a minus sign, or a right parenthesis. These are the only acceptable characters for the beginning of a string. The letters and numbers can be the beginning of a name; the decimal point and minus sign can be the beginning of a numeric quantity. If an acceptable character is encountered, it is placed as the first character in the string buffer; if the character is not acceptable, it is ignored. Two other characters are checked, the right and left curly brackets. If the left curly bracket is encountered, the comment flag is set to one; if the right, zero. Once the flag is set, all characters are ignored until the flag is reset, so that any comments between curly brackets are ignored.

Once an acceptable starting character is encountered, the function loops to read up to 30 more characters. If the initial character was a right parenthesis, the string is terminated. Each character read is converted to upper case and checked to see if it is a letter, a number, an underscore, or a period. These are the only acceptable characters for the part of a string other than the first character. If the character is acceptable, it is added to the string; if not, the string is terminated.

Next, the function checks the string it has created against an array of acceptable strings. If a match is encountered, the function terminates, returning the number of the matching string in the array. If no match is found, the last number (which doesn't correspond to any matching string location) is returned.

Finally, there is a display message of the string and its type. This message is normally commented out, but if you are having real trouble getting a data file to read, you can recompile with this message in the program and locate exactly where your difficulty is.

Loading the World

Now that we have a working parser, we are ready to load the computer's world.

At the beginning of the *input.cpp* file, you will see the function *LoadWorld*, but it is not very interesting. All it does is call the function *get_data*, place the return address from this function in *WORLD.stack*, and return a TRUE.

The *get_data* function scans right down through the entire scene data file, collecting inputs and processing them, until an error occurs or the file comes to an end. The first thing that this function does is to return a NULL if the file end has already been encountered (the file is empty). If there is some file data, the function goes into a *while* loop and begins its work by using the parser to read the first data string from the file. It then sets the parameter *found* to FALSE.

As we progress through the remainder of this loop, we check to determine whether the type of string we obtained corresponds to any of the recognized types that we expect to see. Whenever we encounter a match, *found* is set to TRUE. If we get to the end of the loop and *found* is still FALSE, we print out a syntax error message and exit from the program. We have already pointed out that we are going to quit this loop if we come to the end of the data file. However, we will sometimes be using *get_data* when we want it to cease operation before we hit the end of file. In this case, we place a NULL at the appropriate place in the data file. So the first thing we do after getting a string with the parser is check whether it is a NULL string. If it is, we return from the *get_data* function immediately.

The *get_data* function is going to process four different kinds of inputs. The first of these is *attribute*. This type of input includes lamp characteristics, observer characteristics, patterns, etc. The second type of input is an *instance*. An *instance* is a user-defined object, consisting of a group of primitive objects used at different places in the scene. The third kind of data concerns *bounding boxes*. When the data specifies a bounding box, the program must generate a box around all the objects listed within the box. The fourth kind of data is *objects*. These are the primitives that compose the scene.

Figure 8-1. The input.cpp File*

```
/*
        input.cpp = Functions to read data from disk file

                By Roger T. Stevens - 3/22/90
*/

#include <ctype.h>
#include <string.h>
#include <stdio.h>
#include <stdlib.h>
#include <math.h>
#include <conio.h>
#include "render.hpp"

char string_types[128][32] =
{"PATT_HEADER","LINE","SPHERE","PARALLELOGRAM","TRIANGLE","LAMP",
    "OBSERVER","GROUND","SKY","BBOX","RING","QUADRATIC","BEGIN_BBO
    ","END_BBOX","BEGIN_INSTANCES","END_INSTANCES","AMB","DIFF",
    "MIRROR","TRANS","DENSITY","INDEX","DITHER","SREFLECT",
    "REFLECT","LOC","RADIUS","PATTERN","REMOVE","XMULT","YMULT",
    "NAME","DIST","LOOKAT","V1","V2","ZENITH","HORIZ","RAD_1",
    "RAD_2","A","B","C","D","E","XMAX","YMAX","ZMAX","XMIN","YMIN"
    ,"ZMIN","DIR","FOC_LENGTH","FIRST_SCAN","DEFAULT","FILE_NAME",
    "LAST_SCAN","XRES","YRES","X_SIZE","Y_SIZE","START_X","START_Y
    ","END_X","END_Y",")","NO_SHADOW","NO_LAMP","THRESHOLD","UP",
    "INSTANCE_OF","SCALE","RECTANGLE","CIRCLE","POLYGON","COLOR",
    "POINT","CONE","HEIGHT","FRACTAL","DIMENSION","SCALAR",NULL};

char string_buf[32];
char name[32];
FILE *fget;

/*
        LoadWorld() = Loads the World with data from stdin
*/
```

```
extern int linenumber;

int LoadWorld()
{
  fget = fopen(file_in,"rb");
  WORLD.stack=get_data();
  return(TRUE);
  fclose(fget);
}
```

```
/*

      get_data() = Gets data from stdin and places it in World

*/
```

```
Object * get_data()
{
  Object * queue, * temp;
  BBox * newobj;
  Vector loc,rad,d,v3, upper, lower;
  int found,type;
  name[0] = NULL; queue=NULL;
  loc = Vector();
  rad = Vector();
  d = Vector();
  v3 = Vector();
  upper = Vector();
  lower = Vector();
  if (feof(fget)) return(NULL);
  while (!feof(fget))
  {
      type = get_string(string_buf);
      if (strcmp(string_buf,NULL)==0)
         return(queue);
      found = FALSE;
      if (GetAttrib(type,string_buf))
      {
          found = TRUE;
        if (name[0] == NULL)
          continue;
```

```
      type = get_string(string_buf);
      if (type != BEGIN_BBOX)
      {
        cout << "Error: Name must be followed << "by
              'BEGIN_BBOX'\n";
        exit(1);
      }
  }
  switch(type)
  {
    case BEGIN_INSTANCES:
      found = TRUE;
      WORLD.instances = get_data();
      break;
    case END_INSTANCES:
      found = TRUE;
      return(queue);
      break;
    case END_BBOX:
      found = TRUE;
      return(queue);
      break;
    case BEGIN_BBOX:
      newobj = new BBox;
      strcpy(newobj->name,name);
      newobj->type = BBOX;
      newobj->child = get_data();
      newobj->nextobj = queue;
      queue = newobj;
      found = TRUE;
      break;
  }
  if (type == FRACTAL)
  {
    if ((temp=Get_Object(type,queue))!=NULL)
    {
      found = TRUE;
      queue = temp;
    }
  }
  else
```

```
    {
      if ((temp=Get_Object(type,queue))!=NULL)
      {
        found = TRUE;
        temp->nextobj=queue;
        queue = temp;
      }
    }
    if (!found && !feof(fget))
    {
        cout << "Syntax error in reading input data: " <<
            string_buf  << "\n";
        exit(1);
    }
  }
  return(queue);
}


/*
```

```
          get_string() = Reads a string of data from fget
```

```
*/

int get_string(char string_buf[])
{
  char ch;
  int flag = 0,i,result,test;

  string_buf[0] = NULL;
  result = last_no;
  while (!feof(fget))
  {
      ch = toupper(fgetc(fget));
      if (flag == 0)
      {
              if ((isalnum(ch)) || (ch == '.') || (ch == '-') ||
                  (ch == ')'))
              {
                  string_buf[0] = ch;
                  break;
              }
```

```
                else
                {
                        if (ch == '{')
                                flag = 1;
                }
        }
        else
                        if (ch == '}')
                                flag = 0;
    }
    for (i=1; i<32; i++)
    {
        if (ch == ')')
        {
                        string_buf[1] = NULL;
                        break;
        }
        ch = toupper(fgetc(fget));
        if ((isalnum(ch)) || (ch == '_') || (ch == '.'))
                        string_buf[i] = ch;
        else
        {
                        string_buf[i] = NULL;
                        break;
        }
    }
    for (i=0; i<last_no; i++)
    {
        if (strcmp(string_buf,string_types[i]) == 0)
        {
                        result = i;
                        break;
        }
    }
//      cout << "String buffer contains: " << string_buf <<
//          " which is type " << result << "\n";

    return(result);
}
```

```
/*
┌─────────────────────────────────────────────────────────┐
│                                                           │
│   Get_Attrib() = Gets attribute other than object from fget │
│                                                           │
└─────────────────────────────────────────────────────────┘
*/

int GetAttrib(int Type,char string_buf[])
{
    int i,type=0,no_param=0,found=TRUE
    Vector loc,look;
    float radius, distance;
    Lamp * lamps;

    switch(Type)
    {
      case SKY:
            found = TRUE;
            while (type != PAREN && !feof(fget))
            {
                type = get_string(string_buf);
                switch(type)
                {
                  case ZENITH:
                    WORLD.skycolor_zenith.get_vector();
                    WORLD.skycolor_zenith =
                        WORLD.skycolor_zenith * (float)CNUM;
                    break;
                  case HORIZ:
                    WORLD.skycolor_horiz.get_vector();
                    WORLD.skycolor_horiz =
                        WORLD.skycolor_horiz * (float)CNUM;
                    break;
                  case DITHER:
                    get_string(string_buf);
                    WORLD.sky_dither =
                        fabs(atof(string_buf));
                    break;
                  case PAREN:
                    break;
                  default:
                    found = FALSE;
                }
```

```
        }
        break;
        case COLOR:
        while (type != PAREN && !feof(fget))
        {
            type = get_string(string_buf);
            found = get_color_data(type,&def.col_data);
            if (type == PAREN)
            {
                found = TRUE;
                break;
            }
            if (!found)
            {
                cout << "Undefined parameter " <<string_buf
                    << "while loading color data in
                    'input.cpp'";
                exit(1);
            }
        }
        break;
        case FOC_LENGTH:
        get_string(string_buf);
        WORLD.flength = fabs(atof(string_buf));
        WORLD.flength *= 5
        break;
    case FILE_NAME:
        get_string(string_buf);
        strcpy(WORLD.outfile,string_buf);
        break;
    case LAMP:
        distance = 150;
        while (type != PAREN && !feof(fget))
        {
            type = get_string(string_buf);
            found = TRUE;
            switch(type)
            {
                case LOC:
                    loc.get_vector();
                    no_param |= 1;
                    break;
```

```
                case RADIUS:
                    get_string(string_buf);
                    radius = fabs(atof(string_buf));
                    break;
                case DIST:
                    get_string(string_buf);
                    distance = fabs(atof(string_buf));
                    break;
                case PAREN:
                    break;
                default:
                    found = FALSE;
            }
            if (!found)
            {
                cout << "Undefined parameter " << string_buf
                    << " while loading lamp in
                        'input.cpp'";
                exit(1);
            }
        }
        if (no_param < 1)
        {
            cout << "Too few parameters for lamp in
                'input.cpp'";
            exit(1);
        }
        lamps = new Lamp;
        lamps->loc = loc;
        lamps->radius = radius;
        lamps->distance = distance;
        lamps->next_lamp = WORLD.lamps;
        WORLD.lamps = lamps;
        WORLD.lampcount++;
        break;
    case OBSERVER:
        look = Vector(200,50,0);
        found = TRUE;
        while (type != PAREN && !feof(fget))
        {
            type = get_string(string_buf);
            switch(type)
```

```
            {
                    case LOC:
                        WORLD.obsloc.get_vector();
                        no_param |= 1;
                        break;
                    case LOOKAT:
                        look.get_vector();
                        no_param |= 2;
                        break;
                    case UP:
                        WORLD.obsup.get_vector();
                        break;
                    case PAREN:
                        break;
                    default:
                        found = FALSE;
            }
        if (!found)
        {
                cout << "Undefined parameter " << string_buf
                  << " while loading observer in
                  'input.cpp'";
                exit(1);
        }
    }
    WORLD.obsdir = look - WORLD.obsloc;
    WORLD.obsdir = ~WORLD.obsdir;
    WORLD.obsright = WORLD.obsup ^ WORLD.obsdir;
    WORLD.obsup = WORLD.obsdir ^ WORLD.obsright;
    WORLD.obsup = ~WORLD.obsup;
    WORLD.obsright = ~WORLD.obsright;
    if (no_param != 3)
    {
        cout << "Too few parameters for observer " << "in
          'input.cpp'";
        exit(1);
    }
    break;
case PAttern:
    GetPattern();
    break;
```

```
        case XRES:
            get_string(string_buf);
            XSIZE = fabs(atof(string_buf));
            CENTERX = XSIZE / 2;
            XSIZE4 = XSIZE / 4;
            break;
        case YRES:
            get_string(string_buf);
            YSIZE = fabs(atof(string_buf));
            WORLD.last_scan = YSIZE - 1;
            CENTERY = YSIZE / 2;
            break;
        case NAME:
            get_string(name);
            break;
        default:
            found = FALSE;
    }
    return(found);
}


/*

      get_color_data = Gets the color information from a file


*/

int get_color_data(int type, color_data * col_data)
{
    int found = TRUE;
    char string_buf[32];
    switch(type)
    {
        case AMB:
            col_data->amb.get_vector();
            col_data->amb = col_data->amb * (float)CNUM;
            break;
        case DIFF:
            col_data->diff.get_vector();
            col_data->diff = (col_data->diff) * (float)CNUM;
            break;
```

```
        case MIRROR:
            col_data->mirror.get_vector();
            col_data->mirror = col_data->mirror * (float)CNUM;
            break;
        case TRANS:
            col_data->trans.get_vector();
            col_data->trans = col_data->trans * (float)CNUM;
            break;
        case DENSITY:
            col_data->density.get_vector();
            col_data->density = col_data->density * (float)CNUM;
            break;
        case INDEX:
            get_string(string_buf);
            col_data->index = fabs(atof(string_buf));
            break;
        case DITHER:
            get_string(string_buf);
            col_data->dither = fabs(atof(string_buf));
            break;
        case SREFLECT:
            get_string(string_buf);
            col_data->sreflect = fabs(atof(string_buf));
            break;
        case REFLECT:
            get_string(string_buf);
            col_data->reflect = atof(string_buf)*CNUM;
            break;
        default:
            found = FALSE;
    }
    return(found);
}

/*
    ┌─────────────────────────────────────────────────────────────────┐
    │ GetSphere()=Load a sphere from fget and return pointer to it      │
    └─────────────────────────────────────────────────────────────────┘
*/

Object * GetSphere()
{
```

```
Sphere * newobj;
int type=0,no_param = 0, found;
float temp;

newobj = new Sphere;
newobj->col_data = new color_data;
*newobj->col_data = def.col_data;
while (type != PAREN && !feof(fget))
{
   type = get_string(string_buf);
   found = get_color_data(type,newobj->col_data);
   if (found == TRUE)
   continue;
   found = TRUE;
   switch(type)
{
     case LOC:
         newobj->loc.get_vector();
         no_param |= 1;
         break;
     case RADIUS:
         get_string(string_buf);
         temp = fabs(atof(string_buf));newobj->vect1 =
             Vector(temp,0,0);
         no_param |= 2;
         break;
     case PAttern:
         newobj->pattern=Attach_Pattern();
         break;
     case REMOVE:
         newobj->remove=Attach_Pattern();
         break;
     case XMULT:
         get_string(string_buf);
         newobj->xmult = fabs(atof(string_buf));
         break;
     case YMULT:
         get_string(string_buf);
         newobj->ymult = fabs(atof(string_buf));
         break;
     case NAME:
         get_string(newobj->name);
```

```
                break;
           case PAREN:
                break;
           default:
                found = FALSE;
     }
     if (!found)
     {
          cout << "Undefined parameter " << string_buf << " while
              loading sphere in 'input.cpp'";
          exit(1);
     }
   }
   if (no_param != 3)
     {
          cout << "Too few parameters for sphere in 'input.cpp'";
          exit(1);
     }
   newobj->n1 = newobj->vect1.x * newobj->vect1.x;
   WORLD.objcount++;
   return(newobj);
}


/*
┌──────────────────────────────────────────────────────────┐
│ GetTriangle() = Load a triangle from fget and return       │
│                    pointer to it                           │
└──────────────────────────────────────────────────────────┘
*/

Object * GetTriangle()
{
    Triangle * newobj;
    int type=0,no_param = 0, found;
    float temp;

    newobj = new Triangle;
    newobj->col_data = new color_data;
    *newobj->col_data = def.col_data;
    while (type != PAREN && !feof(fget))
    {
      type = get_string(string_buf);
      found = get_color_data(type,newobj->col_data);
```

```c
if (found == TRUE)
continue;
found = TRUE;
switch(type)
{
  case LOC:
      newobj->loc.get_vector();
      no_param |= 1;
      break;
  case V1:
      newobj->vect1.get_vector();
      no_param |= 2;
      break;
  case V2:
      newobj->vect2.get_vector();
      no_param |= 4;
      break;
  case PAttern:
      newobj->pattern=Attach_Pattern();
      break;
  case REMOVE:
      newobj->remove=Attach_Pattern();
      break;
  case XMULT:
      get_string(string_buf);
      newobj->xmult = fabs(atof(string_buf));
      break;
  case YMULT:
      get_string(string_buf);
      newobj->ymult = fabs(atof(string_buf));
      break;
  case NAME:
      get_string(newobj->name);
      break;
  case PAREN:
      break;
  default:
      found = FALSE;
}
if (!found)
{
```

```
            cout << "Undefined parameter " << string_buf <<
                " while loading triangle in 'input.cpp'";
            exit(1);
          }
      }
    if (no_param != 7)
        {
            cout << "Too few parameters for triangle in 'input.cpp'";
            exit(1);
        }
    newobj->norm = newobj->vect1 ^ newobj->vect2;
    newobj->norm = ~ newobj->norm;
    newobj->n1 = newobj->norm % newobj->loc;
    newobj->len1 = newobj->vect1 % newobj->vect1;
    newobj->len2 = newobj->vect2 % newobj->vect2;
    WORLD.objcount++;
    return(newobj);
}


/*
    ┌─────────────────────────────────────────────────────────────┐
    │  GetRing() = Load a ring from fget and return pointer to it   │
    │                                                               │
    └─────────────────────────────────────────────────────────────┘
*/

Object * GetRing()
{
  Ring * newobj;
  int type=0,no_param = 0, found;
  float temp;

  newobj = new Ring;
  newobj->col_data = new color_data;
  *newobj->col_data = def.col_data;
  while (type != PAREN && !feof(fget))
  {
     type = get_string(string_buf);
     found = get_color_data(type,newobj->col_data);
     if (found == TRUE)
     continue;
     found = TRUE;
     switch(type)
```

```
{
  case LOC:
      newobj->loc.get_vector();
      no_param |= 1;
      break;
  case V1:
      newobj->vect1.get_vector();
      no_param |= 2;
      break;
  case V2:
      newobj->vect2.get_vector();
      no_param |= 4;
      break;
  case RAD_1:
      get_string(string_buf);
      newobj->vect3.x = fabs(atof(string_buf));
      no_param |= 8;
      break;
  case RAD_2:
      get_string(string_buf);
      newobj->vect3.y = fabs(atof(string_buf));
      no_param |= 16;
      break;
  case PAttern:
      newobj->pattern=Attach_Pattern();
      break;
  case REMOVE:
      newobj->remove=Attach_Pattern();
      break;
  case XMULT:
      get_string(string_buf);
      newobj->xmult = fabs(atof(string_buf));
      break;
  case YMULT:
      get_string(string_buf);
      newobj->ymult = fabs(atof(string_buf));
      break;
  case NAME:
      get_string(newobj->name);
      break;
  case PAREN:
      break;
```

```
        default:
            found = FALSE;
    }
    if (!found)
    {
        cout << "Undefined parameter " << string_buf <<
          " while loading ring in 'input.cpp'";
        exit(1);
    }
}
if (no_param != 31)
{
    cout << "Too few parameters for ring in 'input.cpp'";
    exit(1);
}
newobj->vect3.z = 0;
newobj->vect1 = ~ newobj->vect1;
newobj->vect2 = ~ newobj->vect2;
newobj->norm = newobj->vect1 ^ newobj->vect2;
newobj->norm = ~ newobj->norm;
newobj->n1 = newobj->norm % newobj->loc;
newobj->len1 = newobj->vect1 % newobj->vect1;
newobj->len2 = newobj->vect2 % newobj->vect2;
WORLD.objcount++;
return(newobj);
}


/*
```

```
┌─────────────────────────────────────────────────────────┐
│                                                           │
│     GetParallelogram() = Load a parallelogram from fget and│
│                    return pointer to it                    │
│                                                           │
└─────────────────────────────────────────────────────────┘
```

```
*/

Object * GetParallelogram()
{
  Parallelogram * newobj;
  int type=0,no_param = 0, found;
  float temp;

  newobj = new Parallelogram;
  newobj->col_data = new color_data;
  *newobj->col_data = def.col_data;
```

```
while (type != PAREN && !feof(fget))
{
    type = get_string(string_buf);
    found = get_color_data(type,newobj->col_data);
    if (found == TRUE)
    continue;
    found = TRUE;
    switch(type)
    {
        case LOC:
            newobj->loc.get_vector();
            no_param |= 1;
            break;
        case V1:
            newobj->vect1.get_vector();
            no_param |= 2;
            break;
        case V2:
            newobj->vect2.get_vector();
            no_param |= 4;
            break;
        case PAttern:
            newobj->pattern=Attach_Pattern();
            break;
        case REMOVE:
            newobj->remove=Attach_Pattern();
            break;
        case XMULT:
            get_string(string_buf);
            newobj->xmult = fabs(atof(string_buf));
            break;
        case YMULT:
            get_string(string_buf);
            newobj->ymult = fabs(atof(string_buf));
            break;
        case NAME:
            get_string(newobj->name);
            break;
        case PAREN:
            break;
        default:
            found = FALSE;
```

```
        }
    if (!found)
    {
        cout << "Undefined parameter " << string_buf <<
           " while loading parallelogram in 'input.cpp'";
        exit(1);
    }
  }
  if (no_param != 7)
  {
    cout << "Too few parameters for parallelogram in 'input.cpp'";
    exit(1);
  }
  newobj->norm = newobj->vect1 ^ newobj->vect2;
  newobj->norm = ~ newobj->norm;
  newobj->n1 = newobj->norm % newobj->loc;
  newobj->len1 = newobj->vect1 % newobj->vect1;
  newobj->len2 = newobj->vect2 % newobj->vect2;
  WORLD.objcount++;
  return(newobj);

/*

    GetCone() = Load a cone from fget and return pointer to it

*/

Object *GetCone()
{
  Quadratic * newobj;
  int type=0,no_param = 0, found;
  float temp;
  Vector newdir;

  newobj = new Quadratic;
  newobj->col_data = new color_data;
  *newobj->col_data = def.col_data;
  newobj->vect1 = Vector(0,1,0);
  while (type != PAREN && !feof(fget))
  {
        type = get_string(string_buf);
        found = get_color_data(type,newobj->col_data);
```

```
if (found == TRUE)
continue;
found = TRUE;
switch(type)
{
    case LOC:
        newobj->loc.get_vector();
        no_param |= 1;
        break;
    case RADIUS:
        get_string(string_buf);
        newobj->vect2.x = atof(string_buf);
        no_param |= 2;
        break;
    case HEIGHT:
        get_string(string_buf);
        newobj->vect2.z = atof(string_buf);
        no_param |= 4;
        break;
    case DIR:
        newobj->vect1.get_vector();
        break;
    case PAttern:
        newobj->pattern=Attach_Pattern();
        break;
    case REMOVE:
        newobj->remove=Attach_Pattern();
        break;
    case XMULT:
        get_string(string_buf);
        newobj->xmult = fabs(atof(string_buf));
        break;
    case YMULT:
        get_string(string_buf);
        newobj->ymult = fabs(atof(string_buf));
        break;
    case NAME:
        get_string(newobj->name);
        break;
    case PAREN:
        break;
```

```
            default:
                found = FALSE;
        }
        if (!found)
        {
            cout << "Undefined parameter " << string_buf <<
              " while loading cone in 'input.cpp'";
            exit(1);
        }
    }
    if (no_param != 7)
    {
        cout << "Too few parameters for cone in 'input.cpp'";
        exit(1);
    }
    newobj->cterm = 0;
    newobj->lower.x = - newobj->vect2.x;
    newobj->lower.z = - newobj->vect2.x;
    newobj->lower.y = -newobj->vect2.z;
    newobj->upper.x = newobj->vect2.x;
    newobj->upper.z = newobj->vect2.x;
    newobj->upper.y = 0;
    newobj->vect2.x = newobj->vect2.x * newobj->vect2.x;
    newobj->vect2.z = newobj->vect2.z * newobj->vect2.z;
    newobj->vect2.y = -newobj->vect2.x * newobj->vect2.x;
    newobj->vect2.x = newobj->vect2.x * newobj->vect2.z;
    newobj->vect2.z = newobj->vect2.x;
    newobj->vect1 = ~ newobj->vect1;
    temp = newobj->vect1.x * newobj->vect1.x +newobj->vect1.z *
        newobj->vect1.z;
    if (temp == 0)
        newobj->cos1 = 1;
    else
        newobj->cos1 = newobj->vect1.z/sqrt(temp);
        newobj->sin1 = sqrt(1 - newobj->cos1 * newobj->cos1);
    newdir.x = newobj->vect1.x * newobj->cos1 + newobj->vect1.z *
        -newobj->sin1;
    newdir.y = newobj->vect1.y;
    newdir.z = newobj->vect1.x * newobj->sin1 +
        newobj->vect1.z * newobj->cos1;
    temp = newdir.y * newdir.y + newdir.z * newdir.z;
    if (temp == 0)
```

```
        newobj->cos2 = 1;
   else
        newobj->cos2 = newdir.y/sqrt(temp);
   newobj->sin2 = sqrt(1 - newobj->cos2 * newobj->cos2);
   WORLD.objcount++;
   return(newobj);
}


/*
   ┌─────────────────────────────────────────────────────────┐
   │    GetQuadratic() = Load a quadratic surface from fget and │
   │                     return pointer to it                   │
   └─────────────────────────────────────────────────────────┘
*/

Object *GetQuadratic()
{
   Quadratic * newobj;
   int type=0,no_param = 0, found;
   float temp;
   Vector newdir;

   newobj = new Quadratic;
   newobj->col_data = new color_data;
   *newobj->col_data = def.col_data;
   newobj->vect1 = Vector(0,1,0);
   while (type != PAREN && !feof(fget))
   {
        type = get_string(string_buf);
        found = get_color_data(type,newobj->col_data);
        if (found == TRUE)
        continue;
        found = TRUE;
        switch(type)
        {
             case LOC:
                  newobj->loc.get_vector();
                  no_param |= 1;
                  break;
             case A:
                  get_string(string_buf);
                  newobj->vect2.x = atof(string_buf);
                  no_param |= 2;
```

```
        break;
    case B:
        get_string(string_buf);
        newobj->vect2.y = atof(string_buf);
        no_param |= 4;
        break;
    case C:
        get_string(string_buf);
        newobj->vect2.z = atof(string_buf);
        no_param |= 8;
        break;
    case D:
        get_string(string_buf);
        newobj->cterm = atof(string_buf);
        no_param |= 16;
        break;
    case E:
        get_string(string_buf);
        newobj->yterm = atof(string_buf);
        no_param |= 32;
        break;
    case XMIN:
        get_string(string_buf);
        newobj->lower.x = atof(string_buf);
        break;
    case XMAX:
        get_string(string_buf);
        newobj->upper.x = atof(string_buf);
        break;
    case YMIN:
        get_string(string_buf);
        newobj->lower.y = atof(string_buf);
        break;
    case YMAX:
        get_string(string_buf);
        newobj->upper.y = atof(string_buf);
        break;
    case ZMIN:
        get_string(string_buf);
        newobj->lower.z = atof(string_buf);
        break;
```

```
            case ZMAX:
                get_string(string_buf);
                newobj->upper.z = atof(string_buf);
                break;
            case DIR:
                newobj->vect1.get_vector();
                break;
            case PAttern:
                newobj->pattern=Attach_Pattern();
                break;
            case REMOVE:
                newobj->remove=Attach_Pattern();
                break;
            case XMULT:
                get_string(string_buf);
                newobj->xmult = fabs(atof(string_buf));
                break;
            case YMULT:
                get_string(string_buf);
                newobj->ymult = fabs(atof(string_buf));
                break;
            case NAME:
                get_string(newobj->name);
                break;
            case PAREN:
                break;
            default:
                found = FALSE;
        }
        if (!found)
        {
            cout << "Undefined parameter " << string_buf <<
              " while loading quadric in 'input.cpp'";
            exit(1);
        }
    }
    if ((no_param != 63) && (no_param != 59))
    {
        cout << "Too few parameters for quadric in 'input.cpp'";
        exit(1);
    }
    newobj->vect1 = ~ newobj->vect1;
```

```
    temp = newobj->vect1.x * newobj->vect1.x +newobj->vect1.z *
        newobj->vect1.z;
    if (temp == 0)
        newobj->cos1 = 1;
    else
        newobj->cos1 = newobj->vect1.z/sqrt(temp);
    newobj->sin1 = sqrt(1 - newobj->cos1 * newobj->cos1);
    newdir.x = newobj->vect1.x * newobj->cos1 +  newobj->vect1.z *
        -newobj->sin1;
    newdir.y = newobj->vect1.y;
    newdir.z = newobj->vect1.x * newobj->sin1 +
        newobj->vect1.z * newobj->cos1;
    temp = newdir.y * newdir.y + newdir.z * newdir.z;
    if (temp == 0)
        newobj->cos2 = 1;
    else
        newobj->cos2 = newdir.y/sqrt(temp);
    newobj->sin2 = sqrt(1 - newobj->cos2 * newobj->cos2);
    WORLD.objcount++;
    return(newobj);
}


/*
    ┌─────────────────────────────────────────────────────────┐
    │        GetFractal() = Load a fractal from fget and return │
    │                           pointer to it                  │
    └─────────────────────────────────────────────────────────┘
*/

Object * GetFractal(Object *queue)
{
  Triangle * newobj;
  int type=0,no_param = 0, found;
  Vector temp;

  newobj = new Triangle;
  newobj->col_data = new color_data;
  *newobj->col_data = def.col_data;
  while (type != PAREN && !feof(fget))
  {
    type = get_string(string_buf);
    found = get_color_data(type,newobj->col_data);
    if (found == TRUE)
```

```
continue;
found = TRUE;
switch(type)
{
    case LOC:
        newobj->loc.get_vector();
        no_param |= 1;
        break;
    case V1:
        newobj->vect1.get_vector();
        no_param |= 2;
        break;
    case V2:
        newobj->vect2.get_vector();
        no_param |= 4;
        break;
    case DIMENSION:
        get_string(string_buf);
        WORLD.fractal_dim = atof(string_buf);
        break;
    case SCALAR:
        get_string(string_buf);
        WORLD.fractal scalar = atof(string_buf);
        break;
    case PAttern:
        newobj->pattern=Attach_Pattern();
        break;
    case REMOVE:
        newobj->remove=Attach_Pattern();
        break;
    case XMULT:
        get_string(string_buf);
        newobj->xmult = fabs(atof(string_buf));
        break;
    case YMULT:
        get_string(string_buf);
        newobj->ymult = fabs(atof(string_buf));
        break;
    case NAME:
        get_string(newobj->name);
        break;
```

```
        case PAREN:
            break;
        default:
            found = FALSE;
    }
    if (!found)
    {
        cout << "Undefined parameter " << string_buf <<
          " while loading fractal triangle in 'input.cpp'";
        exit(1);
    }
 }
 if (no_param != 7)
 {
    cout <<"Too few parameters for fractal triangle in 'input.cpp'";
    exit(1);
 }
 Fractal_comp(newobj);
 queue = Make_fractal_triangles(newobj->loc, newobj->vect1,
    newobj->vect2,newobj->vect3, queue, WORLD.level);
 WORLD.objcount++;
 return(queue);
}
```

```
/*
    ┌────────────────────────────────────────────────┐
    │          Get_Object()=Load an object from fget  │
    │                  and return pointer to it        │
    └────────────────────────────────────────────────┘
*/

Object * Get_Object(int type, Object *queue)
 {
    Object * newobj;
    newobj=NULL;
    switch(type)
    {
       case SPHERE:
           newobj=GetSphere();
           break;
       case PARALLELOGRAM:
           newobj=GetParallelogram();
```

```
            break;
        case TRIANGLE:
            newobj=GetTriangle();
            break;
        case RING:
            newobj=GetRing();
            break;
        case QUADRATIC:
            newobj=GetQuadratic();
            break;
        case CONE:
            newobj=GetCone();
            break;
        case FRACTAL:
            newobj = GetFractal(queue);
            break;
        case INSTANCE_OF:
            newobj=Get_Instance_Of();
            break;
    }
    return(newobj);
}


/*
    ┌─────────────────────────────────────────────────────┐
    │  Attach_Pattern() = Finds pattern matching object pattern │
    │              name and returns pointer to it          │
    └─────────────────────────────────────────────────────┘
*/

 Pattern *Attach_Pattern()
 {
    Pattern * pat;

    get_string(string_buf);
    pat=WORLD.patlist;
    while (pat!=NULL)
    {
        if (strcmp(string_buf,pat->name)==0)
            break;
        pat=pat->sibling;
    }
    if (pat==NULL)
```

```
    {
        cout << "Pattern not found\n";
        exit(1);
    }
    return(pat);
}


/*  ┌─────────────────────────────────────────────────────┐
    │                                                       │
 *  │     Get_Circle_Pattern() = Loads a circle sub-pattern │
    │                                                       │
    └─────────────────────────────────────────────────────┘
*/

Pattern *Get_Circle_Pattern()
{
    int type=0,no_param = 0, found;
    Pattern *pattern;
    color_data col_data;

    pattern=new Pattern;
    pattern->name[0] = NULL;
    pattern->child = NULL;
    pattern->sibling = NULL;
    pattern->link = NULL;
    pattern->type = CIRCLE;
    col_data = def.col_data;
    while (type != PAREN && !feof(fget))
    {
        type = get_string(string_buf);
        found = get_color_data(type,&col_data);
        if (type == RADIUS)
        {
            get_string(string_buf);
            pattern->radius = abs(atof(string_buf));
            no_param |= 1;
            found = TRUE;
        }
        if (type == PAREN)
        {
            found = TRUE;
        }
        if (!found)
        {
```

```
        cout << "Undefined parameter " << string_buf <<
          "in getting circle pattern\n";
        exit(1);
     }
  }
  if (no_param != 1)
  {
      cout << "Too few parameters in getting circle pattern\n";
      exit(1);
  }
  pattern->col_data = col_data;
  return(pattern);
}


/*
    ┌─────────────────────────────────────────────────────┐
    │                                                       │
    │       Get_Rect_Pattern() = Load a rectangle sub-pattern │
    │                                                       │
    └─────────────────────────────────────────────────────┘
*/

Pattern *Get_Rect_Pattern()
{
  int type=0, no_param =0, found;
  Pattern *pattern;
  color_data col_data;

  pattern=new Pattern;
  pattern->name[0] = NULL;
  pattern->child = NULL;
  pattern->sibling = NULL;
  pattern->link = NULL;
  pattern->type = RECTANGLE;
  col_data = def.col_data;
  while (type != PAREN && !feof(fget))
  {
     type = get_string(string_buf);
     found = get_color_data(type,&col_data);
        if (found == FALSE)
        found = TRUE;
     else
        continue;
     switch(type)
     {
```

```
        case START_X:
            get_string(string_buf);
            pattern->startx = atof(string_buf);
            no_param |= 1;
            break;
        case START_Y:
            get_string(string_buf);
            pattern->starty = atof(string_buf);
            no_param |= 2;
            break;
        case END_X:
            get_string(string_buf);
            pattern->endx = atof(string_buf);
            no_param |= 4;
            break;
        case END_Y:
            get_string(string_buf);
            pattern->endy = atof(string_buf);
            no_param |= 8;
            break;
        case PAREN:
            break;
        default:
            found = FALSE;
    }
    if (!found)
    {
        cout << "Undefined parameter " << string_buf <<
            " in getting rectangle pattern\n";
        exit(1);
    }
}
if (no_param != 15)
{
    cout << "Too few parameters for rectangular pattern";
    exit(1);
}
pattern->col_data = col_data;
return(pattern);
}
```

```
/*
┌─────────────────────────────────────────────────────────┐
│                                                           │
│        Get_Poly_Pattern() = Load a polygon pattern        │
│                                                           │
└─────────────────────────────────────────────────────────┘
*/

Pattern *Get_Poly_Pattern()
{
  int type=0, no_param = 0, found;
  Pattern *pattern, *pointpatt;
  color_data col_data;
  pattern=new Pattern;
  pattern->name[0] = NULL;
  pattern->child = NULL;
  pattern->sibling = NULL;
  pattern->link = NULL;
  pattern->type = POLYGON;
  col_data = def.col_data;
  while (type != PAREN && !feof(fget))
  {
      found = FALSE;
      type = get_string(string_buf);
      found = get_color_data(type,&col_data);
      if (found == TRUE)
      continue;
      if (type == POINT)
      {
          pointpatt = new Pattern;
          get_string(string_buf);
          pointpatt->startx = atof(string_buf);
          get_string(string_buf);
          pointpatt->starty = atof(string_buf);
          no_param += 1;
          pointpatt->link = pattern->link;
          pattern->link = pointpatt;
          found = TRUE;
      }
      if (type == PAREN)
          break;
      if (!found)
      {
          cout << "Undefined parameter " << string_buf <<
             " in getting polygon pattern\n";
```

```
        exit(1);
    }
}
if (no_param < 3)
{
    cout << "Too few parameters for polygon pattern";
    exit(1);
}
pattern->col_data = col_data;
return(pattern);
}


/*
    ┌─────────────────────────────────────────────────────┐
    │         Get_SubPattern() = Load a sub-pattern         │
    └─────────────────────────────────────────────────────┘
*/

Pattern *Get_SubPattern(int type)
{
  switch (type)
  {
    case RECTANGLE:
        return(Get_Rect_Pattern());
    case CIRCLE:
        return(Get_Circle_Pattern());
    case POLYGON:
        return(Get_Poly_Pattern());
    default:
        return(NULL);
  }
}


/*
    ┌─────────────────────────────────────────────────────┐
    │      GetPattern() = Load a pattern into pattern list  │
    └─────────────────────────────────────────────────────┘
*/

int GetPattern()
{
  int type=0, no_param = 0, found= TRUE;
  Pattern *pattern, *spat;
  pattern = new Pattern;
```

```
pattern->name[0] = NULL;
pattern->child = NULL;
pattern->sibling = NULL;
pattern->link = NULL;
pattern->type = PATT_HEADER;
while (type != PAREN && !feof(fget))
{
    type = get_string(string_buf);
    switch(type)
    {
        case X_SIZE:
            no_param |= 1;
            get_string(string_buf);
            pattern->xsize = atof(string_buf);
            break;
        case Y_SIZE:
            get_string(string_buf);
            pattern->ysize = atof(string_buf);
            no_param |= 2;
            break;
        case NAME:
            get_string(pattern->name);
            no_param |= 4;
            break;
        default:
            found = FALSE;
    }
    if ((spat=Get_SubPattern(type))!=NULL)
    {

        spat->sibling=pattern->child;
        pattern->child=spat;
        no_param |= 8; found = TRUE;
    }
    if (type == PAREN)
    {
        found = TRUE;
    }
    if (!found)
    {
        cout << "Undefined parameter " << string_buf <<
          " in getting pattern\n";
        exit(1);
```

```
        }
    }
    if (no_param != 15)
    {
        cout << "Too few parameters in getting pattern\n";
        exit(1);
    }
    pattern->sibling=WORLD.patlist;
    WORLD.patlist=pattern;
    return(TRUE);
}


/*
┌─────────────────────────────────────────────────┐
│                                                   │
│          Make_Bbox() = Create a bounding box      │
│                                                   │
└─────────────────────────────────────────────────┘
*/

void Make_Bbox(Object * node)
{
    Object * tnode;
    Vector v1,v2;
    if (node->child!=NULL)
        Make_Bbox(node->child);
    if (node->nextobj!=NULL)
        Make_Bbox(node->nextobj);
    if (node->type==BBOX)
    {
        tnode=node->child;
        node->lower = Vector(3e30, 3e30, 3e30);
        node->upper = Vector(-3e30, -3e30, -3e30);
        while (tnode!=NULL)
        {
            tnode->FindBbox(&v1,&v2);
            node->lower = v1.min(node->lower);
            node->upper = v2.max(node->upper);
            tnode=tnode->nextobj;
        }
    }
}
```

BBox defined by 2 corner vectors?

```
/*
     Name_Find() = Finds object in stack with a given name
*/

Object * Name_Find(Object *obj,char *name)
{
  Object *temp;

  if (obj == NULL)
      return(NULL);
  if (obj->name != NULL)
      if (strcmp(name,obj->name) == 0)
            return(obj);
  if (obj->child != NULL)
      if ((temp = Name_Find(obj->child,name)) != NULL)
            return(temp);
  if (obj->nextobj != NULL)
      if ((temp = Name_Find(obj->nextobj,name)) != NULL)
            return(temp);
  return(NULL);
}


/*
     Get_Instance() = Loads an instance of a set of objects
*/

Object * Get_Instance_Of()
{
  char name[32];
  int type = 0,no_param = 0, found=TRUE;
  Vector  offset, mult;
  Object * source, * dest;

  mult = Vector (1,1,1);
  while (type != PAREN && !feof(fget))
  {
     type = get_string(string_buf);
     switch(type)
     {
```

```
            case NAME:
                get_string(name);
                no_param |= 1;
                break;
            case LOC:
                offset.get_vector();
                no_param |= 2;
                break;
            case SCALE:
                mult.get_vector();
                break;
            case PAREN:
                break;
            default:
                found = FALSE;
        }
        if (!found)
        {
            cout << "Undefined parameter " << string_buf <<
              " in getting Instance";
            exit(1);
        }
    }
    if (no_param != 3)
    {
        cout << "Too few parameters in getting Instance";
        exit(1);
    }
    if ((source = Name_Find(WORLD.instances,name))==NULL)
    {
        cout << "Undefined instance name: " << name << "\n";
        exit(1);
    }
    dest = Move_Instance(source,TRUE);
    dest->Scale_Instance(&mult,TRUE);
    Offset_Instance(dest,&offset,TRUE);
    WORLD.objcount++;
    return(dest);
}
```

```
/*
    ┌────────────────────────────────────────────────────┐
    │   Move_Instance() = Moves user defined primitive from│
    │              WORLD.instance to WORLD.stack           │
    └────────────────────────────────────────────────────┘
*/

Object * Move_Instance(Object *obj, int fflag)
{
    Object * newobj;
    if (obj==NULL)
         return(NULL);
    switch(obj->type)
    {
        case SPHERE:
             newobj = new Sphere;
             break;
        case TRIANGLE:
             newobj = new Triangle;
             break;
        case RING:
             newobj = new Ring;
             break;
        case PARALLELOGRAM:
             newobj = new Parallelogram;
             break;
        case QUADRATIC:
             newobj = new Quadratic;
             break;
        case BBOX:
             newobj = new BBox;
             break;
        default:
             newobj = new Object;
    }
    *newobj = *obj;
    newobj->child   = Move_Instance(obj->child,FALSE);
    if (!fflag)
        newobj->nextobj = Move_Instance(obj->nextobj,FALSE);
    else
        newobj->nextobj = NULL;
    return(newobj);
}
```

```
/*
    ┌─────────────────────────────────────────────────┐
    │  Offset_Instance() = Offsets a user defined primitive by │
    │                      vector 'offset'              │
    └─────────────────────────────────────────────────┘
*/

void Offset_Instance(Object *obj, Vector *offset, int fflag)
{
  if (obj==NULL)
      return;
  obj->loc = obj->loc + *offset;
  switch(obj->type)
  {
      case SPHERE:
          obj->n1 = obj->vect1.x * obj->vect1.x;
          break;
      case PARALLELOGRAM:
      case TRIANGLE:
      case RING:
          obj->n1 = obj->norm % obj->loc;
  }
  Offset_Instance(obj->child,offset,FALSE);
  if (!fflag)
      Offset_Instance(obj->nextobj,offset,FALSE);
}
```

We will now describe how these kinds of data are treated.

Processing Attributes

The first type of data checked by the *get_data* function is *attributes*. This is accomplished by calling the *GetAttrib* function. This function consists of a large *switch* statement, which provides the proper actions for every attribute type that might have been returned by the parser. As the function is entered, the local *found* parameter is set to TRUE. At the end of the *switch* statement is the *default* case, which is entered only if there is no match for any of the other cases. The *default* case changes *found* to FALSE. Upon returning, the function returns the value of *found*.

The first type of attribute checked is sky data. If a match is found, the function enters a loop which uses the parser to read strings and processes each with a *switch* statement until a right parenthesis is encountered, at which point the loop terminates. There are three acceptable strings (besides the right parenthesis) for sky data. For the first two, ZENITH and HORIZ, a vector is read into the appropriate place in the *WORLD* data. For the third kind of string, DITHER, a string is read in, converted to a floating-point number, and the absolute value entered into the *WORLD.sky_dither* parameter. This parameter should always be positive. If a negative number is encountered, we might choose to declare this an error, print an error message, and exit. Instead, by taking the absolute value, we ignore the minus sign and assume that the numerical value is correct.

Within the loop for sky parameters, we set the *found* parameter to TRUE before entering the loop and then set it to FALSE if we ever get to the *default* case. This means that when we exit the loop, if any string encountered within the loop is unacceptable, *found* will be FALSE; otherwise it remains TRUE.

Next is the COLOR attribute. There are two different ways of assigning color information to an object. One is a default array of color data stored in the program. Whenever an object is created, all of the color information starts out with the default color values. Then, as object data is entered from the file, various items of color information may be entered; if they are, they replace the default values. The COLOR attribute permits changing of the default color values. Thus, you may enter default color values without object color values and all following objects take on the default values. When you want a different colored object, you change the default values before you define the next object. Alternately, you can leave the default values alone and specify particular color values for each object. This attribute is processed by a repeated loop until an end of file is encountered, or a string is read which is a right parenthesis. The loop begins by getting a string with the parser. The string is then sent to the *get_color_data* function, which checks for legitimate color data and processes it. This function is described below. It returns a TRUE if the item was correct color data or a FALSE. If the string was not a legitimate color parameter, an error message is printed out and the program terminates. Otherwise the loop continues processing color data until it terminates.

If the attribute is FOC_LENGTH, the parser gets the focal length string from the data file. It is converted to a floating-point number, the absolute value of this taken (since negative focal lengths are impossible) and multiplied by five. The result is stored in *WORLD.flength*. The focal length parameter is used as a multiplier to scale the perspective of the scene. With the mathematics in the ray-tracing functions, a parameter five times the focal length of the lens gives the proper perspective for a 35 millimeter camera. We won't go deeply into optics, but be aware that a "normal" lens (which gives the kind of photograph we are used to viewing), has a different focal length for each different film size. If you go above the "normal" value, objects appear closer, but also more compressed. This is the telephoto lens. If you go below the "normal" value, you have a wide-angle lens, which crams more into the picture, but creates distortion. We have set up the mathematics so that the focal length inputs correspond to a 35 mm camera, because it is so widely used and many people are familiar with the photographic effects of the different lenses.

If the attribute is FILE_NAME, the parser reads the next string and it is copied to the parameter *WORLD.outfile,* used in opening the output data file.

The next attribute defines a lamp. Lamps are processed with a loop similar to sky data. Only one parameter is required of a lamp, namely its location. Another parameter, distance, is set to a default parameter of 150 for each new lamp source, but may be changed by data from the file. In addition, a radius parameter may be entered (to remain compatible with QRT), but it is otherwise not essential. When the loop ends, the parameter *no_param* will have a value of one if the location has been entered. If not, an error message will be displayed and the program terminated. This loop also uses the *found* parameter to generate an error message and terminate the program if an undefined parameter is encountered. Once a lamp has successfully been defined, a new lamp structure is created and the data transferred to it. The address of the current *WORLD.lamps* is placed in the lamp variable *next_lamp* and the address of the new lamp structure is placed in *WORLD.lamps*.

Getting observer information is the next attribute. It is processed in a manner similar to sky data, with a loop that gets strings and processes them through a *switch* statement. In addition to the right parenthesis which terminates the loop, there are three vectors that define the observer position. They are the observer's location, direction of view, and the direction that is "up" to the observer. A vector is obtained from the data stream for each of these, and stored in the proper place in the *WORLD*. We use the same procedure with the *found* variable, previously described, to terminate the program with an error message if an incorrect parameter is encountered. The observer "up" direction has an original default value, so it is not absolutely necessary to supply this parameter. However, the other parameters must be specified if the program is to work correctly. Hence we have included a parameter *no_param* which is zeroed at the start of the *GetAttrib* function. It has various bits *or*ed to it for each parameter read. When we finish reading observer data, if both parameters have been read, this test parameter should have a value of 3. If it does not, the program terminates and prints an error message.

The *GetAttrib* function next processes the PATTERN attribute. This is handled by the *GetPattern* function, which will be described later.

The function then processes the XRES and YRES attributes. It uses the parser to read a string for each of these, converts it to a floating-point number, takes the absolute value of this number, and places it in the appropriate *WORLD* parameter.

Finally, if the attribute is NAME, the parser gets the next string and places it in the variable *name*.

Processing Color Data

The *get_color_data* function performs checking and processing for all valid color data parameters with a *switch* statement. The first characteristics to be processed are for ambient lighting, diffuse color, mirror, transmission, and density. Each is a vector. These vectors are specified in the data file as having red, green, and blue components between zero and one. Actually, in the program, they are expected to vary between zero and the maximum number of colors (CNUM).

Hence, each one is processed by using the *get_vector* function to read the data from the stream and convert it into a vector. The vector is then multiplied by CNUM to obtain the proper color range. Color data is stored in a color data array, with address specified by a parameter passed to the function. Next, three floating-point parameters are processed: index of refraction, dither value, and the specular reflection coefficient. These are all positive numbers, so that the string obtained from the data stream by the parser is converted from a floating-point number into an absolute value.

Finally, the reflection coefficient is processed. This is a floating-point number which must be multiplied by CNUM, after the incoming value has been converted to a floating point from the string obtained by the parser.

Processing Instances

All of the instances defined in a file must be placed in a single block which starts with BEGIN_INSTANCES and ends with END_INSTANCES. When this first string is encountered, the *get_data* function is recalled recursively. This results in the generation of a separate list of objects similar to the main list described below. The *get_data* function terminates at the END_INSTANCES string, whereupon the address of the last object added to the linked list is placed in *WORLD.instances*.

Processing Bounding Boxes

When you want a bounding box to surround a set of objects, the string

BEGIN_BBOX is placed before the data of the first set of objects in the data file and the string END_BBOX is placed after the end of the data of the last set of objects. The reason for using a bounding box is to accelerate computations. Instead of checking whether each ray intersects each nearby object, we can first check to see if the ray intersects the bounding box. If it does not (as will happen in most cases), we are through. Only for the few rays that intersect the bounding box do we need to test against each of the enclosed objects for an intersection. When the BEGIN_BBOX string is encountered, we first create an object of the BBOX type. We then copy the current name to its name parameter. We then run *get_data* recursively, putting all of the objects encountered into a separate linked list until the string END_BBOX is encountered. At this point we terminate *get_data* and place the address of the last object entered into the linked list in the *child* of the box we are creating.

Processing Objects

Next, *get_data* calls the function *Get_Object* if the string indicates that object data is to be processed. This function uses a *switch* statement to call the proper function for the object to be created.

Creating a Sphere

If a sphere is to be created, we first allocate memory space. (The call to *new* for class *Sphere* not only assigns the proper amount of memory, but also assures that this object is always of class *Sphere*.) Next the function begins a *while* loop, where it remains until the file ends or a right parenthesis is encountered. At the beginning of each iteration of this loop, the parser gets a string. The parameter *found* is set to TRUE. A *switch* statement is then run to see if the string matches any parameters for the class *Sphere*. Except for the PATTERN string, which we will describe later, each acceptable string generates a vector or number from the data and stores it in the appropriate object variable location.

Some of these variables are optional; others are essential to the creation of a sphere. When an essential variable is processed, the *no_param* variable has a bit set in it so that when the loop is terminated, the parameter will contain a 3 if the essential parameters have been read. If the parameter does not contain a 3 when the loop is finished, an error message is displayed and the program terminates. As in processing several of the attributes, the *default* for the switch statement is to set the found parameter to FALSE. So, upon leaving the loop, if this parameter is FALSE, it indicates that an incorrect string was encountered. In this situation, the program displays an error message and terminates. Otherwise, the function proceeds to precompute any parameters that do not change for the sphere and are needed in the process of computing ray intersections. By computing them at this point and storing them in the object data structure, only one computation is required (rather than one for every ray tested for intersection). In the case of the sphere, the only parameter that is computed is *n1*. Finally, *WORLD.objcount* is incremented, which keeps count of the total number of objects in the scene.

Creating a Triangle

As with a sphere, we allocate the memory space for a triangle by calling *new* (for class *Triangle)* which not only assigns the proper amount of memory, but assures that this object is always of class *Triangle*. Next, the function begins a *while* loop, where it remains until the file ends or a right parenthesis is encountered. At the beginning of each iteration of this loop, the parser gets a string. The parameter *found* is set to TRUE and a *switch* statement runs to see if the string matches any of the acceptable parameters for the class *Triangle*. Except for the PATTERN string, each acceptable string causes a vector or number to be read from the data and stored in the appropriate object variable location. Some of these variables are optional; others are essential to the creation of a triangle. When an essential variable is processed, the *no_param* variable has a bit set in it in such a manner that when the loop is terminated, the parameter will contain a 7 if the essential parameters have been read in. If the parameter does not contain a 7 when the loop is finished, an error message is displayed and the program terminates. As in processing several of the attributes, the *default* for the *switch* statement is to set the *found* parameter to FALSE. So, on leaving the loop, if this parameter is FALSE, it indicates that an incorrect string was encountered. In this situation, the program displays an error message and terminates. The critical parameters for the triangle are: *loc,* which is the location of one of the vertices of the triangle in system coordinates; *v1* (stored as *vect1*), which is in a coordinate system centered at the first vertex; and *v2* (stored as *vect2*), the third vertex of the triangle which is also in a coordinate system centered at the first vertex. The triangle processing function precomputes *norm, n1, len1,* and *len2,* which are used in the intersection computations. Finally, this function also increments the object count.

Creating a Ring

If a ring is to be created, we first allocate the memory space for a ring. (The call to *new* for class *Ring* not only assigns the proper amount of memory, but also assures that this object is forevermore known to be of class *Ring*.) Next, the function begins a *while* loop, in which it remains until the file ends or a right parenthesis is encountered. At the beginning of each iteration of this loop, the parser is used to get a string. The parameter *found* is set to TRUE. A *switch* statement is then run to see if the string matches any of the acceptable parameters for the class *Ring*. Except for the PATTERN string, which we will describe later, each acceptable string causes a vector or number to be read from the data and stored in the appropriate object variable location. Some of these variables are optional; others are essential to the creation of a ring. When an essential variable is processed, the *no_param* variable has a bit set in it in such a manner that when the loop is terminated, the parameter will contain a 31 if the essential parameters have been read in. If the parameter does not contain a 31 when the loop is finished, an error message is displayed and the program terminates.

As in processing several of the attributes, the *default* for the *switch* statement is to set the *found* parameter to FALSE. So, upon leaving the loop, if this parameter is FALSE, it indicates that an incorrect string was encountered. In this situation, the program displays an error message and terminates. The ring processing function precomputes *norm, n1, len1,* and *len2,* which are used in the intersection computations. It also sets *vect3.z* to zero and normalizes *vect1* and *vect2*. Finally, this function also increments the object count.

Creating a Parallelogram

If a parallelogram is to be created, we first allocate the memory space for a parallelogram. (The call to *new* for class *Parallelogram* not only assigns the proper amount of memory, but also assures that this object is forevermore known to be of class *Parallelogram.*) Next the function begins a *while* loop, in which it remains until the file ends or a right parenthesis is encountered. At the beginning of each iteration of this loop, the parser is used to get a string. The parameter *found* is set to TRUE. A *switch* statement is then run to see if the string matches any of the acceptable parameters for the class *Parallelogram.* Except for the PATTERN string, which we will describe later, each acceptable string causes a vector or number to be read from the data and stored in the appropriate object variable location. Some of these variables are optional; others are essential to the creation of a parallelogram. When an essential variable is processed, the *no_param* variable has a bit set in it in such a manner that when the loop is terminated, the parameter will contain a 7 if the essential parameters have been read in. If the parameter does not contain a 7 when the loop is finished, an error message is displayed and the program terminates. As in the processing of several of the attributes, the *default* for the *switch* statement is to set the *found* parameter to FALSE. So, upon leaving the loop, if this parameter is FALSE, it indicates that an incorrect string was encountered. In this situation, the program displays an error message and terminates. The critical parameters for the parallelogram are *loc,* which is the location of the first vertex of the parallelogram in system coordinates; *v1* (stored as *vect1*), which is a vertex of the parallelogram adjacent to the first vertex in a coordinate system centered at the first vertex; and *v2* (stored as *vect2*), which is the other vertex of the parallelogram that is adjacent to the first vertex in a coordinate system centered at the first vertex. From these three vertices, the function computes the location of the fourth vertex and stores the information necessary to be able to make a test of whether an intersection between a ray and the parallelogram occurs. If you modify the software so that a fourth vertex can be entered as an input, the parallelogram object can become a generalized quadralateral. The parallelogram processing function precomputes *norm, n1, len1,* and *len2,* which are used in the intersection computations. Finally, this function also increments the object count.

Creating a Quadratic

If a quadratic is to be created, we first allocate the memory space for a quadratic. (The call to *new* for class *Quadratic* not only assigns the proper amount of memory, but also assures that this object is forevermore known to be of class *Quadratic.*) Next the function begins a *while* loop, in which it remains until the file ends or a right parenthesis is encountered. At the beginning of each iteration of this loop, the parser is used to get a string. The parameter found is set to TRUE. A *switch* statement is then run to see if the string matches any of the acceptable parameters for the class *Quadratic.* Except for the PATTERN string, which we will describe later, each acceptable string causes a vector or number to be read from the data and stored in the appropriate object variable location.

Some of these variables are optional; others are essential to the creation of a quadratic. When an essential variable is processed, the *no_param* variable has a bit set in it in such a manner that when the loop is terminated, the parameter will contain a 31 if the essential parameters have been read in. If the parameter does not contain a 31 when the loop is finished, an error message is displayed and the program terminates. As in the processing of several of the attributes, the *default* for the *switch* statement is to set the *found* parameter to FALSE. So, upon leaving the loop, if this parameter is FALSE, it indicates that an incorrect string was encountered. In this situation, the program displays an error message and terminates. The quadratic preprocessing function normalizes *vect1* and precomputes *cos1* and *sin1*. It then computes the direction vector *newdir,* using *vect1* and *cos1* and *sin1*. Using this new vector, it precomputes *cos2* and *sin2.* Finally, this function also increments the object count.

Creating a Cone

The function for creating a Quadratic can produce a wide variety of shapes, depending on the coefficients assigned to the terms of the equation. However, the coefficient values needed for a shape are not always evident. Consequently, you may want to create some new shape names, which use the quadratic equation. A cone is an example of how such functions are created.

To begin with, you need to add the shape name at the beginning of the *input.cpp* listing, and an appropriate *define* statement in the header file.

You need to do this for any new parameter names you will use. Now look at the *GetCone* function to see how it is written. It is similar to the other functions for getting objects except that it creates a new object of class *Quadratic*. The terms processed within the *switch* statement used to define the cone are: *radius* (at the base of the cone), cone *height,* and *direction* (which is the same as the curve direction used in getting a quadratic).

After all input data is collected, we convert the *radius* and *height* parameters into the proper coefficients for the quadratic equation to produce a cone. Nothing else has to be done; all of the additional parts of the ray-tracing program treat this cone in the same way as any other object of class *Quadratic*. You can use this technique to create any shapes defined by a quadratic, such as a cylinder.

Attaching a Pattern to an Object

The PATTERN string can occur in two contexts: preceding the definition of the pattern characteristics, or within the definition of an object (to indicate the name of the pattern associated with this object). It is the latter situation that we are discussing here.

When the PATTERN string is encountered within an object, the function *Attach_Pattern* is called. This function first uses the parser to get the next string, which is the name of the pattern, then the address of the pattern at the top of the pattern list, *WORLD.patlist*. A *while* loop begins by comparing the name of this pattern with the name of the pattern that was read in for the object. If there is a match, the function terminates and the address of the pattern is returned to the object function where it is saved as part of the object data structure. If there is no match, the function obtains the address of the next pattern in the list and reiterates the loop. If a NULL address is obtained, it indicates that the entire list has been read without a match being found. In this case, an error message is displayed and the program terminates.

Processing Pattern Data

When the PATTERN string is outside of an object definition, the *GetAttrib* function calls *GetPattern* to process the data. The data for a pattern must first specify three parameters: the pattern name, and size in the x and y directions. Then data for at least one of three acceptable pattern types (rectangle, circle, and polygon) must appear. The function begins by creating a new pattern variable and initializing its parameters. Then a *while* loop reiterates until the file ends or until a right parenthesis is encountered. At the beginning of each loop iteration, the function uses the parser to get the next data string. A *switch* statement determines if the string is an acceptable one for pattern data; if it is, the next string is read, converted to a floating-point number if it's not a name, and put into the appropriate data slot in the pattern structure. The function makes use of *no_param*, as was done with objects, to assure that all of the required parameters exist.

The *found* parameter is used a little differently. It starts out as TRUE. After passing through the *switch* statement, if the string is not one of the three that must occur initially in the pattern definition, the *default* case sets it to FALSE. After leaving the *switch* statement, the function calls the *Get_SubPattern* function to process data for one of three pattern types. If this function is successful, the *no_param* parameter has the appropriate bit added to it, the *found* parameter is reset to TRUE, and the address of the sub-pattern put into a list pointed to by the *child* parameter.

When the loop is completed, the function displays an error message and terminates the program if *found* is false. Otherwise, it checks the value of *no_param* to make sure all required parameters were read from the file. If so, the parameter should be 15. If not, an error message is displayed and the program terminates. Otherwise, the pattern address is linked to the pattern list and the function ends.

The *Get_SubPattern* function is simply a *switch* statement which calls the appropriate function to process one of three types of pattern data or returns a NULL if the type is not one of three acceptable ones.

The *Get_Circle_Pattern* function processes pattern data for a circle pattern. It sets up a new pattern and initializes the parameters. A *while* loop begins, which is iterated until the end of file occurs or a right parenthesis is encountered. Then the parser gets the next string. The only acceptable ones are RADIUS, one of the color data strings, or the right parenthesis. If RADIUS is encountered, the string is converted to the absolute value of a floating-point number and stored in the pattern radius parameter. When the loop is complete, the appropriate error message is displayed if the radius was not found or if an undefined parameter occurs, and the program terminates. Otherwise, the color data is transferred to the pattern structure and the function returns the address of the sub-pattern.

The *Get_Rect_Pattern* function processes pattern data for a rectangle. It sets up a new pattern and initializes the parameters. A *while* loop begins, which is iterated until end of file occurs or a right parenthesis is encountered. The parser is then used to get the next string. The acceptable strings are START_X, START_Y, END_X, END_Y, the color data strings, and the right parenthesis. For each acceptable parameter (other than the color data and the right parenthesis) the next string is read, converted to a floating-point number, and stored in the appropriate variable in the sub-pattern data structure. When the loop is complete, the appropriate error message is displayed if the rectangular coordinates were not found or if an undefined parameter occurs, and the program terminates. Otherwise, the color data is transferred to the pattern structure and the function returns the address of the sub-pattern.

The *Get_Poly_Pattern* function processes pattern data for a polygon. It first sets up a new pattern and initializes the parameters. Then a *while* loop is begun, which is iterated until the end of file occurs or a right parenthesis is encountered. The parser is then used to get the next string. The only acceptable strings are POINT, the color data strings, and the right parenthesis. For each POINT parameter a new pattern is created. Then the next two strings are read by the parser, converted to floating-point numbers, and stored as the x and y coordinates of a point on the polygon in the new pattern data structure. This pattern is added to the pattern linked list by properly setting up the addresses in the *pointpatt->link* and *pattern->link* variables. The *no_param* variable is also incremented. If the type was not POINT or a right parenthesis, an error message is displayed and the program terminates. When the right parenthesis is encountered, the loop terminates. When the loop is complete, there must be at least three points defined for a polygon to have been created. Thus if *no_param* is less than 3, there aren't enough points so an error message is displayed and the program is terminated. Otherwise, the color data is copied to the pattern color data and the function ends, returning the pattern address.

Transferring an Instance to the Object List

When the string INSTANCE_OF is encountered in the data stream, the function *Get_Instance_Of* is called. The first thing that this function does is to set the multiplier vector *mult* to a default value of (1, 1, 1). Next, a *while* loop iterates until the file ends or a right parenthesis is encountered. Each iteration of the loop begins by the parser reading a string from the data stream.

Two parameters are mandatory: the name of the instance, and the location at which the instance is to be generated. A *switch* statement is used to check for these mandatory parameters (using the *no_param* variable to assure that both occur) for the multiplier vector (which is optional), and for the right parenthesis. The *found* parameter is used to cause the program to display an error message and terminate if an undefined parameter is encountered. At the completion of the loop, if both mandatory parameters are not present, the program displays an error message and terminates. Otherwise, the function *Name_Find* is called.

This function checks the name just read against every instance name in the list of instances. If no match occurs, an error message is displayed and the program terminates. If a match does occur, the function calls *Move_Instance*. This function first sets up a new object to match the object in the instances file. It copies all of the data for that object from the instances file to the new object. It then calls itself recursively to perform the same operations for any *child* objects or succeeding objects in the instances list that are part of the named instance. Then, the *Get_Instance_Of* function calls the *Scale_Instance* function to apply the multiplier vector to the object. This function differs for each different type of object under consideration. It will be discussed in detail in Chapter 10. Finally, the *Get_Instance_Of* function calls the *Offset_Instance* function which moves the object location from that specified in the instance to that read in above for this particular instance. It recursively does the same for all objects associated with this instance.

Making Bounding Boxes

We have completed loading the world and will return to the main rendering program (described in Chapter 6). You will note, however, that while we created a bounding box each time the BEGIN_BBOX string was encountered, and set up the list linking to the bounding box, we did not establish any parameters for the size of the bounding box. Consequently, before anything else, the main program needs to run the function *Make_BBox* to establish these bounds. This function runs recursively for every object contained in the bounding box. It starts out with a high value for the lower bound and a low value for the upper bound, then runs the function *FindBbox*. This function, which differs for each type of object, sets an upper and lower bound for the box surrounding the object.

The *Make_BBox* function then applies the minimum function to the object lower bounding box and the new lower bound and the maximum function to the object upper bound and the new upper bound. Here, minimum and maximum mean that we take the minimum or maximum of each coordinate to create a new set of coordinates. When the process is completed, all objects are encompassed within the bounding box.

CHAPTER 9

Using the Ray Tracing Definition Language

Now that we have described how this part of the program creates a scene, we will regress a bit and describe how to write a data file containing scene data. First, take a look at the sample data files given in Appendix A. These are formatted similar to the QRT input language, but are simplified without violating the relaxed requirements of the parser developed above. Note that the use of parentheses, equals signs, etc. provide a clear understanding of what is being done. However, the program described in this chapter is more flexible in the data structure it requires. In the sections that follow, you'll see the bare minimum that must be included in each data file for the particular property being described. You can insert any optional characters you desire to enhance program readability. Furthermore, you can add any comments you need by enclosing them in curly brackets. (Note that the parser converts all letters of the alphabet to upper case so you can use any combination of upper and lower case to enhance readability. They are treated the same, and will end up as capital letters after being parsed.) String type characters are defined as all alphanumerics plus the underscore character(_) and the decimal point(.). The minus(-), and right parenthesis ()) characters are also considered string type characters, but only if they are at the beginning of a string.

FILE_NAME

In order to specify the name of the output file for the scene data, the string FILE_NAME must appear in the data stream. It must be followed by at least one non-string type character and may be followed by as many non-string type characters as desired. The next string must be an MS-DOS compatible type file name.

PATTERN

The PATTERN string is used to initiate the description of a pattern. (The pattern is projected onto the surface of whatever object has a pattern of this name.) The string must be followed by at least one string type character and may be followed by as many non-string type characters as desired. The following strings may follow the PATTERN string:

X_SIZE This denotes the size of the pattern in the x direction. It must be followed by one or more non-string type characters, followed by a number representing the x pattern size, then followed by one or more non-string type characters.

Y_SIZE This denotes the size of the pattern in the y direction. It must be followed by one or more non-string type characters, followed by a number representing the y pattern size, and followed by one or more non-string type characters.

NAME This denotes the name of the pattern. It must be followed by one or more non-string type characters, followed by a string giving the pattern name, which must be followed by one or more non-string type characters.

The above three strings are mandatory for the PATTERN description. Following them one or more groups of strings must occur to provide a description of the pattern. The first entry in each group must be one of the following three strings RECTANGLE, which denotes a rectangle pattern, CIRCLE, which denotes a circle pattern, or POLYGON, which denotes a polygon pattern. The string must be followed by one or more non-string type characters. Following all of the information that makes up one of these three types of patterns, a right parenthesis must occur to complete the pattern data.

The following strings may follow the RECTANGLE string.

START_X This denotes the beginning x position of the rectangle pattern. It must be followed by one or more non-string type characters, which must be followed by a number corresponding to the x pattern beginning position, which must be followed by one or more non-string type characters.

START_Y This denotes the beginning y position of the rectangle pattern. It must be followed by one or more non-string type characters, which must be followed by a number corresponding to the y pattern beginning position, which must be followed by one or more non-string type characters.

END_X This denotes the end x position of the rectangle pattern. It must be followed by one or more non-string type characters, which must be followed by a number corresponding to the x pattern ending position, which must be followed by one or more non-string type characters.

END_Y This denotes the end y position of the rectangle pattern. It must be followed by one or more non-string type characters, which must be followed by a number corresponding to the y pattern ending position, which must be followed by one or more non-string type characters.

Color Information Any of the items which make up the color data may be specified in the rectangle pattern data. These are described in the next section. Note that there is no specific order in which the acceptable strings need to be listed. You may arrange them at your convenience. After all information for the rectangle has been supplied, a right parenthesis must occur to terminate the rectangle pattern data.

The following strings may follow the CIRCLE string.

RADIUS This denotes the radius of the circle pattern. It must be followed by one or more non-string type characters, which must be followed by a number corresponding to the x pattern beginning position, which must be followed by one or more non-string type characters.

Color Information Any of the items which make up the color data may be specified in the circle pattern data. These are described in the next section. Note that there is no specific order in which the acceptable strings need to be listed. You may arrange them at your convenience. After all information for the circle has been supplied, a right parenthesis must occur to terminate the rectangle pattern data.

The following strings may follow the POLYGON string.

POINT This denotes that the coordinates of one point of the polygon pattern will follow. It must be followed by one or more non-string type characters, which must be followed by a number corresponding to the x coordinate of the polygon, which must be followed by one or more non-string type characters, which must be followed by a number corresponding to the y coordinate of the polygon, which must be followed by one or more non-string type characters. The POINT string and its associated numbers must occur at least three times to define a polygon.

Color Information Any of the items which make up the color data may be specified in the polygon pattern data. These are described in the next section. Note that there is no specific order in which the acceptable strings need to be listed. You may arrange them at your convenience. After all information for the polygon has been supplied, a right parenthesis must occur to terminate the rectangle pattern data.

COLOR

Color information may be supplied in two ways. First, there is a default set of color information which will be used for an object or pattern if other color information is not furnished. This default color information may be set by placing the string COLOR in the data file. Any of the items of color information shown below may then occur. When all color information is complete, the color section must be completed by a right parenthesis. The other way of supplying color information is to include it in the description of an object or pattern. Any of the color information items shown below may be included in an object or pattern description and will then supersede the default information for this object or pattern only. The strings that may be included as color information are as follows (the order is immaterial):

AMB This denotes the character of the ambient light impinging upon the object or pattern. It must be followed by one or more non-string type characters, which must be followed by three numbers (separated by one or more non-string type characters) which make up the ambient light red, green, and blue components. The last number must be followed by one or more non-string type characters.

DIFF This denotes the character of the light diffused by the object or pattern. It must be followed by one or more non-string type characters, which must be followed by three numbers (separated by one or more non-string type characters) which make up the diffused light red, green, and blue components. The last number must be followed by one or more non-string type characters.

MIRROR This denotes the amount of light directly reflected by the object or pattern. It must be followed by one or more non-string type characters, which must be followed by three numbers (separated by one or more non-string type characters) which make up the reflecting red, green, and blue characteristics. The last number must be followed by one or more non-string type characters.

TRANS This denotes the light transmission characteristics of a transparent or semi-transparent object or pattern. It must be followed by one or more non-string type characters, which must be followed by three numbers (separated by one or more non-string type characters) which make up the transmission red, green, and blue components. The last number must be followed by one or more non-string type characters.

DENSITY This denotes the density characteristics of an object or pattern. It must be followed by one or more non-string type characters, which must be followed by three numbers (separated by one or more non-string type characters) which make up the density red, green, and blue components. The last number must be followed by one or more non-string type characters.

INDEX This denotes the index of refraction of the object or pattern. It must be followed by one or more non-string type characters which must be followed by a floating-point number which is the index of refraction, which must be followed by one or more non-string type characters.

DITHER This denotes the dither to be applied to an object or pattern. It must be followed by one or more non-string type characters which must be followed by a floating-point number which is the amount of dither between two different colors, which must be followed by one or more non-string type characters.

SREFLECT This denotes the specular reflection coefficient for an object or pattern. It must be followed by one or more non-string type characters which must be followed by a floating-point number which is the specular reflection coefficient, which must be followed by one or more non-string type characters.

REFLECT This denotes the specular reflection for an object or pattern. It must be followed by one or more non-string type characters, which must be followed by a floating-point number that is the specular reflection, which must be followed by one or more non-string type characters.

BEGIN_BBOX

The BEGIN_BBOX string marks the beginning of a box that will enclose several objects. It must be followed by at least one non-string type character. It is followed by descriptions of all of the objects which are to be enclosed within the box. The box is terminated by the string END_BBOX, which is followed by one or more non-string type characters.

BEGIN_INSTANCES

The BEGIN_INSTANCES string marks the beginning of an object or group of objects that are to appear as a group at several places throughout a scene. It must be followed by one or more non-string type characters. This must be followed by the descriptions of one or more objects which make up the instance. The instance description is terminated by the string END_INSTANCES, followed by one or more non-string type characters. The BEGIN_INSTANCES and END_INSTANCES strings may occur only once in a data file. All instances to be used in the scene must be included between these two strings in their one occurrence.

SPHERE

The SPHERE string denotes data for an object which is a sphere. It is followed by one or more non-string type characters. This is followed by any of the sphere descriptive items shown below. Finally, the sphere description is terminated by a right parenthesis. The legitimate strings for a sphere are:

LOC This denotes the location of the sphere. It must be followed by one or more non-string type characters, which must be followed by three numbers (separated by one or more non-string type characters) which make up the location vector. The last number must be followed by one or more non-string type characters.

RADIUS This denotes the radius of the sphere. It must be followed by one or more non-string type characters, which must be followed by a floating-point number which is the sphere radius, which must be followed by one or more non-string type characters.

PATTERN This denotes that a pattern is to be applied to the surface of the sphere. It must be followed by one or more non-string type characters, which are followed by a string which is the name of the pattern to be used, which must be followed by one or more non-string type characters.

REMOVE This denotes a type of pattern that is used to remove a part of an object. It must be followed by one or more non-string type characters, which are followed by a string which is the name of the remove pattern to be used, which must be followed by one or more non-string type characters.

XMULT This denotes a multiplier for the size of the sphere. It must be followed by one or more non-string type characters, which must be followed by a floating-point number which is the x multiplier, which must be followed by one or more non-string type characters.

YMULT This denotes a multiplier for the size of the sphere. It must be followed by one or more non-string type characters, which must be followed by a floating-point number which is the y multiplier, which must be followed by one or more non-string type characters.

NAME This denotes a name for the sphere. It is used only when the sphere is part of an instance. It must be followed by one or more non-string type characters, which are followed by a string which is the name of the sphere, which must be followed by one or more non-string type characters.

PAREN This is the right parenthesis which terminates the sphere description.

Color Information Any of the items which make up the color data may be specified in the sphere object data. These are described in the previous section. Note that there is no specific order in which the acceptable strings need to be listed. You may arrange them at your convenience. After all information for the sphere has been supplied, a right parenthesis must occur to terminate the rectangle pattern data.

TRIANGLE

The TRIANGLE string denotes data for an object which is a triangle. It is followed by one or more non-string type characters. This is followed by any of the triangle descriptive items shown below. Finally, the triangle description is terminated by a right parenthesis. The legitimate strings for a triangle are:

LOC This denotes the location of the triangle. It must be followed by one or more non-string type characters, which must be followed by three numbers (separated by one or more non-string type characters) which make up the location vector. The last number must be followed by one or more non-string type characters.

V1 This denotes one of the apexes of the triangle. It is assumed that the first apex of the triangle is indicated by the location vector. This is the second apex. Its position is given with respect to the first apex. It must be followed by one or more non-string type characters, which must be followed by three numbers (separated by one or more non-string type characters) which make up the apex coordinates. The last number must be followed by one or more non-string type characters.

V2 This denotes one of the apexes of the triangle. It is assumed that the first apex of the triangle is indicated by the location vector. This is the third apex. Its position is given with respect to the first apex. It must be followed by one or more non-string type characters, which must be followed by three numbers (separated by one or more non-string type characters) which make up the apex coordinates. The last number must be followed by one or more non-string type characters.

PATTERN This denotes that a pattern is to be applied to the surface of the triangle. It must be followed by one or more non-string type characters, which are followed by a string which is the name of the pattern to be used, which must be followed by one or more non-string type characters.

REMOVE This denotes a type of pattern that is used to remove a part of an object. It must be followed by one or more non-string type characters, which are followed by a string which is the name of the remove pattern to be used, which must be followed by one or more non-string type characters.

XMULT This denotes a multiplier for the size of the triangle. It must be followed by one or more non-string type characters, which must be followed by a floating-point number which is the x multiplier, which must be followed by one or more non-string type characters.

YMULT This denotes a multiplier for the size of the triangle. It must be followed by one or more non-string type characters, which must be followed by a floating-point number which is the y multiplier, which must be followed by one or more non-string type characters.

NAME This denotes a name for the triangle. It is used only when the sphere is part of an instance. It must be followed by one or more non-string type characters, which are followed by a string which is the name of the triangle, which must be followed by one or more non-string type characters.

PAREN This is the right parenthesis which terminates the triangle description.

Color Information Any of the items which make up the color data may be specified in the triangle object data. These are described in a previous section. Note that there is no specific order in which the acceptable strings need to be listed. You may arrange them at your convenience. After all information for the triangle has been supplied, a right parenthesis must occur to terminate the triangle pattern data.

RING

The RING string denotes data for an object which is a ring. It is followed by one or more non-string type characters. This is followed by any of the ring descriptive items shown below. Finally, the ring description is terminated by a right parenthesis. The legitimate strings for a ring are:

LOC This denotes the location of the ring. It must be followed by one or more non-string type characters, which must be followed by three numbers (separated by one or more non-string type characters) which make up the location vector. The last number must be followed by one or more non-string type characters.

V1 This denotes one of two vectors which define the plane of the ring. Its position is given with respect to location vector. It must be followed by one or more non-string type characters, which must be followed by three numbers (separated by one or more non-string type characters) which make up the vector. The last number must be followed by one or more non-string type characters.

V2 This denotes the second of two vectors which define the plane of the ring. Its position is given with respect to location vector. It must be followed by one or more non-string type characters, which must be followed by three numbers (separated by one or more non-string type characters) which make up the vector. The last number must be followed by one or more non-string type characters.

RAD_1 This denotes the inner radius of the ring. It must be followed by one or more non-string type characters, which must be followed by a floating-point number which is the inner ring radius, which must be followed by one or more non-string type characters.

RAD_2 This denotes the outer radius of the ring. It must be followed by one or more non-string type characters, which must be followed by a floating-point number which is the outer ring radius, which must be followed by one or more non-string type characters.

PATTERN This denotes that a pattern is to be applied to the surface of the ring. It must be followed by one or more non-string type characters, which are followed by a string which is the name of the pattern to be used, which must be followed by one or more non-string type characters.

REMOVE This denotes a type of pattern that is used to remove a part of an object. It must be followed by one or more non-string type characters, which are followed by a string which is the name of the remove pattern to be used, which must be followed by one or more non-string type characters.

XMULT This denotes a multiplier for the size of the ring. It must be followed by one or more non-string type characters, which must be followed by a floating-point number which is the x multiplier, which must be followed by one or more non-string type characters.

YMULT This denotes a multiplier for the size of the ring. It must be followed by one or more non-string type characters, which must be followed by a floating-point number which is the y multiplier, which must be followed by one or more non-string type characters.

NAME This denotes a name for the ring. It is used only when the ring is part of an instance. It must be followed by one or more non-string type characters, which are followed by a string which is the name of the ring, which must be followed by one or more non-string type characters.

PAREN This is the right parenthesis which terminates the ring description.

Color Information Any of the items which make up the color data may be specified in the ring object data. These are described in a previous section. Note that there is no specific order in which the acceptable strings need to be listed. You may arrange them at your convenience. After all information for the ring has been supplied, a right parenthesis must occur to terminate the ring pattern data.

PARALLELOGRAM

The PARALLELOGRAM string denotes data for an object which is a parallelogram. It is followed by one or more non-string type characters. This is followed by any of the parallelogram descriptive items shown below. Finally, the parallelogram description is terminated by a right parenthesis. The legitimate strings for a parallelogram are:

LOC This denotes the location of the parallelogram. It must be followed by one or more non-string type characters, which must be followed by three numbers (separated by one or more non-string type characters) which make up the location vector. The last number must be followed by one or more non-string type characters.

V1 This denotes one of the corners of the parallelogram. It is assumed that the first corner of the parallelogram is indicated by the location vector. This is the next adjacent corner on one side of the first corner. Its position is given with respect to the first corner. It must be followed by one or more non-string type characters, which must be followed by three numbers (separated by one or more non-string type characters) which make up the corner coordinates. The last number must be followed by one or more non-string type characters.

V2 This denotes another of the corners of the parallelogram. It is assumed that the first corner of the triangle is indicated by the location vector and an adjacent corner to the first corner by V1. This is the adjacent corner on the other side of the first corner. Its position is given with respect to the first corner. It must be followed by one or more non-string type characters, which must be followed by three numbers (separated by one or more non-string type characters) which make up the corner coordinates. The last number must be followed by one or more non-string type characters.

PATTERN This denotes that a pattern is to be applied to the surface of the parallelogram. It must be followed by one or more non-string type characters, which are followed by a string which is the name of the pattern to be used, which must be followed by one or more non-string type characters.

REMOVE This denotes a type of pattern that is used to remove a part of an object. It must be followed by one or more non-string type characters, which are followed by a string which is the name of the remove pattern to be used, which must be followed by one or more non-string type characters.

XMULT This denotes a multiplier for the size of the parallelogram. It must be followed by one or more non-string type characters, which must be followed by a floating-point number which is the x multiplier, which must be followed by one or more non-string type characters.

YMULT This denotes a multiplier for the size of the parallelogram. It must be followed by one or more non-string type characters, which must be followed by a floating-point number which is the y multiplier, which must be followed by one or more non-string type characters.

NAME This denotes a name for the parallelogram. It is used only when the parallelogram is part of an instance. It must be followed by one or more non-string type characters, which are followed by a string which is the name of the parallelogram, which must be followed by one or more non-string type characters.

PAREN This is the right parenthesis which terminates the parallelogram description.

Color Information Any of the items which make up the color data may be specified in the parallelogram object data. These are described in a previous section. Note that there is no specific order in which the acceptable strings need to be listed. You may arrange them at your convenience. After all information for the parallelogram has been supplied, a right parenthesis must occur to terminate the parallelogram pattern data.

QUADRATIC

The QUADRATIC string denotes data for an object which is expressed by a quadratic equation. The equation to denote this object is: $A x^2 + B y2 + C z^2 + Ez = D$ (Equation 9-1). The string is followed by one or more non-string type characters. This is followed by any of the quadratic descriptive items shown below. Finally, the quadratic description is terminated by a right parenthesis. The legitimate strings for a quadratic are:

LOC This denotes the location of the quadratic. It must be followed by one or more non-string type characters, which must be followed by three numbers (separated by one or more non-string type characters) which make up the location vector. The last number must be followed by one or more non-string type characters.

A This denotes the coefficient of x^2 in the quadratic equation. It must be followed by one or more non-string type characters, which must be followed by a floating-point number which is the A coefficient value, which must be followed by one or more non-string type characters.

B This denotes the coefficient of y^2 in the quadratic equation. It must be followed by one or more non-string type characters, which must be followed by a floating-point number which is the B coefficient value, which must be followed by one or more non-string type characters.

C This denotes the coefficient of z^2 in the quadratic equation. It must be followed by one or more non-string type characters, which must be followed by a floating-point number which is the C coefficient value, which must be followed by one or more non-string type characters.

D This denotes the constant term in the quadratic equation. It must be followed by one or more non-string type characters, which must be followed by a floating-point number which is the D constant value, which must be followed by one or more non-string type characters.

E   This denotes the coefficient of *y* in the quadratic equation. It must be followed by one or more non-string type characters, which must be followed by a floating-point number which is the C coefficient value, which must be followed by one or more non-string type characters. Note that the program does not allow the equation to contain both a y and a y^2 term for any given object. If you try to include both, the program will terminate with an error message.

XMIN   This denotes the minimum value for the x coordinate in the quadratic equation. It must be followed by one or more non-string type characters, which must be followed by a floating-point number which is the minimum x value, which must be followed by one or more non-string type characters.

XMAX   This denotes the maximum value for the x coordinate in the quadratic equation. It must be followed by one or more non-string type characters, which must be followed by a floating-point number which is the maximum x value, which must be followed by one or more non-string type characters.

YMIN   This denotes the minimum value for the y coordinate in the quadratic equation. It must be followed by one or more non-string type characters, which must be followed by a floating-point number which is the minimum y value, which must be followed by one or more non-string type characters.

YMAX   This denotes the maximum value for the y coordinate in the quadratic equation. It must be followed by one or more non-string type characters, which must be followed by a floating-point number which is the maximum y value, which must be followed by one or more non-string type characters.

ZMIN   This denotes the minimum value for the z coordinate in the quadratic equation. It must be followed by one or more non-string type characters, which must be followed by a floating-point number which is the minimum z value, which must be followed by one or more non-string type characters.

ZMAX This denotes the maximum value for the z coordinate in the quadratic equation. It must be followed by one or more non-string type characters, which must be followed by a floating-point number which is the maximum z value, which must be followed by one or more non-string type characters.

DIR This denotes a vector which indicates the direction of the axis of the quadratic. It must be followed by one or more non-string type characters, which must be followed by three numbers (separated by one or more non-string type characters) which make up the direction vector. The last number must be followed by one or more non-string type characters.

PATTERN This denotes that a pattern is to be applied to the surface of the quadratic. It must be followed by one or more non-string type characters, which are followed by a string which is the name of the pattern to be used, which must be followed by one or more non-string type characters.

REMOVE This denotes a type of pattern that is used to remove a part of an object. It must be followed by one or more non-string type characters, which are followed by a string which is the name of the remove pattern to be used, which must be followed by one or more non-string type characters.

XMULT This denotes a multiplier for the size of the quadratic. It must be followed by one or more non-string type characters, which must be followed by a floating-point number which is the x multiplier, which must be followed by one or more non-string type characters.

YMULT This denotes a multiplier for the size of the quadratic. It must be followed by one or more non-string type characters, which must be followed by a floating-point number which is the y multiplier, which must be followed by one or more non-string type characters.

NAME This denotes a name for the quadratic. It is used only when the quadratic is part of an instance. It must be followed by one or more non-string type characters, which are followed by a string which is the name of the quadratic, which must be followed by one or more non-string type characters.

PAREN This is the right parenthesis which terminates the quadratic description.

Color information Any of the items which make up the color data may be specified in the quadratic object data. These are described in a previous section. Note that there is no specific order in which the acceptable strings need to be listed. You may arrange them at your convenience. After all information for the quadratic has been supplied, a right parenthesis must occur to terminate the quadratic pattern data.

CONE

The CONE string denotes data for an object which is expressed by a quadratic equation of the form:

$$h^2x^2 - 2r^2y^2 + h^2z^2 = 0 \quad \text{(Equation 9-2)}$$

where r is the radius of the cone at its base and h is the height of the cone. The string is followed by one or more non-string type characters. This is followed by any of the cone descriptive items shown below. Finally, the cone description is terminated by a right parenthesis. The legitimate strings for a cone are:

LOC This denotes the location of the cone. It must be followed by one or more non-string type characters, which must be followed by three numbers (separated by one or more non-string type characters) which make up the location vector. The last number must be followed by one or more non-string type characters.

RADIUS This denotes the radius of the cone at its base. It must be followed by one or more non-string type characters, which must be followed by a floating-point number which is the radius value, which must be followed by one or more non-string type characters.

HEIGHT This denotes the height of the cone. It must be followed by one or more non-string type characters, which must be followed by a floating point number which is the height value, which must be followed by one or more non-string type characters.

DIR This denotes a vector which indicates the direction of the axis of the cone. It must be followed by one or more non-string type characters, which must be followed by three numbers (separated by one or more non-string type characters) which make up the direction vector. The last number must be followed by one or more non-string type characters.

REMOVE This denotes a type of pattern that is used to remove a part of an object. It must be followed by one or more non-string type characters, which are followed by a string which is the name of the remove pattern to be used, which must be followed by one or more non-string type characters.

XMULT This denotes a multiplier for the size of the cone. It must be followed by one or more non-string type characters, which must be followed by a floating-point number which is the x multiplier, which must be followed by one or more non-string type characters.

YMULT This denotes a multiplier for the size of the cone. It must be followed by one or more non-string type characters, which must be followed by a floating-point number which is the y multiplier, which must be followed by one or more non-string type characters.

NAME This denotes a name for the cone. It is used only when the cone is part of an instance. It must be followed by one or more non-string type characters, which are followed by a string which is the name of the cone, which must be followed by one or more non-string type characters.

PAREN This is the right parenthesis which terminates the cone description.

Color Information Any of the items which make up the color data may be specified in the quadratic object data. These are described in a previous section. Note that there is no specific order in which the acceptable strings need to be listed. You may arrange them at your convenience. After all information for the cone has been supplied, a right parenthesis must occur to terminate the cone pattern data.

SKY

The SKY string denotes data for color of the sky. It is followed by one or more non-string type characters. This is followed by any of the sky descriptive items shown below. Finally, the sky description is terminated by a right parenthesis. The legitimate strings for the sky are:

ZENITH This denotes the color of the sky at the zenith. It must be followed by one or more non-string type characters, which must be followed by three numbers (separated by one or more non-string type characters) which make up the red, green, and blue components of the color. The last number must be followed by one or more non-string type characters.

HORIZ This denotes the color of the sky at the horizon. It must be followed by one or more non-string type characters, which must be followed by three numbers (separated by one or more non-string type characters) which make up the red, green, and blue components of the color. The last number must be followed by one or more non-string type characters.

DITHER This denotes the dither to be applied to the sky. It must be followed by one or more non-string type characters which must be followed by a floating-point number which is the amount of dither between two type characters.

PAREN This is the right parenthesis which terminates the sky description.

FOC_LENGTH

The FOC_LENGTH string denotes the focal length of a 35 millimeter lens to give the equivalent perspective to the picture. It must be followed by one or more non-string type characters, which are followed by a floating-point number giving the focal length of the lens, which is followed by one or more non-string type characters.

LAMP

The LAMP string denotes data for a light source. It is followed by one or more non-string type characters. This is followed by any of the lamp descriptive items shown below. Finally, the lamp description is terminated by a right parenthesis. The legitimate strings for the lamp are:

LOC This denotes the location of the light source. It must be followed by one or more non-string type characters, which must be followed by three numbers (separated by one or more non-string type characters) which make up the location vector. The last number must be followed by one or more non-string type characters.

RADIUS This denotes the radius of the light source. It must be followed by one or more non-string type characters, which must be followed by a floating-point number which is the radius of the light source, which must be followed by one or more non-string type characters.

DIST This denotes the distance from the light source at which the lighting of objects will be at a normal intensity. Objects closer than this will be overlit (washed out) while objects farther away will be darker than normal. The string must be followed by one or more non-string type characters, which must be followed by a floating-point number which is the distance of the light source, which must be followed by one or more non-string type characters.

PAREN This is the right parenthesis which terminates the light source description.

OBSERVER The OBSERVER string denotes data for the observer. It is followed by one or more non-string type characters. This is followed by any of the observer descriptive items shown below. Finally, the observer description is terminated by a right parenthesis. The legitimate strings for the observer are:

LOC This denotes the location of the observer. It must be followed by one or more non-string type characters, which must be followed by three numbers (separated by one or more non-string type characters) which make up the location vector. The last number must be followed by one or more non-string type characters.

LOOKAT This denotes the direction in which the observer is looking. It must be followed by one or more non-string type characters, which must be followed by three numbers (separated by one or more non-string type characters) which make up the direction vector. The last number must be followed by one or more non-string type characters.

UP This denotes the direction for the observer. It must be followed by one or more non-string type characters, which must be followed by three numbers (separated by one or more non-string type characters) which make up the UP vector. The last number must be followed by one or more non-string type characters.

PAREN This is the right parenthesis which terminates the observer description.

XRES

The XRES string denotes the x resolution of the display. It must be followed by one or more non-string type characters, which are followed by a floating-point number giving the x resolution, which is followed by one or more non-string type characters.

YRES

The YRES string denotes the y resolution of the display. It must be followed by one or more non-string type characters, which are followed by a floating-point number giving the y resolution, which is followed by one or more non-string type characters.

NAME

The NAME string denotes a name. It must be followed by one or more non-string type characters, which are followed by a string designating a name, which is followed by one or more non-string type characters.

Sample Files

Figure 9-1 is a small sample file of data for a scene written in the QRT language format. This file can be read and processed with the ray-tracing program described in this book. For comparison, Figure 9-2 lists the same file, showing the minimum that is required for processing the file with the input functions described in this chapter. You can see that you have a lot of flexibility with adding non-string type characters to create a format that you are comfortable with and which still can be read with these functions.

```
FILE_NAME = Sphere.RAW

PATTERN ( x_size = 60,
          y_size = 60,
          name = CHECK,
            RECTANGLE (
                start_x = 0,
                start_y = 0,
                end_x = 30,
                end_y = 30,
                diff = (.1,1.0,.1),
                dither = 0,
                        )
            RECTANGLE (
                start_x = 30,
                start_y = 30,
```

```
                        end_x = 60,
                        end_y = 60,
                        diff = (.1,1.0,.1),
                        dither = 0,
                              )
          )


PARALLELOGRAM  (   loc = ( -10000, 0, -10000),
                        v1  = (20000, 0, 0),
                        v2 = (0, 0, 20000),
                        diff = (.8, .8, 0),
                        dither = 0,
                        pattern = CHECK
                        xmult = 2
                        ymult = 2
                    )


SPHERE  (     loc   = (200, 90, 80),
              radius   = 35,
              diff      = (.3, .3, .8),
              amb   = (.32, .32, .32),
              reflect   = .60,
              sreflect = 20
              xmult   = 1.0,
              ymult   = 1.0,
            )


LAMP    (loc = (120, 120, -50),
          radius = 5,
          dist = 80
          )


LAMP    (loc = (120, 150, 80),
          radius = 5,
          dist = 70
          )


SKY     (horiz = (.2, .2, .55),
          zenith = (.1, .1, .25),
          dither = 1
          )
```

```
XRES = 320
YRES = 200

FOC_LENGTH = 80
```

Figure 9-1. Sample QRT Data File

```
FILE_NAME Sphere.RAW

PATTERN ( x_size 60
          y_size 60
          name CHECK
            RECTANGLE (
                start_x 0
                start_y 0
                end_x 30
                end_y 30
                diff .1 1.0 .1
                dither 0
                        )
            RECTANGLE )
                start_x 30
                start_y 30
                end_x 60
                end_y 60
                diff .1 1.0 .1
                dither 0
                        )
        )

PARALLELOGRAM (
     loc -10000 0 -10000
     v1 20000 0 0
     v2 0 0 20000
     diff .8 .8 0
     dither  0
     pattern CHECK
     xmult 2
     ymult 2
            )
```

```
SPHERE (
     loc 200 90 80
     radius 35
     diff .3 .3 .8
     amb .32 .32 .32
     reflect .60
     sreflect 20
     xmult 1.0
     ymult 1.0
        )

LAMP (
     loc 120 120 -50
     radius  5
     dist 80
        )

LAMP (
     loc 120 150 80
     radius 5
     dist 70
        )
SKY (
     horiz .2 .2 .55
     zenith .1 .1 .25
     dither 1
        )

XRES 320
YRES 200

FOC_LENGTH 80
```

Figure 9-2. Sample Simplified Data File

CHAPTER 10

Functions that Match an Object: The Concept of Virtual Functions

One of the most critical things to the philosophy of object-oriented programming is to have a function that can be applied to objects of several different classes and will automatically perform the appropriate action for whatever class the object belongs to. For example, suppose we have the classes *Sphere, Cone,* and *Cube*. We want to have a function *Test* and be able to say:

object.Test();

Now, if *object* is a member of class *Sphere* we want the function to perform one set of test operations, but if the object is of class *Cone* we want a different set of operations performed and if the object is of class *Cube,* we want another set performed that is totally different from those performed for either *Sphere* or *Cone*. The C++ language provides the capability for doing this through the use of *Virtual* functions. It works in this manner:

First, define a base class.

```
class Shape
{
    ... class member definitions;
    ...;
```

```
    virtual int Test(int a, float b);
      ...;
};
```

The virtual function is a prototype as a part of the class definition. It begins with the word *Virtual,* followed by the variable that is to be returned by the function, followed by the function name which is followed by the types and names of parameters passed by the function, enclosed in parentheses. Thus, except for being preceded by the word *Virtual* the function definition is the same used for any function. Next, we define a derived class for each type of object we want available. For example:

```
class Sphere: public Shape
{
      ...class member definitions;
      ...;
      int Test(int a, float b);
      ...;
};
```

The fact that the name of the class is followed by a colon, the word public, and the name of a previously defined class, makes this class a derived class, which inherits all of the characteristics of the base class and may include various special members of its own. If you want to use the common function (*Test* in the example) you must include in the definition of *Sphere* a prototype of the function which is the same as that for the *Virtual* function in the base class, except that the word *Virtual* is omitted. The same procedure for the definition of the classes is the *Cone* and *Cube*.

Next, you must have a definition for each of the functions. This includes a definition for the function for the base class, which must be defined, even if there is nothing in it. For example,

```
int Shape :: Test(int a, float b)
{};

int Sphere :: Test(int a, float b)
{
        operation a;
        operation b;
        ...;
}

int Cone :: Test(int a, float b)
{
        operation c;
        operation d;
        ...;
}

int Cube :: Test(int a, float b)
{
        operation e;
        operation f;
        ...;
}
```

Note the format for the first line of each function definition. The type of the variable returned by the function comes first. It must be the same as it was in the prototype definition. Next comes the name of the particular class for which the function is being defined. It is followed by two colons, the name of the function and the variables that are passed by it. This part of the definition must be the same for each definition of the function and match the prototype definition. Finally comes the body of the definition which may be different for each of the definitions. Once you have done this groundwork, you can use this function throughout your program as we discussed at the beginning of the chapter. Call the function by preceding the normal function call with the name of an object, followed by a dot. The function will have access to the members of the named object. The program will automatically look at the object, determine to what class it belongs, and use the definition of the function which matches that class to perform the function operations.

The *objects.cpp* File

In the ray-tracing program, all the functions that make use of the virtual-function technique to provide different actions for each class of objects are grouped in the file called *objects.cpp*. This file is listed in Figure 10-1. Although the functions are used at various places throughout the program, they are all described in this chapter.

Constructors

The *constructor* is a special kind of function automatically called by the program to initialize an object, each time an object is defined. It is identified by the same name as the class. Thus, a typical *constructor* would look like:

```
Sphere :: Sphere()
{
member definitions.;
}
```

The *objects.cpp* file begins with the definition of a *constructor* for each of the five different types of objects. You can look at them in the listing of Figure 10-1. There is nothing particularly unusual about them. They simply specify the initial values the members of the object should have. Mostly they are NULLS. The type in each case corresponds to the proper number for the type of object. The multipliers are set to default values of one. The color information is set to the default values.

Destructors

Whenever you define a class member, the required memory space remains assigned to that class member forever unless you deallocate it. If you want to deallocate the memory assigned to this class member when you are through using it, you must call a *destructor* function. Similarly, if you assign space for a class member with *new*, this memory will be reserved forever unless you deallocate it with the function *delete*. Since almost all of our class members in this program are allocated using *new*, we don't use destructors. If you need them for your program, refer to the C++ manual for details on how to create them.

Figure 10-1. The objects.cpp File

```
/*

        objects.c = Functions belonging to each of the classes
                    derived from the Object class.

                    By Roger T. Stevens 3/1/90

*/

#include "render.hpp"

/*

                        Sphere Constructor

*/

Sphere::Sphere()
{
  type = SPHERE;
  nextobj = NULL;
  child = NULL;
  pattern = NULL;
  remove = NULL;
  name[0] = NULL;
  xmult = 1;
  ymult = 1;
  upper = Vector();
  lower = Vector();
}
```

```
/*
  ┌─────────────────────────────────────────────────────────┐
  │                                                           │
  │                    Triangle Constructor                   │
  │                                                           │
  └─────────────────────────────────────────────────────────┘
*/

Triangle::Triangle()
{
  type = TRIANGLE;
  nextobj = NULL;
  child = NULL;
  pattern = NULL;
  remove = NULL;
  name[0] = NULL;
  xmult = 1;
  ymult = 1;
  upper = Vector();
  lower = Vector();
}

/*
  ┌─────────────────────────────────────────────────────────┐
  │                                                           │
  │                     Ring Constructor                      │
  │                                                           │
  └─────────────────────────────────────────────────────────┘
*/

Ring::Ring()
{
  type = RING;
  nextobj = NULL;
  child = NULL;
  pattern = NULL;
  remove = NULL;
  name[0] = NULL;
  xmult = 1;
  ymult = 1;
  upper = Vector();
  lower = Vector();
}
```

```
/*
```

```
                      Parallelogram Constructor
```

```
*/
```

```
Parallelogram::Parallelogram()
{
  type = PARALLELOGRAM;
  nextobj = NULL;
  child = NULL;
  pattern = NULL;
  remove = NULL;
  name[0] = NULL;
  xmult = 1;
  ymult = 1;
  upper = Vector();
  lower = Vector();
  vect3 = Vector();
}
/*
```

```
                        Quadratic Constructor
```

```
*/
```

```
Quadratic::Quadratic()
{
  type = QUADRATIC;
  nextobj = NULL;
  child = NULL;
  pattern = NULL;
  remove = NULL;
  name[0] = NULL;
  cterm = 0;
  yterm = 0;
  xmult = 1;
  ymult = 1;
  upper = Vector();
  lower = Vector();
```

```
}
```

```
/*
┌──────────────────────────────────────────────────┐
│            Normal finder for generic object        │
└──────────────────────────────────────────────────┘
*/

void Object::FindNorm(Vector * normal, Vector * position)
{
}
```

```
/*
┌──────────────────────────────────────────────────┐
│              Normal finder for sphere               │
└──────────────────────────────────────────────────┘
*/

void Sphere::FindNorm(Vector * normal, Vector * position)
{
        * normal = *position - loc;   vector from centr to surface pt
        * normal = ~ *normal;
}
```

```
/*
┌──────────────────────────────────────────────────┐
│            Normal finder for parallelogram          │
└──────────────────────────────────────────────────┘
*/

void Parallelogram::FindNorm(Vector * normal, Vector * position)
{
  *normal = norm;
}
```

```
/*
┌──────────────────────────────────────────────────┐
│             Normal finder for triangle              │
└──────────────────────────────────────────────────┘
*/
```

```
void Triangle::FindNorm(Vector * normal, Vector * position)
{
  *normal = norm;
}


/*
┌─────────────────────────────────────────────────────────┐
│                                                           │
│                 Normal finder for ring                    │
│                                                           │
└─────────────────────────────────────────────────────────┘
*/

void Ring::FindNorm(Vector * normal, Vector * position)
{
  *normal = norm;
}


/*
┌─────────────────────────────────────────────────────────┐
│                                                           │
│                Normal finder for quadratic                │
│                                                           │
└─────────────────────────────────────────────────────────┘
*/

void Quadratic::FindNorm(Vector * normal, Vector * position)
{
  Vector newpos,newdir;

  newpos = *position - loc;
  if ((vect1.x == 0) && (vect1.y == 1) && (vect1.z == 0))
 {
  *normal = vect2 * newpos;
  *normal = ~ *normal;
 }
 else
 {
  newpos = newpos.Rotate(cos1, sin1, cos2, sin2);
  newdir = vect2 * newpos;
  *normal = newdir.Rev_Rotate(cos1, sin1, cos2, sin2);
 }
}
```

```
/*
        +--------------------------------------------------+
        |      Find Bounding Box for Generic Object        |
        +--------------------------------------------------+
*/

void Object::FindBbox(Vector * v1, Vector * v2)
{}

/*
        +--------------------------------------------------+
        |         Find Bounding Box for Sphere             |
        +--------------------------------------------------+
*/

void Sphere::FindBbox(Vector * v1, Vector * v2)
{
  v1->x=loc.x-vect1.x;
  v2->x=loc.x+vect1.x;
  v1->y=loc.y-vect1.x;
  v2->y=loc.y+vect1.x;
  v1->z=loc.z-vect1.x;
  v2->z=loc.z+vect1.x;
}

/*
        +--------------------------------------------------+
        |       Find Bounding Box for Parallelogram        |
        +--------------------------------------------------+
*/

void Parallelogram::FindBbox(Vector * v1, Vector * v2)
{
  Vector point2, point3, point4;
  point2 = loc + vect1;
  point3 = loc + vect2;
  point4 = point3 + vect1;
  v1->x=MIN(point2.x,point3.x);
  v1->x=MIN(v1->x,point4.x);
  v1->x=MIN(v1->x,loc.x);
  v1->y=MIN(point2.y,point3.y);
  v1->y=MIN(v1->y,point4.y);
```

```
    v1->y=MIN(v1->y,loc.y);
    v1->z=MIN(point2.z,point3.z);
    v1->z=MIN(v1->z,point4.z);
    v1->z=MIN(v1->z,loc.z);
    v2->x=MAX(point2.x,point3.x);
    v2->x=MAX(v2->x,point4.x);
    v2->x=MAX(v2->x,loc.x);
    v2->y=MAX(point2.y,point3.y);
    v2->y=MAX(v2->y,point4.y);
    v2->y=MAX(v2->y,loc.y);
    v2->z=MAX(point2.z,point3.z);
    v2->z=MAX(v2->z,point4.z);
    v2->z=MAX(v2->z,loc.z);
}


/*
        ┌──────────────────────────────────────────────┐
        │                                              │
        │        Find Bounding Box for Triangle        │
        │                                              │
        └──────────────────────────────────────────────┘

*/

void Triangle::FindBbox(Vector * v1, Vector * v2)
{
    Vector point2, point3;

    point2 = loc + vect1;
    point3 = loc + vect2;
    v1->x=MIN(point2.x,point3.x);
    v1->x=MIN(v1->x,loc.x);
    v1->y=MIN(point2.y,point3.y);
    v1->y=MIN(v1->y,loc.y);
    v1->z=MIN(point2.z,point3.z);
    v1->z=MIN(v1->z,loc.z);
    v2->x=MAX(point2.x,point3.x);
    v2->x=MAX(v2->x,loc.x);
    v2->y=MAX(point2.y,point3.y);
    v2->y=MAX(v2->y,loc.y);
    v2->z=MAX(point2.z,point3.z);
    v2->z=MAX(v2->z,loc.z);
}
```

195

```
/*
   +------------------------------------------------+
   |          Find Bounding Box for Bounding Box    |
   +------------------------------------------------+
*/

void BBox::FindBbox(Vector * v1, Vector * v2)
{
  *v1 = lower;
  *v2 = upper;
}

/*
   +------------------------------------------------+
   |              Find Bounding Box for Ring        |
   +------------------------------------------------+
*/

void Ring::FindBbox(Vector * v1, Vector * v2)
{
  v1->x = loc.x-vect3.y;
  v2->x = loc.x+vect3.y;
  v1->y = loc.y-vect3.y;
  v2->y = loc.y+vect3.y;
  v1->z = loc.z-vect3.y;
  v2->z = loc.z+vect3.y;
}

/*
   +------------------------------------------------+
   |           Find Bounding Box for Quadratic      |
   +------------------------------------------------+
*/

void Quadratic::FindBbox(Vector * v1, Vector * v2)
{
  *v1 = lower;
  *v2 = upper;
  *v1 = *v1 + loc;
  *v2 = *v2 + loc;
}
```

```
/*
    ┌──────────────────────────────────────────────────────────┐
    │                                                            │
    │          Change scale of user defined generic Object       │
    │                                                            │
    └──────────────────────────────────────────────────────────┘
*/

void Object::Scale_Instance(Vector * mult,int fflag)
{
}

/*
    ┌──────────────────────────────────────────────────────────┐
    │                                                            │
    │          Change scale of user defined Sphere               │
    │                                                            │
    └──────────────────────────────────────────────────────────┘
*/

void Sphere::Scale_Instance(Vector * mult, int fflag)
{
  float size;

  size = Min(mult->x,mult->y,mult->z);
  loc = loc * *mult;
  vect1.x *= size;
  child->Scale_Instance(mult,FALSE);
  if (!fflag)
    nextobj->Scale_Instance(mult,FALSE);
}

/*
    ┌──────────────────────────────────────────────────────────┐
    │                                                            │
    │          Change scale of user defined Parallelogram        │
    │                                                            │
    └──────────────────────────────────────────────────────────┘
*/

void Parallelogram::Scale_Instance(Vector * mult, int fflag)
{

  loc = loc * *mult;
  vect1 = vect1 * *mult;
  vect2 = vect2 * *mult;
  child->Scale_Instance(mult,FALSE);
```

```
  if (!fflag)
  nextobj->Scale_Instance(mult,FALSE);
}


/*  ┌──────────────────────────────────────────────┐
    │                                              │
    │         Change scale of user defined Ring     │
    │                                              │
    └──────────────────────────────────────────────┘

*/

void Ring::Scale_Instance(Vector * mult, int fflag)
{
  float size;

  size = Min(mult->x,mult->y,mult->z);
  loc = loc * *mult;
  vect1 = vect1 * *mult;
  vect2 = vect2 * *mult;
  vect3.x *= size;
  vect3.y *= size;
  child->Scale_Instance(mult,FALSE);
  if (!fflag)
  nextobj->Scale_Instance(mult,FALSE);
}


/*  ┌──────────────────────────────────────────────┐
    │                                              │
    │       Change scale of user defined Triangle   │
    │                                              │
    └──────────────────────────────────────────────┘

*/

void Triangle::Scale_Instance(Vector * mult, int fflag)
{

  loc = loc * *mult;
  vect1 = vect1 * *mult;
  vect2 = vect2 * *mult;
  child->Scale_Instance(mult,FALSE);
  if (!fflag)
  nextobj->Scale_Instance(mult,FALSE);
}
```

```
/*
┌─────────────────────────────────────────────────────────────┐
│              Change scale of user defined Quadratic           │
└─────────────────────────────────────────────────────────────┘
*/

void Quadratic::Scale_Instance(Vector * mult, int fflag)
{
  float size;

  upper = upper * *mult;
  lower = lower * *mult;
  loc = loc * *mult;
  child->Scale_Instance(mult,FALSE);
  if (!fflag)
  nextobj->Scale_Instance(mult,FALSE);
}

/*
┌─────────────────────────────────────────────────────────────┐
│           Determine position variables for generic object     │
└─────────────────────────────────────────────────────────────┘
*/

void Object :: Position(float * pos1, float *pos2, Vector *
  location)
{
}

/*
┌─────────────────────────────────────────────────────────────┐
│              Determine position variables for sphere          │
└─────────────────────────────────────────────────────────────┘
*/

void Sphere :: Position(float * pos1, float *pos2, Vector *
  location)

{
    Vector delta;

    delta = * location - loc;
```

```
    *pos1 = atan2(delta.x,delta.y) * vect1.x;
    *pos2 = atan2(sqrt((delta.x * delta.x) + (delta.y * delta.y)),
        delta.z) * vect1.x;
}

/*
┌─────────────────────────────────────────────────────┐
│                                                       │
│         Determine position variables for triangle     │
│                                                       │
└─────────────────────────────────────────────────────┘

*/

void Triangle :: Position(float * pos1, float *pos2, Vector *
  location)
{
    Vector delta;
    float length1, length2;

    delta = * location - loc;
    length1 = sqrt(vect1 % vect1);
    length2 = sqrt(vect2 % vect2);
    *pos1 = (delta % vect1)/length1;
    *pos2 = (delta % vect2)/length2;
}

/*
┌─────────────────────────────────────────────────────┐
│                                                       │
│       Determine position variables for parallelogram  │
│                                                       │
└─────────────────────────────────────────────────────┘

*/

void Parallelogram :: Position(float * pos1, float *pos2, Vector *
  location)
{
    Vector delta;
    float length1, length2;

    delta = * location - loc;
    length1 = sqrt(vect1 % vect1);
    length2 = sqrt(vect2 % vect2);
    *pos1 = (delta % vect1)/length1;
    *pos2 = (delta % vect2)/length2;
```

```
}

/*
┌─────────────────────────────────────────────────────────┐
│              Determine position variables for ring        │
└─────────────────────────────────────────────────────────┘
*/

void Ring :: Position(float * pos1, float *pos2, Vector *
  location)
{
    Vector delta;
    float length1, length2;

    delta = * location - loc;
    length1 = sqrt(vect1 % vect1);
    length2 = sqrt(vect2 % vect2);
    *pos1 = (delta % vect1)/length1;
    *pos2 = (delta % vect2)/length2;
}


/*
┌─────────────────────────────────────────────────────────┐
│            Determine position variables for quadratic     │
└─────────────────────────────────────────────────────────┘
*/

void Quadratic :: Position(float * pos1, float *pos2, Vector *
  location)
{
  Vector newpos;

  newpos = *location - loc;
  *pos1 = newpos.x;
  *pos2 = newpos.y;
}

/*
┌─────────────────────────────────────────────────────────┐
│                  Generic intersection test                │
└─────────────────────────────────────────────────────────┘
```

```
*/

int Object :: CollisionTest(Line * line, float *t)
{
  return(0);
}

/*
```

```
              Test for intersection of line with sphere
```

```
*/

int Sphere :: CollisionTest(Line * line, float *t)
{
  float a,b,c,d,t1;
  Vector temp;

  temp = loc - line->loc;
  c = (temp % temp) - n1;
  b = -2*(line->dir % temp);
  a = line->dir % line->dir;
  d = b*b - 4.0*a*c;
  if (d<=0)
        return(FALSE);
  d=sqrt(d); *t=(-b+d)/(a+a);
  t1=(-b-d)/(a+a);
  if (*t<=SMALL && t1 <=SMALL)
        return(FALSE);
  if (t1 > *t)
  {
        if (*t < SMALL)
                *t = t1;
  }
  else
        if (t1 > SMALL)
                *t = t1;
  return(TRUE);
}
```

```
/*
       ┌─────────────────────────────────────────────────┐
       │                                                 │
       │      Test for intersection of line with triangle │
       │                                                 │
       └─────────────────────────────────────────────────┘

*/

  int Triangle :: CollisionTest(Line * line, float *t)
{
  Vector delta, location;
  float dot, pos1, pos2,gu[3],gv[3];
  int i,j,crossing_no;

  dot = norm % line->dir;
  if (fabs(dot)<SMALL)
        return(FALSE);
  pos1 = n1;
  pos2 = norm % line->loc;
  *t=(pos1-pos2)/dot;
  location = line->loc + (line->dir * *t);
  delta = location - loc;
  if ((fabs(norm.x) > fabs(norm.y)) && (fabs(norm.x) >
        fabs(norm.z)))
     {
        gu[0] = - delta.y;
        gv[0] = - delta.z;
        gu[1] = vect1.y - delta.y;
        gv[1] = vect1.z - delta.z;
        gu[2] = vect2.y - delta.y;
        gv[2] = vect2.z - delta.z;
     }
  else
     {
        if (fabs(norm.y) > fabs(norm.z))
           {
                gu[0] = - delta.x;
                gv[0] = - delta.z;
                gu[1] = vect1.x - delta.x;
                gv[1] = vect1.z - delta.z;
                gu[2] = vect2.x - delta.x;
                gv[2] = vect2.z - delta.z;
           }
```

203

```
        else
        {
                gu[0] = - delta.x;
                gv[0] = - delta.y;
                gu[1] = vect1.x - delta.x;
                gv[1] = vect1.y - delta.y;
                gu[2] = vect2.x - delta.x;
                gv[2] = vect2.y - delta.y;
        }
}

crossing_no = 0;
for (i=0; i<3; i++)
{
    j = (i + 1) % 3;
    if ((((gv[i] < 0) && (gv[j] >= 0)) || ((gv[j] < 0) && (gv[i]
            >= 0)))
    {
            if ((gu[i]>=0) && (gu[j] >= 0))
                    crossing_no++;
            else
            {
                    if((gu[i]>=0) || (gu[j] >= 0))
                    {
                            if (gu[i] - gv[i] * (gu[j] - gu[i]) /
                                    (gv[j] - gv[i]) > 0)
                                    crossing_no++;
                    }
            }
    }
}
if ((crossing_no % 2) == 0)
        return(FALSE);
return(TRUE);
}
```

```
/*
    ┌─────────────────────────────────────────────────────┐
    │                                                       │
    │   Test for intersection of line with parallelogram    │
    │                                                       │
    └─────────────────────────────────────────────────────┘

*/

int Parallelogram :: CollisionTest(Line * line, float *t)
{
    Vector delta, location;
    float dot,pos1,pos2,gu[4],gv[4];
    int i,j,crossing_no;

    dot = norm % line->dir;
    if (fabs(dot)<SMALL)
        return(FALSE);
    pos1 = n1;
    pos2 = norm % line->loc;
    *t=(pos1-pos2)/dot;
    location = line->loc + (line->dir * *t);
    delta = location - loc;
    if ((fabs(norm.x) > fabs(norm.y)) && (fabs(norm.x) >
        fabs(norm.z)))
    {
       gu[0] = - delta.y;
       gv[0] = - delta.z;
       gu[1] = vect1.y - delta.y;
       gv[1] = vect1.z - delta.z;
       gu[2] = vect2.y + vect1.y - delta.y;
       gv[2] = vect2.z + vect1.z - delta.z;
       gu[3] = vect2.y - delta.y;
       gv[3] = vect2.z - delta.z;
    }
       else
       {
         if (fabs(norm.y) >= fabs(norm.z))
         {
            gu[0] = - delta.x;
            gv[0] = - delta.z;
            gu[1] = vect1.x - delta.x;
            gv[1] = vect1.z - delta.z;
            gu[2] = vect2.x + vect1.x - delta.x;
            gv[2] = vect2.z + vect1.z - delta.z;
```

205

```
                gu[3] = vect2.x - delta.x;
                gv[3] = vect2.z - delta.z;
        }
        else
        {
                gu[0] = - delta.x;
                gv[0] = - delta.y;
                gu[1] = vect1.x - delta.x;
                gv[1] = vect1.y - delta.y;
                gu[2] = vect2.x + vect1.x - delta.x;
                gv[2] = vect2.y + vect1.y - delta.y;
                gu[3] = vect2.x - delta.x;
                gv[3] = vect2.y - delta.y;
        }
}
crossing_no = 0;
for (i=0; i<4; i++)
{
        j = (i + 1) % 4;
        if (((gv[i] < 0) && (gv[j] >= 0)) || ((gv[j] < 0) &&
                        (gv[i]>= 0)))
        {
                        if ((gu[i]>=0) && (gu[j] >= 0))
                                crossing_no++;
                        else
                        {
                                if((gu[i]>=0) || (gu[j] >= 0))
                                        {
                                        if (gu[i] - gv[i] * (gu[j]
                                          gu[i]) /(gv[j] - gv[i])
                                          >0)crossing_no++;
                                        }
                        }
        }
}
if ((crossing_no % 2) == 0)
        return(FALSE);
```

```
  return(TRUE);
}

/*  ┌─────────────────────────────────────────────────┐
    │                                                 │
    │        Test for intersection of line with ring  │
    │                                                 │
    └─────────────────────────────────────────────────┘
*/

int Ring :: CollisionTest(Line * line, float *t)
{
  Vector delta, location;
  float dot, rad, pos1, pos2;
  dot  = norm % line->dir;
  if (fabs(dot)<SMALL)
        return(FALSE);
  pos1 = n1;
  pos2 = norm % line->loc;
  *t=(pos1-pos2)/dot;
  location = line->loc + (line->dir * *t);
  delta = location - loc;
  rad = sqrt(delta % delta);
  if (rad<(vect3.x) || rad>(vect3.y))
  return(FALSE);
  return(TRUE);
}

/*  ┌─────────────────────────────────────────────────────┐
    │                                                       │
    │       Test for intersection of line with quadratic    │
    │                                                       │
    └─────────────────────────────────────────────────────┘
*/

int Quadratic :: CollisionTest(Line * line, float *t)
{
  float a,b,c,d, t1;
  Vector location, loc1, tempdir;
  Line newline;

  newline.loc = line->loc - loc;
  if ((vect1.x == 0) && (vect1.y == 1) && (vect1.z == 0))
        newline.dir = line->dir;
```

207

```
else
{
        newline.dir = line->dir.Rotate(cos1, sin1, cos2, sin2);
        newline.loc = newline.loc.Rev_Rotate(cos1, sin1, cos2,
                    sin2);
}
if (yterm == 0)
{
    c = -(cterm) + vect2.x * newline.loc.x * newline.loc.x +
            vect2.y * newline.loc.y * newline.loc.y +
            vect2.z * newline.loc.z * newline.loc.z;
    b = 2*(vect2.x * newline.loc.x * newline.dir.x +
            vect2.y * newline.loc.y * newline.dir.y +
    vect2.z * newline.loc.z * newline.dir.z);
    a = vect2.x * newline.dir.x * newline.dir.x +
    vect2.y * newline.dir.y * newline.dir.y +
            vect2.z * newline.dir.z * newline.dir.z;
}
else
{
    c = -(cterm) + vect2.x * newline.loc.x * newline.loc.x -
            yterm * newline.loc.y +
            vect2.z * newline.loc.z * newline.loc.z;
    b = 2*(vect2.x * newline.loc.x * newline.dir.x -
            yterm * newline.dir.y +
    vect2.z * newline.loc.z * newline.dir.z);
    a = vect2.x * newline.dir.x * newline.dir.x +
    vect2.z * newline.dir.z * newline.dir.z;
}
d = b * b - 4.0*a*c;
if (d<0)
    return(FALSE);
d = sqrt(d);
*t = (-b+d)/(a+a);
t1 = (-b-d)/(a+a);
location = newline.loc + (newline.dir * *t);
loc1 = newline.loc + (newline.dir * t1);
if ((location.x < lower.x) ||
    (location.x > upper.x) ||
    (location.y < lower.y) ||
    (location.y > upper.y) ||
    (location.z < lower.z) ||
```

```
            (location.z > upper.z))
            *t = -1;
   if ((loc1.x < lower.x) ||
        (loc1.x > upper.x) ||
        (loc1.y < lower.y) ||
        (loc1.y > upper.y) ||
        (loc1.z < lower.z) ||
        (loc1.z > upper.z))
        t1 = -1;
   if (*t<=SMALL && t1 <=SMALL)
        return(FALSE);
   if (t1 > *t)
   {
        if (*t < SMALL)
                *t = t1;
   }
   else
        if (t1 > SMALL)
                *t = t1;
   return(TRUE);
}

/*
   ┌──────────────────────────────────────────────┐
   │                                                │
   │    Test for intersection of line with bounding box │
   │                                                │
   └──────────────────────────────────────────────┘

*/

int BBox :: CollisionTest(Line * line, float *t)
{
   float tminx, tmaxx, tminy, tmaxy,
   tminz, tmaxz, tmin, tmax, t1,t2;

   *t=10;
   if (fabs(line->dir.x) < SMALL)
   {
        if ((lower.x < line->loc.x) &&
            (upper.x > line->loc.x))
            {
                    tminx = -3e30;
                    tmaxx = 3e30;
     }
```

```
        else
            return(FALSE);
    }
    else
    {
        t1 = (lower.x-line->loc.x)/line->dir.x;
        t2 = (upper.x-line->loc.x)/line->dir.x;
        tminx = MIN(t1,t2);
        tmaxx = MAX(t1,t2);
        if (tmaxx<0)
            return(FALSE);
    }
    if (fabs(line->dir.y) < SMALL)
    {
        if ((lower.y < line->loc.y) &&
            (upper.y > line->loc.y))
        {
            tminy = -3e30;
            tmaxy=3e30;
        }
        else
            return(FALSE);
    }
    else
    {
        t1 = (lower.y-line->loc.y)/line->dir.y;
        t2 = (upper.y-line->loc.y)/line->dir.y;
        tminy = MIN(t1,t2);
        tmaxy = MAX(t1,t2);
        if (tmaxy<0)
            return(FALSE);
    }
    if (fabs(line->dir.z) < SMALL)
    {
        if ((lower.z < line->loc.z) &&
            (upper.z > line->loc.z))
        {
            tminz = -3e30;
            tmaxz=3e30;
        }
        else
            return(FALSE);
```

```
    }
    else
    {
        t1 = (lower.z-line->loc.z)/line->dir.z;
        t2 = (upper.z-line->loc.z)/line->dir.z;
        tminz = MIN(t1,t2);
        tmaxz = MAX(t1,t2);
        if (tmaxz<0)
            return(FALSE);
    }
        tmin = Max(tminx,tminy,tminz);
        tmax = Min(tmaxx,tmaxy,tmaxz);
        if (tmax<tmin)
            return(FALSE);
            return(TRUE);
}
```

Finding the Normal to an Object

Three of the object classes, the *Triangle, Ring,* and *Parallelogram* are plane figures. Their normal at any point is the same; it is the normal to the plane. This normal is calculated once at the time the figure is read in from the data file and stored within the object structure. Hence, the function *FindNorm* for these three classes of object simply gets the precomputed normal and puts it into the variable *normal.* The *Sphere* class has a normal that differs, depending upon the point on the sphere where you are located. This position is represented by the variable *position.* The normal is a vector drawn from the center of the sphere (represented by the vector *loc*) to the position. This has to be normalized.

For the surfaces represented by quadratic equations, things are a little more complicated. Usually, the quadratic surfaces are oriented around the y axis. If any other orientation is desired, it is specified in the vector *vect1.* We first define a vector *newpos,* which is the vector from the center (*loc*) of the object to the position where we are on the surface. Then check *vect1;* if it is a unit vector in the y direction, the normal vector is the normalized value of a vector which is the cross product of the vector *vect2* (a vector created from the coefficients of x^2, y^2, and z^2 in the quadratic equation) and the vector *newpos*. If *vect1* indicates that the quadric is rotated in some direction other than normal, first rotate the *newpos* vector to correspond with the normal orientation of the solid then find the normal, and reverse rotate it back to get the actual normal for the rotated solid.

Generating Bounding Boxes

This next series of functions generates bounding boxes that encompass various objects. The first function is empty for the base class . For the *Sphere* class, the bounding box has x, y, and z maximums which are the coordinates of the sphere center plus the radius, and x, y, and z minimums which are coordinates of the sphere center minus the radius. The function passes the addresses of two vectors, whose contents are changed by the function action. The first, *v1*, represents the corner of the box corresponding to the minimums, and the second, *v2*, the corner of the box corresponding to the maximums.

The parallelogram is defined by the *loc* vector, which marks the set of coordinates for the first corner of the parallelogram, and by two other vectors, *vect1* and *vect2*, which represent the location of two other corners of the parallelogram with respect to the first corner. The fourth corner is defined from the other three and the fact that pairs of sides of the figure are parallel. The function to find the bounding box computes the second, third, and fourth corners of the parallelogram in absolute coordinates (not referenced to *loc*) and then takes the maximum and minimum values of each of the three coordinates for the box corners.

The function to find the bounding box for the triangle works exactly the same as for the parallelogram, except there are only three corners for the figure instead of four.

The function to find the bounding box for the ring simply adds the outer radius of the ring to each of the three coordinates to obtain the maximum box corner and subtracts it from the coordinates to obtain the minimum box corner. This is not too efficient, since it generates a box which will hold the ring, no matter which direction it is oriented in. Taking into consideration the actual orientation of the ring, a much tighter bounding box can be generated. You may want to attempt this improvement.

For the quadratic, the upper and lower bounds of x, y, and z are specified at the time when data for the quadratic is entered. These bounds are simply taken to generate the bounding box.

Changing the Scale of a User-Generated Object

User-defined objects are created by the statement *BEGIN_INSTANCES* followed by definitions of one or more objects, and ending with the statement *END_INSTANCES*. When a named instance is called for by the appropriate command, its description is first transferred to new objects within the list of objects processed by the ray-tracing program. The instance may then be modified, scaled, and/or relocated. Usually, the location for a single-object instance is given as a *loc* vector of (0, 0, 0). When relocation occurs, the *loc* vector is changed to the new location of the object. If an instance consists of several objects, the center of the group is usually considered to be the location (0, 0, 0) and the *loc* vector for each object shows the displacement of that object from the center of the group.

An object is scaled by one of the functions *Scale_Instance*. For each of the scaling functions, a parameter is passed to the function which is a vector showing the multiplication factors for scaling in each of the three coordinates. The scaling function for each class of object treats the *loc* vector in the same way, namely by multiplying each coordinate by the multiplier for that coordinate. Scaling of other parameters differs, depending upon the class of object. For an object of class *Sphere,* the minimum multiplier for the three coordinates is used to scale the radius of the sphere, *vect1.x*. For an object of class *Parallelogram,* the vector *loc* defines the first corner of the parallelogram, and the vectors *vect1* and *vect2* define two other corners with respect to the first corner. The scaling function simply multiplies these two vectors by the multiplier vector. For an object of class *Triangle,* the function is the same as for the *Parallelogram* class. For an object of class *Ring,* vectors *vect1* and *vect2* define the plane of orientation of the ring, with respect to the *loc* vector, and these are multiplied by the multiplier vector. The parameter *vect3.x* is the inner radius of the ring and *vect3.y* is the outer radius. Both are scaled by multiplying by the minimum of the three coordinate multipliers. For an object of class *Quadratic,* the upper and lower limits are scaled by multiplying by the multiplier vector. Finally, each *Scale_Instance* function recursively calls itself to scale any child functions and if a flag is passed to the function, it also recursively calls itself to scale any function addressed in the *nextobj* parameter.

Determining Position Variables for an Object

Once the ray tracing functions described in Chapter 12 have established an intersection between the ray being traced and an object, we need to project a pattern (if one has been specified) onto the object surface to determine whether the pattern color should be substituted for the native color of the object. This is described in detail later. At this point, only two position variables, *pos1* and *pos2,* are required for the process and these variables are different for each type of object. For the sphere, the angle of the vector from the center of the object coordinate system to the point of intersection in the x-y plane is multiplied by the radius of the sphere to give *pos1.* For *pos2,* the angle is that between the z coordinate of the above vector and the projection of it onto the x-y plane. Again, the angle is multiplied by the radius of the sphere.

For the *Ring, Parallelogram,* and *Triangle* objects, the *pos1* value is the projection of the vector from the center of the object-oriented coordinate system to the intersection on one of the vectors that defines the plane of the object. *Pos2* is the projection of that same vector upon the other vector that defines the object plane. Finally, for the *Quadratic* object, *pos1* and *pos2* are simply the x and y coordinates at the point of intersection in the object-oriented coordinate system.

CHAPTER 11

Finding Where the Ray Hits an Object

Here we describe the *ray.cpp* file, which traces each ray throughout the picture. Before doing that, however, we need to discuss how to determine where a ray actually hits an object. Given that we are working backwards, starting at the observer's eye and tracing a ray of light back to the screen, we determine at some point in our computations exactly where on an object's surface the ray may be hitting. A function for this action is found in *ray.cpp,* while the functions that determine the exact intersection for each class of object are a part of *objects.cpp,* which was described in the previous chapter. However, at that time, we deliberately neglected these functions, choosing to describe the whole operation here in a separate chapter.

The Intersect Function

The function *Intersect* controls the intersect point with an object. It is listed as part of Figure 10-1. The principal inputs are the address of line, the current ray being traced, and the address of *CurrObj,* the object in the object list that is being tested for intersection with the ray. This function is going to return the address of the closest object intersected, which is locally stored in the static object address *Closest_object*. It is not destroyed, since it is a static address. The function loops, calling *CollisionTest* for each object in the object list. This latter function usually solves a quadratic equation, saving the closest object intersection of the two roots obtained. When *Intersect* finishes, it returns the address of the closest object intersected. The function also updates a variable called *Shortest_time,* which is the time travelled along the ray to the closest

215

object. The first thing the function does is reinitialize the closest-object address and the shortest-time variable, if necessary. A value of TRUE in *init_flag* is the criterion for reinitialization. The time is initialized to a very large value and the address of the closest object to a null.

Next, the function starts a loop through every object in the object list. At the beginning of the loop, we call *CollisionTest,* which determines whether an intersection occurs. If there is no intersection, this function returns a FALSE; otherwise, it returns TRUE and the variable *t* contains the time when the intersection takes place. (Throughout our consideration of intersections, we use a parametric method wherein we follow the ray from its beginning along the direction in which it is oriented until an intersection occurs. Since the ray-direction vector is normalized, multiplying this vector by the time provides the coordinates of the position we have reached by following the ray.)

After this, we increment a statistics variable that tracks the number of intersection tests made. Next, if an intersection occurred, we check to make sure that the time parameter *t* returned was not too small. This eliminates a computation problem that occurs when we start a ray at the surface of some object, intending to follow reflected or refracted light from that point on. If our computer had absolute precision, we could compute our next intersection without a problem. When precision is not absolute, we may find that the next intersection is very close by, where in fact we are just finding the intersection that we started from all over again. This not only wastes time, it can become an infinite loop where we keep finding the same intersection and never escape. To avoid this, we specify a minimum length of the ray before the intersection is considered valid. This minimum is greater than the possible computation error, thus eliminating erroneous cases.

If we have a valid intersection, we next check to see whether the intersection is with a bounding box. If so, we run *Intersect* recursively to find the closest intersection (if any) with an object within the bounding box. If there is a valid intersection with an object (not a bounding box), we first check to see if the *remove* parameter for that object is active. If so, we compute the point of intersection and put it in the vector *loc* and call the function *Find_Color*. Normally, this function determines whether a pattern color must be used to replace the usual color of the object. In this case, the pattern is actually a part of the object to be removed. If the function returns to a pattern intersection, we eliminate this object from consideration, set the address of the object to be checked to the next object in the list, and start another iteration of the loop. If the *remove* parameter was not active or if it was active but we intersected a part of the object that is not to be removed, we increment the statistical variable that counts the number of ray intersections with objects that are not bounding boxes.

There are two kinds of rays whose intersections may be investigated with the *Intersect* function. One of these is called *shadow rays*, which go from the object to a light source. The other kind of ray goes from the observer to the screen to the object. We distinguish between the two cases by passing the parameter *shadow_flag* as TRUE for shadow rays and FALSE for the other types of rays. For the shadow rays, if *t* is less than one and the transmission characteristics of the object are all less than the threshold values, we assign this object to be the closest object and terminate the function. Otherwise, the light-attenuation factor increases according to the transmission characteristic for the object.

If the ray is from the observer to an object, we compare the value of *t* returned for this object with the value in *Shortest_time*. If *t* is smaller than the previously shortest time, we put this value into *Shortest_time* and put the address of this object into *Closest_object*. We then set the object address to that of the next object in the list and continue with another iteration of the loop. When the loop is done, an intersection of the ray with every object in the list has been checked. If any intersections occurred, *Shortest_time* contains the time to the closest object and *Closest_object* contains the address of the closest object. This address is returned by the function when it terminates.

General Intersection Math

We mentioned in passing that in ray tracing we use the equation of the ray in a parametric form. In particular, the equations for the coordinates of the ray are:

$$x = x_1 t + x_0 \qquad \text{(Equation 11-1)}$$

$$y = y_1 t + y_0 \qquad \text{(Equation 11-2)}$$

$$z = z_1 t + z_0 \qquad \text{(Equation 11-3)}$$

The coordinates (x_0, y_0, z_0) are the coordinates of the starting point of the ray; the coordinates (x_1, y_1, z_1) represent a unit vector in the direction in which the ray is travelling. The parameter t can be taken as time. Thus, at zero time, the ray is at its origin. As time passes, the ray travels farther along its path. We are interested in determining the time at which the ray intersects an object; in particular, if we scan through a list of objects, we would like to know which object the ray hits first (the intersection for which t is the smallest). We compute the intersection of the ray with an object by inserting the ray equation into the equation for the object's surface and solving the resulting equation. For this computation, we'll use a coordinate system that is referenced in some convenient way to the surface of the object we are testing.

Intersection with a Sphere

The function *CollisionTest* is different for each type of object for which an intersection with the ray must be tested. As described in the previous chapter, using virtual functions, the program automatically selects the proper version of the function for the type of object being tested. The versions of the function are listed in Table 11-1. For a sphere, we determine the intersection as follows. The equation of a sphere, centered at $(0, 0, 0)$ and having a radius r, is:

$$x^2 + y^2 + z^2 - r^2 = 0 \qquad \text{(Equation 11-4)}$$

If we substitute the parametric equations of the ray into this equation (using for the ray the coordinate system whose origin is the center of the sphere) we obtain the following:

$$(x_1{}^2 + y_1{}^2 + z_1{}^2)t^2 + 2(x_0 x_1 + y_0 y_1 + z_0 z_1)t + (x_0{}^2 + y_0{}^2 + z_0{}^2) - 1 = 0$$

(Equation 11-5)

We begin by converting the line origin to the sphere's coordinate system and storing the result in the vector *temp*. We have precomputed the square of the sphere's radius; it is stored in *nl*. Next, we use some vector mathematics to determine the coefficients of t^2 (*a* in the function), *t* (*b* in the function), and the constant term (*c* in the function). We then perform a straightforward solution of the quadratic equation to obtain two roots, one of which is *tl* and the other placed in the space addressed by *t*. (The address of *t* is passed to the function so that the final value is available to the calling program rather than only being local to this function.)

We are going to return a TRUE if there is a legitimate intersection and a FALSE if there is not. A legitimate intersection yields at least one root that is greater than a specified minimum value. The minimum protects us from thinking that a ray starting at the sphere's surface (such as a reflected ray) has an intersection at the surface ($t = 0$).

We first check to see whether *tl* is both greater than the minimum and smaller than the contents of *t*. If it meets these conditions, we replace it as the contents of *t,* then check that the contents of *t* are greater than the minimum. (This check is necessary in case we didn't make a switch in the above test.) If the contents meet the condition, we have a legitimate root and we return TRUE, with the time corresponding to the closest root stored in the location pointed to by *t*. Otherwise, we return a FALSE to indicate that there is no legitimate root and we don't really care what time it is.

Intersecting a Quadric Curve

The next consideration is intersecting with a quadric curve. This is similar to our sphere intersection, since the sphere is a degenerate case of the general quadric curve. The most common quadric shapes are cylinder, elliptic paraboloid, hyperbolic paraboloid, elliptic cone, hyperboloid of one sheet, hyperboloid of two sheets, and ellipsoid. These shapes are shown in Plate 9. All of these shapes are represented by the following generalized equation:

$$ax^2 + 2bxy + 2cxz + 2dxw + ey^2 + 2fyz + 2gyw + hz^2 + 2izw + jw^2 = 0$$

(Equation 11-6)

Although the above equation covers every possible kind of quadric curve, it is too complex to be handled easily by this simple ray-tracing program. Fortunately, most of the common quadric surfaces can be treated by a subset of this equation, namely:

$$Ax^2 + By^2\ Cz^2 + Ey = D \qquad \text{(Equation 11-7)}$$

Table 11-1. Parameters of Quadric Shapes

Shape	A	B	C	D	E	Color
Elliptic cone	+	-	+	0	—	Cyan
Cylinder	+	0	+	+	—	Green
Elliptic paraboloid	+	—	+	0	-	Purple
Hyperbolic paraboloid	+	—	-	0	-	Blue
Hyperboloid of one sheet	+	-	+	+	—	Orange
Hyperboloid of two sheets	-	-	+	+	—	Red
Ellipsoid	+	+	+	+	—	White

We further impose the restriction that only one y term may occur in the equation for any given surface (there may be either a y term or a y^2 term, but not both). Table 11-1 lists the various shapes and gives the sign of each coefficient required for that particular shape, along with the color of the shape in Plate 9.

We are going to use the same technique of substituting the parametric ray equations into the equation of the quadric and then solving the resulting quadratic equation. The equation for the quadric containing a y^2 term is:

$$t^2(Ax_1^2 + By_1^2 + Cz_1^2) + 2t(Ax_0x_1 + By_0y_1 + Cz_0z_1) + (Ax_0^2 + By_0^2 + Cz_0^2 - D) = 0$$

(Equation 11-8)

For the quadric that has y term instead of a y^2 term, the corresponding equation is:

$$t^2(Ax_1^2 + Cz_1^2) + 2t(Ax_0x_1 - Ey_1 + Cz_0z_1) + (Ax_0^2 - Ey_0 + Cz_0^2) = 0$$

(Equation 11-9)

Look at the function listed in Table 11-1. It first converts the origin of the ray to the quadric-centered coordinate system and places the result in *newline.loc*. Next, it checks the orientation of the quadric by looking at the contents of *vect1*. If this is a unit vector pointed in the y direction, the orientation of the quadric is standard, so the ray direction is placed in *newline.dir*. If the vector in *vect1* indicates a different orientation for the quadric, the ray direction is rotated to correspond to the orientation of the quadric coordinate system. This is done with the function *Rotate,* using the sines and cosines for rotation precomputed for the particular quadric. The result, after rotation, is placed in *newline.dir.*

The function next uses vector mathematics to generate the coefficients for the quadratic equation of the intersection. This equation is then solved to obtain two roots. Next, the location of each root is computed in terms of the quadric coordinate system. The upper and lower limits for each coordinate of the quadric are stored in terms of its own coordinate system. The location of each intersection is compared with these limits. If the root falls within the limits, it is an acceptable intersection; if not, set the time parameter for that root to -1 to assure that it will not be considered a valid intersection in the tests that follow, then proceed with the testing process. As with the sphere, the goal is to find the smaller of the two intersection times, providing that the time selected must exceed the threshold parameter *SMALL*. The function returns TRUE for a valid intersection and FALSE if there is no valid intersection. If there is a valid intersection, *t* points to the time for that intersection.

Intersection with a Ring

Next, we consider an intersection with a ring. This is the first of three surfaces that are actually sections of a plane. The first thing the intersection function, *CollisionTest*, does in this case is to determine whether the ray intersects with the plane containing the ring. The initial step is to take the dot product of the line (ray) direction vector and the normal to the plane (which was precomputed and stored in norm). If this is zero or very small, the ray is hitting the plane on its edge. But a plane doesn't really have an edge (the edge is infinitely thin), so we might as well forget this case and return FALSE to indicate that an intersection does not take place. The equation for a plane is:

$$ax + by + cz + d = 0 \qquad \text{(Equation 11-10)}$$

The intersection of the ray with the plane is obtained, as before, by substituting the parametric equations of the ray into the equation of the plane, giving:

$$t = \frac{ax_0 + by_0 + cz_0 + d}{ax_1 + by_1 + cz_1 + d} \qquad \text{(Equation 11-11)}$$

This is a general equation, but we use a coordinate system centered at the middle of the plane so that the parameter *d* will always be zero. Observe that the vector (a, b, c) is the normal to the plane. Consequently, the denominator of the equation is the dot product of the normal to the plane and the line direction. As for the numerator, it is the dot product of the normal to the plane with the difference between the origin of the plane coordinate system and the origin of the line. We have already computed the dot product of the normal and the origin of the plane coordinate system; it is stored in *n1,* so all that needs to be done is to subtract from *n1* the dot product of the normal to the plane and the line origin, then plug the results into the intersection equation and obtain a value for the time until intersection.

Next, determine the point on the ray at which it intersects the plane, called the *location,* then find the vector *delta,* which is the vector from the plane coordinate origin to the point of intersection. The length of this vector is the square root of the dot product of the vector and itself. We call this length *rad.* If *rad* falls between the values of the inner radius of the ring and the outer radius of the ring, we have a valid intersection with the ring and return TRUE. Otherwise, there is no valid intersection and we return FALSE.

Intersection of the Ray with a Parallelogram

The function for determining whether there is a valid intersection with a parallelogram begins like the function for obtaining an intersection with a ring. We first reject cases where the ray intersects the edge of the plane, then, for the remaining cases, determine the intersection of the ray with the plane. Again, we compute the exact point of intersection of the ray with the plane and store this location in the vector *location.* In *delta,* the location of the intersection is stored in terms of the parallelogram coordinate system.

We are now ready to determine whether the intersection is actually inside the parallelogram. This turns out to be a lot more work than determining whether the intersection with the plane occurs, and more work than doing the same thing for the ring (which is a rather trivial case). We are going to use the Jordan curve theorem, which states that if we project a line from the intersection point in an arbitrary direction and the line has an odd number of intersections with the line segments that are the sides of the parallelogram, the intersect point is inside the parallelogram. If there is an even number of intersections, the intersect point is outside the parallelogram.

To make things easier, we first project both the parallelogram and the intersect point onto a plane defined by two axes of the coordinate system. We must decide which of the three coordinate axes should be discarded, namely the one with the largest value for any of the vertices of the parallelogram. This is the dominant axis. We then perform the projection onto the plane formed by the other two coordinates by throwing away the values of the dominant coordinate for each of the parallelogram's vertices, then compute the location of each vertex in the new system with respect to the parallelogram coordinate system. The first vertex is always at (0, 0) by definition.

In the *CollisionTest* function, we take into consideration the dominant axis and compute the coordinates of each vertex in terms of a coordinate system centered at the intersect point. These are stored in ($gu[n]$, $gv[n]$), where n is the vertex number from 0 to 3. The new coordinate system will have the axes u and v. We can project the test line in an arbitrary direction; we choose to project it along the u axis. We initialize *crossing_no,* which contains the number of crossings of a parallelogram line segment, then enter a loop that checks the test line against the line segment between each pair of adjacent vertices. We can only have an intersection of the test line and the line segment connecting adjacent vertices if $gv[i]$ and $gv[j]$ have opposite signs. (This puts one vertex on one side of the u axis and the other on the opposite side, which assures a crossing of the u axis.)

If both $gu[i]$ and $gu[j]$ are positive, then we know that the crossing of the u axis is also a crossing of the test line, and we therefore increment *crossing_no.* If one of the vertex u coordinates is positive and the other is negative, we must compute the value of the u coordinate for the intersection of the line segment with the u axis. If this is positive, we have an intersection with the test line and therefore increment the number of crossings; if negative, there is no intersection with the test line, so the number of crossings is unchanged.

Plate 1. Newton's Method for $x^5 - 1 = 0$

Plate 2. Newton's Method for $x^7 - 1 = 0$

Plate 15. Quarternion Julia Set

Plate 16. Quaternion Dragon Curve

After completing the loop for all adjacent line segment pairs, we take the value of *crossing_no* modulo 2, which gives us a zero for an even number of crossings and a one for an odd number of crossings. If the number of crossings is odd, we know that the intersection is within the parallelogram and return TRUE when the function terminates; if the number of crossings is even, there is no intersection within the parallelogram so we return FALSE when the function terminates.

This function will work equally well for any quadrilateral. It is restricted to parallelograms because of the way we handle the input data, namely inputting the location of the parallelogram (which is one vertex) and then the location of two other vertices in relation to the first vertex. The fourth vertex of the parallelogram is computed internally. You might want to create a new type called QUADRILATERAL, which allows three arbitrary vertices to be entered rather than two. After input and the proper initial calculations, the new object is considered a type PARALLELOGRAM.

Intersection with a Triangle

The function *Collision_Test* for finding the intersection of a ray with a triangle is exactly the same as the function for finding the intersection of a ray with a parallelogram except that only three vertices are specified, the loop to check line segment only tests for three line segments, and the modulus arithmetic statement that makes sure the second vertex of the pair rolls around to zero on the last check uses modulo three rather than modulo four. In fact, this whole method of determining if a line that intersects a plane is also within a figure will work equally well for any polygon, regardless of the number of sides. You can set up a more generalized version in which objects of different numbers of sides are treated; however, you need to make sure you have room to generate the number of line segments needed to create the polygon.

Intersection with a Bounding Box

In addition to the intersection tests of the ray with various types of objects, we need to have a version of the intersection function *CollisionTest* with the bounding box, which may be set up around an object or group of objects to reduce the number of intersection tests needed. The ray-tracing part of the program is set up so that unless an intersection with the bounding box occurs, further tests for intersection with the objects contained in the box are unnecessary.

The function begins by determining whether the x component of the ray direction is greater than the minimum value *SMALL*. If not, the function determines whether the ray origin is between the x limits of the box. If so, the minimum time in this direction is set to a very low value and the maximum to a very high value; otherwise, the function terminates, reporting no intersection.

If the component exceeds the threshold *SMALL,* times are calculated for the ray to hit the upper and lower x limits of the box. If the maximum time is less than zero, the function terminates, reporting no intersection. The same procedure takes place for the y and z components of the ray. Overall maximum and minimum times are taken, the maximum time being the minimum of the three maximum components and the minimum time being the maximum of the three minimum components. If the overall maximum is less than the overall minimum, the function terminates and reports no intersection; otherwise, it reports that an intersection did occur.

CHAPTER 12

Tracing the Ray

We have completed the portions of our ray-tracing program that support the main task: tracing the path of each ray of light that makes up the picture. This job is done by the functions that make up the file called *ray.cpp*. This file is listed in Figure 12-1. Bear in mind that each light source emits rays that illuminate all of the objects in the picture. The objects, in turn, absorb, reflect, or refract the light rays, and some return through the viewing screen to the observer. The rays of light striking the observer's eyes determine the appearance of the scene. These rays are a small fraction of the actual light rays in the world. In the interest of reducing our computer processing to a reasonable amount, rather than trace each ray of light from the light source, we trace backwards only those rays that strike the observer's eyes.

We start at the observer's eye and follow a ray to a pixel on the screen. We then continue to follow the ray in a straight line until it finally hits some object. Then we follow reflected and refracted rays, as necessary, to their sources and combine all that information to determine the color that this particular light ray has when it reaches the eye. In doing ray tracing in this reverse manner, we avoid the multitude of rays that don't contribute to the light seen by the observer or to the picture.

The Overall Scene-Tracing Function

In Chapter 6, we noted that the main program called *Trace_Scene* performed the ray-tracing operation. Of course, it isn't all that simple: The *Trace_Scene* function begins by defining a new line and putting it into the list of lines. It then goes into a *for* loop, which repeats for each line of the display from *WORLD.first_scan* to *WORLD.last_scan*. Usually these scan limits are the first and last lines of the display screen. Next, the number of the line being scanned is displayed, giving the user some idea of how far the program has progressed, since ray tracing takes a considerable amount of time. Then the function determines the parameter *yf,* which is the *y* coordinate for the current scan line in *WORLD* coordinates. It enters another *for* loop, which reiterates for each pixel on the line. At each iteration, this loop begins by calculating *xf,* which is the equivalent value of x in *WORLD* coordinates for the pixel being processed. The function then computes the vector giving the direction of the ray *(line->dir)* from the observer to the *WORLD* coordinates of the current pixel at the screen. The function *Trace_Ray* is run to follow the ray for the rest of its path and return the colors of the ray. These are stored in character arrays of *red, green,* and *blue.* After the inner *for* loop has been completed, the function *Dump_Line* is called to send all of the data for the colors of one line to the output file. When the outer *for* loop is finished, *Trace_Scene* terminates and returns to the main program.

```
/*

    ray.cpp = Functions related to ray tracing

            By Roger T. Stevens 2-12-90


*/

#include <stdlib.h>
#include <math.h>
#include "render.hpp"

int level;

/*

        Trace_Scene() = Ray tracing of entire scene


*/

void Trace_Scene()
{
   int x,y;
   char red[max_pixel], green[max_pixel], blue[max_pixel];
```

```
    Vector color;
    Line line;
    float xf, yf;

    for (y=WORLD.first_scan; y<=WORLD.last_scan; y++)
    {
            cout << "Tracing line #: " << y << "\n";
            yf=((float)(CENTERY-y))/(WORLD.flength);
            for (x=0; x<XSIZE; x++)
            {
                xf=((float)(CENTERX-x))/(WORLD.flength*ASPECT);
                line.loc = WORLD.obsloc;
                line.dir = WORLD.obsdir;
                line.dir = line.dir + WORLD.obsright * xf +
                        WORLD.obsup * yf;
                level = 0;
                Trace_Ray(&line,&color,1.0);
                WORLD.primary_traced++;
                red[x] = color.x;
                green[x] = color.y;
                blue[x] = color.z;
            }
    Dump_Line(y,red,green,blue);
    }
}


/*
        ┌─────────────────────────────────────────────────┐
        │                                                 │
        │     Trace_Ray() = Ray traces for a line of display │
        │                                                 │
        └─────────────────────────────────────────────────┘
*/

int Trace_Ray(Line * line,Vector * color,float multiplier)
{
    Vector new_position, new_direction, close_obj_loc, close_obj_norm;
    float Shortest_time, divisor;
    Object * Closest_object;
    color_data col_data;

    *color = Vector();
    level++;
    if (level > 48)
            return(FALSE);
```

```
  if (multiplier < WORLD.threshold)
      return(FALSE);
  Closest_object=Intersect(WORLD.stack,line,&Shortest_time,FALSE,
      TRUE, NULL);
  if (Closest_object!=NULL)
  {
      close_obj_loc = line->loc + (line->dir * Shortest_time);
      Closest_object->FindNorm(&close_obj_norm,&close_obj_loc);
      if ((close_obj_norm % line->dir) >0)
            close_obj_norm  = -close_obj_norm;
      Find_Color(Closest_object,Closest_object->pattern,
            &close_obj_loc,&col_data,
      Closest_object->xmult,Closest_object->ymult);
      AmbientColor(color,&col_data,&close_obj_norm,
            &close_obj_loc);
      DiffuseColor(color,&col_data,&close_obj_norm,
            &close_obj_loc,line);
      TransparentColor(color,&col_data,&close_obj_norm,
            &close_obj_loc,line,multiplier);
      ReflectColor(color,&col_data,&close_obj_norm,
            &close_obj_loc,line,multiplier);
      Dither(color,&col_data);
  }
  else
      SkyColor(line,color);
  if (color->x > CNUM || color->y > CNUM || color->z > CNUM)
  {
      divisor = (float)Max(color->x,color->y,color->z) /
            (float)CNUM;
      *color = *color / divisor;
  }
  return(Closest_object!=NULL);
}


/*

      Intersect() = Finds first object hit by ray

*/

Object * Intersect(Object * CurrObj,Line * line,float *Shortest_time,
      short shadow_flag, short init_flag,Vector * atten)
{
```

```
static Object * Closest_object;
Vector loc;
Object * obj;
short collision;
static short stop;
float t;
obj = CurrObj;
if (init_flag)
{
     *Shortest_time=3e30;
     Closest_object=NULL;
     stop=FALSE;
}
while (obj!=NULL && !stop)
{
     collision = obj->CollisionTest(line,&t);
     WORLD.intersect_tests++;
     if (collision && (t>SMALL))
     {
          if (obj->type == BBOX)
          {
              WORLD.bbox_intersects++;
              Intersect(obj->child,line,Shortest_time,
                 shadow_flag,FALSE,atten);
          }
          else
          {
              if(obj->remove != NULL)
              {
                 loc = line->loc + line->dir * t;
                 if (Find_Color(obj,obj->remove, &loc,NULL, 1.0,
                   1.0))
                 obj=obj->nextobj;
                 continue;
              }
              WORLD.ray_intersects++;
              if (shadow_flag && t<1)
              {
                  if ((obj->col_data->trans.x <
                    WORLD.int_threshold) &&
                    (obj->col_data->trans.y <
                    WORLD.int_threshold) &&
```

```
                            (obj->col_data->trans.z <
                            WORLD.int_threshold))
                    {
                        Closest_object = obj;
                        return(obj);
                    }
                    else
                    {
                        if (atten != NULL)
                        {
                            *atten = *atten *
                            (obj->col_data->trans *
                            obj->col_data->trans) /
                            (float)(CNUM * CNUM);
                        }
                    }
                }
                if ((!shadow_flag) && (t<*Shortest_time))
                {
                    *Shortest_time  = t;
                    Closest_object = obj;
                }
            }
        }
        obj=obj->nextobj;
    }
    return(Closest_object);
}


/*
```

┌───┐
│   │
│   AmbientColor() = Add ambient color   │
│   │
└───┘

```
*/

void AmbientColor(Vector * color, color_data * col_data, Vector *
                                            norm,
        Vector * loc)
{
        *color = *color + col_data->amb * (col_data->diff /
                                            float)CNUM);
}
```

```
/*
    ┌─────────────────────────────────────────────────┐
    ║                                                   ║
    ║   DiffuseColor() = Computes specular reflections and color
    ║                    emitted by object             ║
    ║                                                   ║
    └─────────────────────────────────────────────────┘
*/

void DiffuseColor(Vector * color,color_data * col_data,Vector *
  norm,Vector * loc, Line * oline)
{
  Line  line;
  Object * CurrObj;
  Lamp * lamp;
  float dot, distance, time, t1, t2;
  Vector reflect, attenuate;

  line.loc = *loc;
  lamp = WORLD.lamps;
  while (lamp!=NULL)
  {
      line.dir = lamp->loc - *loc;
      attenuate = Vector(1,1,1);
      CurrObj-Intersect(WORLD.stack,&line,&time,TRUE,
            TRUE,&attenuate);
      WORLD.to_lamp++;
      if (CurrObj==NULL)
      {
            distance = line.dir % line.dir;
            line.dir = ~ line.dir;
            if (col_data->diff.x>0 || col_data->diff.y>0 ||
                col_data->diff.z>0)
            {
                t1 = *norm % line.dir;
                if (t1>0)
                {
                    t2 = lamp->distance*t1/sqrt(distance);
                    *color = *color + ((attenuate *
                        col_data->diff) * t2);
                }
            }
            if (col_data->sreflect>0)
            {
```

```
                dot = line.dir % *norm;
                reflect = -line.dir + *norm * dot + *norm * dot;
                t1 = -(reflect % oline->dir);
                if (t1>0.6)
                {
                    t2 = pow(t1,col_data->sreflect)
                    *lamp->distance/sqrt(distance);
                    t2 *= (float)col_data->reflect;
                    *color = *color + attenuate * t2;
                }
            }
        }
        lamp=lamp->next_lamp;
    }
}


/*
    ┌─────────────────────────────────────────────────────────┐
    │                                                           │
    │ TransparentColor() = Traces ray through transparent medium│
    │                                                           │
    └─────────────────────────────────────────────────────────┘
*/

void TransparentColor(Vector * color, color_data * col_data,Vector *
  norm,Vector * loc, Line * line,float inmult)
{
  Line newline;
  Vector col1, refract, distance, displacement, attenuation;
  float glassdist,current_index, multiplier, side1;
  int maxtrans;
  static Vector old_position;

  if ((col_data->trans.x < WORLD.int_threshold) &&
  (col_data->trans.y < WORLD.int_threshold) &&
      (col_data->trans.z < WORLD.int_threshold))
      return;
  if (line->flag)
  {
      current_index = col_data->index/WORLD.globindex;
      displacement = *loc - old_position;
      glassdist = sqrt(displacement % displacement);
  }
  else
  {
```

```
       current_index = WORLD.globindex/col_data->index;
       old_position = *loc;
  }
  newline.loc = *loc;
  side1 = *norm % (-line->dir);
  refract = -(*norm * side1) - line->dir;
  refract = refract * (1-current_index);
  newline.dir = line->dir + refract;
  newline.dir = ~ newline.dir;
  maxtrans = Max(col_data->trans.x,col_data->trans.y,
       col_data->trans.z);
  newline.flag = !(line->flag);
  multiplier = inmult * (float)maxtrans/(float)CNUM;
  Trace_Ray(&newline,&col1,multiplier);
  WORLD.refl_trans++;
  *color = *color + col1;
  if (line->flag)
  {
       attenuation = col_data->density * (*color * glassdist);
       *color = *color - attenuation.min(*color);
  }
}


/*
         ┌─────────────────────────────────────────────┐
         │      ReflectColor() = Traces ray bounced off object │
         │                                               │
*/       └─────────────────────────────────────────────┘


void ReflectColor(Vector * color,color_data * col_data,Vector *
  norm,Vector * loc, Line * line,float inmult)
{
  Vector col1;
  Line newline;
  float multiplier,dot;
  int maxmirror;

  if ((col_data->mirror.x < WORLD.int_threshold) &&
  (col_data->mirror.y < WORLD.int_threshold) &&
       (col_data->mirror.z < WORLD.int_threshold)) return;
  newline.loc = *loc;
  dot = -(line->dir % *norm);
  newline.dir = line->dir + *norm * dot + *norm * dot;
```

```
   maxmirror = Max(col_data->mirror.x,col_data->mirror.y,
       col_data->mirror.z);
   multiplier = inmult * (float)maxmirror/CNUM;
   Trace_Ray(&newline,&col1,multiplier);
   WORLD.refl_trans++;
   *color = *color + col1 * (col_data->mirror / (float)CNUM);
}


/*
                    SkyColor() = Computes sky color

*/

void SkyColor(Line * line,Vector * color)
{
   float length, horiz, zenith;

   length = line->dir % line->dir;
   zenith = line->dir.y * line->dir.y / length;
   horiz  = (line->dir.x * line->dir.x + line->dir.z * line->dir.z)/
        length;
   *color = *color + WORLD.skycolor_zenith * zenith +
        WORLD.skycolor_horiz * horiz;
   Dither(color,WORLD.sky_dither);
}


/*
                    Dither() = Color dithering functions

*/

#define MINCOL 10

void Dither(Vector * color,float dither)
{
   float r,g,b;

   if (dither==0) return;
   if (dither>0)
   {
        r=((float)rand()/16383) - 1;
        g=((float)rand()/16383) - 1;
```

```
            b=((float)rand()/16383) - 1;
            if (color->x<MINCOL)
            r=fabs(r);
            if (color->y<MINCOL)
                  g=fabs(g);
            if (color->z<MINCOL)
                  b=fabs(b);
            *color= *color + Vector(r*dither,g*dither,b*dither);
      }
}

void Dither(Vector * color,color_data * col_data)
{
   float r,g,b;
   if (col_data->dither==0)
      return;
   if (col_data->dither>0)
   {
         r=((float)rand()/16383) - 1;
         g=((float)rand()/16383) - 1;
         b=((float)rand()/16383) - 1;
         if (color->x<MINCOL)
               r=fabs(r);
         if (color->y<MINCOL)
               g=fabs(g);
         if (color->z<MINCOL)
               b=fabs(b);
         *color= *color + Vector(r*col_data->dither,
               g*col_data->dither,b*col_data->dither);
   }
   else
   {
         r=((float)rand()/16383) - 1;
         if ((color->x+color->y+color->z)>(3*MINCOL))
         r=fabs(r);
         *color= *color + Vector(r*col_data->dither,
         r*col_data->dither,
         r*col_data->dither);
   }
}
```

```
/*
        ┌─────────────────────────────────────────────────┐
        │                                                 │
        │    Dump_Line() = Sends a line of data to disk file │
        │                                                 │
*/      └─────────────────────────────────────────────────┘


void Dump_Line(int lineno, char *red, char *green, char *blue)
{
  fwrite(&lineno,sizeof(int),1,WORLD.filept);
  fwrite(red,sizeof(char),XSIZE,WORLD.filept);
  fwrite(green,sizeof(char),XSIZE,WORLD.filept);
  fwrite(blue,sizeof(char),XSIZE,WORLD.filept);
}


/*
        ┌─────────────────────────────────────────────────┐
        │  Find_Color () = Finds the color of a point on an object │
        │                  surface, returning either pattern or │
        │                  default color information         │
        │                                                 │
*/      └─────────────────────────────────────────────────┘

int Find_Color(Object * obj, Pattern *pattern, Vector * location,
  color_data * c_data,float x_mult, float y_mult)
{
  Pattern *patt;
  float x,y, pos1, pos2;
  int modx, mody;
  float radius_sq, x_cir, y_cir, x1, x2, y1, y2;
  Pattern *line_segment;
  int number = 0;

  if (pattern==NULL)
  {
        *c_data = *(obj->col_data);
        return(FALSE);
  }
  obj->Position(&pos1, &pos2, location);
  pos1 /= x_mult;
  pos2 /= y_mult;
  modx = (int)(pos1 / (pattern->xsize));
  if (pos1<0)
        modx-;
```

```
mody = (int)(pos2 / (pattern->ysize));
if (pos2<0)
        mody-;
x = pos1 - ((float)modx * pattern->xsize);
y = pos2 - ((float)mody * pattern->ysize);
patt = pattern->child;
while (patt!=NULL)
{
     WORLD.pattern_matches++;
     switch(patt->type)
     {
             case RECTANGLE:
                 if ((x>patt->startx) && (x<patt- endx) &&
                   (y>patt->starty) && (y<patt->endy))
                 {
                   *c_data = patt->col_data;
                   return(TRUE);
                 }
                 break;
             case CIRCLE:
                 x_cir = x  patt->radius;
                 y_cir = y - patt->radius;
                 radius_sq = x_cir*x_cir + y_cir*y_cir;
                 if (radius_sq <= (patt- >radius*patt->radius))
                 {
                   *c_data = patt->col_data;
                   return(TRUE);
                 }
                 break;
             case POLYGON:
                 while (line_segment->link != NULL)
                 {
                     x1 = line_segment->startx - x;
                     x2 = line_segment->link- >startx - x;
                     y1 = line_segment->starty - y;
                     y2 = line_segment->link- >starty - y;
                     if ((x1<=0) && (x2<=0))
                     {
                         if ((y1==0) && (y2==0))
                             number++;
                         else
                         {
```

```
                          if (y1*y2 <= 0)
                             if (x1 - (y1*(x2-x1)/(y2-y1))> 0)
                                number++;
                       }
                    }
                    line_segment = line_segment->link;
                 }
                 if ((number % 2) == 0)
                       break;
                 else
                 {
                       *c_data = patt->col_data;
                       return(TRUE);
                 }
             }
          patt = patt->sibling;
       }
    *c_data = *(obj->col_data);
    return(FALSE);
}
```

Figure 12-1. Listing of the ray.cpp File

Tracing a Ray

The function *Trace_Ray* performs the actual ray-tracing operation for a single ray. It begins by zeroing the vector *color*, which will contain the color information for this ray. Next, the function looks at the parameter *multiplier*, which has been passed to it, and compares it with the threshold *WORLD.threshold*.

The *multiplier* parameter is set to one when the *Trace_Ray* function is first entered. It is used to multiply the color parameters. It darkens the colors during repeated reflections and transmissions through a transparent medium. The parameter decreases with each reflection or refraction, thereby darkening the colors. When the parameter is reduced below the threshold, any further ray contributions are unimportant, so the ray-tracing function ceases. Obviously, this never happens when the *Trace_Ray* function is called by *Trace_Scene*. However, *Trace_Ray* is also called recursively by some of the functions that are subsequently called in the *Trace_Ray* function. To reduce computing time, these need to be omitted when the color contribution is negligible. Next, the function calls *Intersect,* which scans the list of objects and determines where the intersection with the nearest object occurs. This was described in Chapter 11. If objects are identified as being intersected by the ray, the function computes the location of the closest object. We then find the normal for the closest object at the point of intersection and, if necessary, reverse it so that it is projecting out from the intersected surface.

The *Trace_Ray* function then calls the function *Find_Color*. This function, described below, determines whether a pattern is superimposed upon the object surface. If there is, and our intersection occurs at a point that should be the pattern color rather than the native color of the object, the function changes the color accordingly. The functions *AmbientColor, DiffuseColor, TransparentColor,* and *ReflectColor* are then called to trace reflected and refracted rays and add in their color contributions. Finally, we call the function *Dither*, which dithers the color information if necessary. If no intersection with an object is found, the function calls the function *SkyColor* and colors the pixel with the appropriate color for the sky. Finally, the function verifies that none of the color components exceeds the maximum allowable color number. If so, the color information for that pixel is scaled within the color limits. The function then terminates.

Determining the Background Color

Observe that at the start of the *Trace_Ray* function, a color vector for the pixel was initialized to zero. What happens if the ray from the observer to the pixel on the screen continues on through the scene without intersecting any objects at all? When this happens, the function *SkyColor* is called. The parameters passed to this function are the address of the object of class *Line*, which contains the parameters of the ray being traced and the address of the vector *color*. *Color* represents the pixel color, which, up to this point, is zero.

WORLD stores two colors for the background (or sky), one at the horizon and one at the zenith (directly overhead). The *SkyColor* function determines from these what color to use for the sky-colored pixel. It squares the length of the ray being traced (from the observer to the screen), then uses this to normalize the components of the ray direction in the *y* and *x-z* plane directions. The color for the zenith is multiplied by the square of the *y* component, horizon color is multiplied by the square of the *x-z* component, and the result is added to give the final background color. Try a few examples to satisfy yourself that if you use the same color for both horizon and zenith, this process will result in that same color, regardless of the direction of the normalized direction vector.

The function finally calls *Dither* with the color vector address and the *World.sky_dither* value as parameters. *Dither* begins with three random numbers between -1 and +1. For each component of the sky color, if the component is less than a minimum value of 10, the random number is made positive. Finally, each random number is multiplied by the dither parameter and the results are added to the three color components.

Ambient Color

Suppose we have a collision between the light ray and an object. At the moment, our color vector is still set to zero. The first thing we do is call the function *AmbientColor*. The ambient color is the general light illuminating the scene; it does not come from any of the light sources. We multiply this light color by the diffuse color, which is the natural color of the object, and the result is scaled to the number of permitted color shades (64). The product is added to the current color vector value of the pixel.

Specular Reflections and Color Emitted by an Object

The function *DiffuseColor* determines the color emitted by an object intersected by the ray being traced. This color is influenced by inherent color of the object itself and by the light striking it from various light sources. This function begins by creating a line whose origin is the point of intersection of the light ray and object. Next, the function begins a *while* loop that scans the list of light sources (lamps). For each light source, the direction of the new line is set up to point at the light source.

242

The vector *attenuate* is then set to (1,1,1) or no attenuation. Next, the *Intersect* function determines whether this new line intersects any of the objects in the scene. If it does, that object blocks any contribution from the light source under consideration, so no action is necessary. If there is no intervening object, the function determines the distance of the new line to the light source, normalizes the line direction vector, and checks to see whether the color vector of the object is greater than zero for any of its components. If so, the current object color is multiplied by the *attenuate* vector and by a factor representing the diffuse reflection of the light from the light source being checked by the object under test. This factor is the cosine of the angle between the normal-to-object surface and direction-of-light (found by taking the dot product of the line direction vector and the object normal vector) multiplied by *lamp->distance* and divided by distance-to-lamp. The *lamp->distance* parameter indicates the distance from the lamp at which the illumination is considered to be 100 percent. The overall color obtained from this procedure is added to the *color* vector.

Specular reflection produces highlights on curved surfaces. It is particularly noticeable when you look at an illuminated ball and see a spot of bright, reflected light. This type of reflection is sometimes called Phong shading because the model was first proposed by Phong. The function determines the cosine of the angle between the surface normal of the object and the direction of a microfacet of the surface, which would result in perfect specular reflection of the light in the direction of the observer. We propose to raise this cosine to some power; for values less than 0.6, any power that we would normally use would cause the contribution to become negligibly small, so we can ignore it and avoid making any calculations. If the cosine is greater than 0.6, we raise it to the *sreflect* power, where *sreflect* is a Phong coefficient that is input as part of the object data. This is then multiplied by *lamp->distance* and divided by the distance from the object to the lamp, giving a light intensity coefficient. We multiply this coefficient by *reflect,* the reflection factor that was input for the object. The product is multiplied by *attenuate* and that product added to the color vector.

This procedure for diffuse and specular color reflection repeats for each light source in the list. When all light sources are exhausted, the loop terminates and the function ends.

Tracing a Ray through a Transparent Medium

The function *TransparentColor* traces a ray through a transparent or semi-transparent medium, shifting the ray angle as needed at the junction of surfaces and attenuating it in accordance with medium characteristics. The function begins by testing the *col_data->trans* vector to see if all components are below a preset threshold. If they are, the light ray extinguishes. No further processing is needed, and the function returns to the caller. Otherwise, the function continues by checking *line->flag,* which indicates whether the light ray is currently inside or outside a transparent object. If it is inside the object, we determine a new index of refraction and compute *glassdist,* the distance travelled within the glass. Otherwise, we compute the index of refraction outside the object and set *old_position* to the current line position.

The function then creates a new line, with its beginning at the point of intersection. The angle of refraction determines the direction of the line as it continues from the point of intersection. Based on the transparency characteristics of the *trans* vector of the object, a *multiplier* is computed. The *flag* for this new line is the opposite of the current flag. In other words, if the flag indicates that we are outside a transparent object, we are inside after the intersection, and vice versa. *Trace_Ray* is called recursively to trace the new ray. The returned color information is added to the *color* vector. Finally, if we have been travelling inside the transparent object, a new *attenuation* vector is calculated as the product of the distance travelled within the transparent object and the *density* vector, which is part of the object information.

Reflections

The function *ReflectColor* determines the reflections on a mirrored surface and begins by determining whether any of the coefficients of the object's *mirror* vector are above the preset threshold. If none are, there is no reflection and the function returns without further action. If there is some reflection, a new line is set up with its origin at the point of intersection. We then calculate the direction at which the ray we are tracing reflects off the surface. A *multiplier* is computed based upon the maximum *mirror* coefficient of the object. The function *Trace_Ray* then recursively traces this new ray. The result, multiplied by the *mirror* vector, is added to the *color* vector.

Sending a Line to the Data File

During the tracing of a scene, one full line of data is accumulated in the color arrays. When the line is complete, the function *Dump_Line* is called. This function first writes the line number out to the data file and then writes a full line of red data, a full line of green data, and a full line of blue data.

Pattern Effects on Color

The function *Find_Color* determines whether the application of a pattern affects the inherent color of an object. It begins by checking if the pattern address passed to it is a NULL (indicating no pattern) or a legitimate address. If a NULL is found, the color data to be used by the calling program is set to the object's color data, and FALSE is returned by the function to indicate that no pattern information was used. Otherwise, the *Position* function for the particular object is called, returning position data on the object intersection point. This data is scaled by the *x_mult* and *y_mult* parameters to determine *x* and *y* coordinate positions on a pattern. The function then scans the pattern elements, checks for the type of pattern, and performs the necessary computations to determine whether the coordinates fall upon a pattern area. If so, the color data to be used by the calling program is set to the pattern color data and a TRUE is returned; if not, the color data is set to the object's color data and a FALSE is returned.

CHAPTER 13

Putting it All Together With the Make Capability

We now have all of the files necessary for ray tracing. (An additional file for fractals is in Chapter 15 and is included in the *make* files discussed in this chapter, but is not necessary for ordinary scene rendering.) Tying these files together could be a complicated job but is simplified by using the *make* capability that is available in many languages including most versions of C, and in Zortech C++ and Turbo C++. There is, however, a difference between them.

The advantage of the *make* capability is that it tracks the date and time when each file was created. (You need to make sure your system clock is working and is set to the correct time.) When you use *make*, the program automatically checks each object file that you link together to make up the finished program to assure that it is the latest version. If so, it is linked without recompiling. If you have performed editing since an object file was last generated, it will be recompiled. Thus, only the minimum amount of recompiling is necessary. You don't need to recompile everything to be safe. If you really want to recompile a file, you first type:

```
touch filename
```

where *filename* is the name of the file you're interested in recompiling, and a flag is set that forces recompilation of this file when you next run *make*. With our ray-tracing program, *render.hpp* is a header file associated with every other file, so if you use *touch* on it, every file will be recompiled when *make* is run.

There are two ways to run *make*. The first method applies if you intend to use *make* on only one set of program data. You may then store all of the data required by the *make* facility in a file called *makefile*, then invoke the capability by typing:

```
make
```

The program automatically searches out the *makefile* and uses the data to perform its functions. Alternately, if you have several programs that require the *make* capability, you can give the data file a different name, such as *zraymake.mak*. The *make* capability is then invoked by typing:

```
make -fzraymake.mak
```

where the name following the *-f* is that of the file where your *make* data is stored.

Creating the Ray-Tracing Program with Zortech C++

All of the programs in this book were written and debugged using Zortech C++, version 2.06. They should work well with this compiler. Earlier versions of Zortech C++ have a bug in the *make* capability that prevents this program from compiling. Figure 13-1 is the *makefile* for use with Zortech C++.

The first line of the file begins by specifying the name of the executable file to be created, followed by the name of each object file to make up the program. This data must not exceed 127 characters because of DOS limitations. Then there's the statement to define linking of the program. It must be indented; otherwise, *make* may think it is part of the previous data. It too is limited to 127 characters and begins by *blink* followed by a space, followed by the names of all the object files to be linked by + signs. At the end of the line is the option */noi*, which tells the linker to be case-sensitive. Each object file created by the *make* capability is followed by two lines of code. At the beginning of the first line for each object file is the name of the object file followed by a colon. The *.c* or *.cpp* file is compiled to produce the object file followed by the names of all other source files. The second line begins with *ztc*, invoking the compiler, followed by any desired options and the name of the source file to be compiled.

```
render.exe: render.obj vmath.obj input.obj objects.obj
                                          fractal.obj ray.obj

          blink render+vmath+input+fractal+objects+ray/noi

render.obj:         render.cpp        render.hpp
    ztc -w-  -o -c -ml -f render.cpp

vmath.obj:          vmath.cpp  render.hpp
    ztc -w-  -o -c -ml -f vmath.cpp

input.obj:          input.cpp       render.hpp
    ztc -w-  -o -c  -ml -f input.cpp

fractal.obj:        fractal.cpp     render.hpp
    ztcpp1 fractal -w-  -ml -f
           ztc2b fractal

objects.obj:    objects.cpp render.hpp
    ztc -w-  -c -ml -f objects.cpp

ray.obj:        ray.cpp        render.hpp
    ztc -w-  -c -ml -f ray.cpp
```

Figure 13-1. Listing of Zortech C++ Make File

Let's take a look at the options used in compiling programs. The *-c* option is needed for each compile statement, since it tells the compiler to compile only and not link. This is necessary because we will do the linking with a separate link command line once all of the necessary updated object modules are identified by the *make* facility. The *-f* option tells the compiler to generate in-line instructions for the math coprocessor. If you have a math coprocessor, you need this option for every compile; if not, it should not be included.

The *-ml* option indicates that the large memory model should be used. This is necessary for all modules for this program because it is large and complex and uses a lot of memory for data storage. The *-o* option tells the compiler to use the global optimizer to optimize the code. Ideally, this should be used for every module to obtain optimum code for the final program. However, the complexities of some files caused the global optimizer to become confused and, for example, reject a simple *if* statement as illegal. If you use the optimizer option only for those files shown, you'll be safe. You may want to try it on additional files one at a time, but you do so at your own peril.

Finally, the *-w-* option turns off warnings from the compiler. Since the compiler tends to generate a warning every time it encounters an external variable, there can be quite a stack of warning messages, most of them useless. If you get into trouble trying to compile, you may want to remove this option and display the warning messages for your review.

Look at the instructions for compiling the *fractal* file. Although this file is not too big, it has some complicated multiple recursion in it. As a result, if you use the normal Zortech *ztc* compile command, you are apt to get an *out of memory* message. Zortech has a more complex but slower compiler that must be invoked in two steps, as shown. This compiler is able to handle the *fractal* module without difficulty.

Once you run the *make* facility, you should have a fully compiled program that will perform whatever ray tracing you desire.

Running Programs with Turbo C++

The Newton's method programs have been compiled and run with Turbo C++. This is the first version of Turbo C++ released by Borland. The ray tracing program has also been compiled with Turbo C++ and the *wsphere.ray* data file successfully traced. The other data files were not checked with Turbo C++.

There are some differences that have to be considered for Turbo C++. First, where Zortech C++ uses the include file *stream.hpp,* Turbo C++ uses the file *iostream.h,* so you will have to go through the files and change this statement wherever it occurs—hopefully, once, in the *render.hpp* file. If there were a few other places I missed, you will find them quickly enough when you try to compile.) Figure 13-2 lists the *makefile* for Turbo C++. First, look at the linking command, and note that while the Zortech command line linker automatically finds any library files needed and links them in, the Turbo C++ command line linker does not. Instead, you have to specify several of these library files on the linker command line. The Turbo C++ command line linker doesn't recognize any instructions for the location of include or library files in the integrated environment, so you have to specify the full path for each library file if it is not in the same directory with the rest of your program. When you installed Turbo C++, your linker and compiler were put in the sub-directory *bin,* whereas the library files were put into the subdirectory *lib.* Unfortunately, if you include a full path command for each library file, such as:

```
c:\tcplus\lib\cl
```

you are likely to find that when you attempt to link, you get an error message like:

```
command line too long
```

because you have exceeded a DOS limitation of 127 characters in a single command line. You can get around this limitation by using a response file to contain your extra data as described in the Turbo C++ manual, but it's just as easy to copy the needed library files to your *bin* directory. That is why there are no paths given for the library files in the make file.

Note that the compile statements use a compiler *tcc* instead of the *ztc* compiler used by Zortech. All of the compile options used are the same, except for the additional ones *Y* and *Yo* used by Turbo C++. Now we get to the good and bad aspects of Turbo C++. The Zortech C++ compiler is apparently much more efficient than the Turbo C++ compiler, since the ray tracing program compiles to a little over 100k bytes with Zortech while Turbo C++ requires 122k

memory model ???
If 22K breaks your book, you
most be in any-mod XT

bytes. Unfortunately, we need all that extra memory consumed by Turbo C++ for our data, so the program runs out of memory. That's the bad side. The good side is that Turbo C++ has a sophisticated overlay capability that reduces the amount of memory required by the program at any given time. Note the use of /o in the link command which separates the program modules that remain resident at all times from those that may be overlaid. In addition, in the compile section, -Y is used with each module that is to remain resident and -Yo with each module that may be overlaid. Once the program is compiled and linked with these overlay options specified, it is capable of tracing the sample pictures without difficulty.

```
render.exe: render.obj vmath.obj input.obj objects.obj
                                              fractal.obj ray.obj

        tlink c0l render vmath /o input objects fractal
                                    ray,,,overlay emu mathl cl

render.obj:          render.cpp          render.hpp
          tcc -c  -Y -ml -f render.cpp

vmath.obj:          vmath.cpp  render.hpp
          tcc -c -Y -ml -f vmath.cpp

input.obj:          input.cpp    render.hpp
          tcc -c -Yo -ml -f input.cpp

fractal.obj:          fractal.cpp    render.hpp
          tcc -c -Yo -ml -f fractal.cpp

objects.obj:    objects.cpp render.hpp
          tcc -w- -Yo -c   -ml -f objects.cpp

ray.obj:          ray.cpp          render.hpp
          tcc -c  -Yo -ml -f ray.cpp
```

Figure 13-2. Listing of Turbo C++ Make File

252

Ray-Tracing Pictures

Pictures generated by the ray-tracing program are shown in Plates 4 to 16 in the color section. The input data used to specify these pictures is listed in Appendix A. You should be able to process any one of these pictures and create the same picture, or modify the data to create a new picture according to your own design.

CHAPTER 14

Displaying and Saving Screens

The result of using the ray-tracing program is a disk file which contains a lot more detailed color information than we can ever use with the VGA monitor on a personal computer. Because of the large amount of information in the file, it takes a lot of space; in fact, we can only get one of these files onto a standard 360k floppy disk. This chapter looks at how we convert from the file generated by the ray tracer to the best possible VGA display, how that display is stored in a reasonably sized disk file, and how to restore that disk file to a screen display. If you're lucky enough to have a color printer, you may want to make some printouts of these displays. There is a program commercially available called Pizazz Plus, which can capture any display screens you will generate and print to many different color printers with reasonably good quality.

Creating a VGA Color Display

The file generated by the ray tracer provides three bytes of data for each pixel of the color display. Each byte contains a number from 0 to 63 representing a shade of color. One byte gives the shade of red, another the shade of green, and the third the shade of blue. Together, each set of bytes can represent 262,144 different shades of color. This is adequate to color any scene with more precision than the human eye can discern. Unfortunately, the VGA display card, in the mode which displays the largest number of colors, can only display 256 different colors at any one time. It might seem hopeless to attempt to create a realistic scene from our original data file with such a limited number of available colors. Actually, the situation is not as bad as it appears. In the first place, most scenes don't even come close to requiring the full range of colors. The program described below tallies the number of color shades in a scene. The number of colors for scenes in this book ranges from 350 to 3500, even when realistic shading, reflections, and shadows are included. This is a much greater number than the 256 handled by the VGA, but fortunately many of these colors are used in shading a surface and are thus very close to each other, so that the number of colors can be reduced to 256 without major degradation of the picture. Of course, we could have a prettier, more realistic picture if we had more colors to work with, but by using a few tricks we can make the VGA display look pretty good.

The program for this operation is listed in Figure 14-1. We first need to halve the number of color shades from 0 to 63 to 0 to 31. Since we can only display 256 out of a possible 262,144 colors, it doesn't matter if we cut the number of possible values of each color in half. Fortunately, this results in a total maximum number of color shades of 32,768, which is a size we can contain within an array in a C program. Every set of three bytes represents a color in the file. Each time we encounter a color, we'll increment the member of the array representing this color so that when we are finished the array contains the total number of occurrences for each of the 32,768 shades of color. We sort these according to the number of occurrences and assign the 256 VGA colors to the 256 shades that occur most often. This is all very well, but what do we do about the colors not in the first 256 in frequency of occurrence? It is instructive to look at the number of occurrences for these remaining colors. If you want to do this for several typical files, you can modify the program of Figure 14-1 so that after it completes the sort, it prints out the values in the array instead of generating the color picture. You'll find that many of the colors below the first 256 occur only once, so that if we get them wrong only a single pixel is affected. Even the ones that occur most frequently do so 20 or 30 times, which is not a very big section of a picture. Nevertheless, we want to do the best we can, so we compare each of these colors with the 256 selected for display and assign each color to whichever of the 256 is closest to the actual color.

```
/*
        ┌─────────────────────────────────────────────────┐
        │    colproc = Program to Process Color Data for VGA │
        └─────────────────────────────────────────────────┘
                                                                */

#include <dos.h>
#include <stdio.h>

void gotoxy(int x, int y);
void plot(int x, int y, int color);
void setMode(int mode);
void setVGApalette(unsigned char *buffer);
void sort(unsigned int start, unsigned int end);

typedef struct
{
    char Red;
    char Green;
    char Blue;
}
RGB;

enum { red=0,grn=1,blu=2 };

union REGS reg;
struct SREGS inreg;

#define   MAXXRES        800    /* set max horiz coord expected */

unsigned int Col_Array[256][2];
unsigned char Pal_Array[256][3];
RGB Color,Color2;

int i,k,xres, yres, last_color,scanline,r1,r2,g1,g2,b1,b2;
unsigned char r[MAXXRES], g[MAXXRES], b[MAXXRES];
FILE *file_1;
unsigned char far *color_hist;
long int color_no;
unsigned int j;
unsigned char frequency[8192];
unsigned int hues[8192];

void main(argc,argv)
```

```
int argc;
char *argv[];

{
    int index;
    int rgbindex;
    int y1;
    unsigned int d1, temp_d;
    unsigned char d2;

    setMode(3);
    if (argc != 2)
    {
            printf("VGA Color Processor by Roger Stevens\n");
            printf("Usage: %s filename.RAW\n",argv[0]);
            exit(1);
    }
    if ((file_1 = fopen(argv[1],"rb"))==NULL)
    {
            printf("Couldn't open file %s\n",argv[1]);
            exit(1);
    }

    color_hist = farmalloc(32768);
    for (i=0;i<256;i++)
            {
            Pal_Array[i][red] = 0;
            Pal_Array[i][grn] = 0;
            Pal_Array[i][blu] = 0;
            }
            for (j=0; j<32768; j++)
            color_hist[j] = 0;
    xres = yres = 0;
    fread(&xres,sizeof(int),1,file_1);
    fread(&yres,sizeof(int),1,file_1);
    printf("VGA color post-processor by Roger Stevens\n");
    printf("Image file resolution is: %d  by  %d\n",xres,yres);
    y1 = 0;
    printf("Collecting color data [    ]");
    while (!feof(file_1))
    {
```

open data file for binary reading

read image resolution

```
fread(&scanline,sizeof(int),1,file_1);
        if (scanline >= yres)
            {
                        printf("Faulty data file.\n");
                        exit(1);
            }
gotoxy(24,3);
printf("%d",scanline);
fread(&r[0],sizeof(char),xres,file_1);
fread(&g[0],sizeof(char),xres,file_1);
fread(&b[0],sizeof(char),xres,file_1);
for (index=0;index<xres;index++)
    {
            Color.Red   = (r[index] & 0x3e);
            Color.Green = (g[index] & 0x3e);
            Color.Blue  = (b[index] & 0x3e);
            color_no =  (Color.Red >> 1) | (Color.Green
                << 4) | (Color.Blue << 9);
            if (color_hist[color_no] < 255)
                color_hist[color_no]++;
    }
    y1 += 1;
}
last_color = -1;
for (j=0; j<32768; j++)
{
        if (color_hist[j] > 0)
            {
                    last_color++;
                    hues[last_color] = j;
                    frequency[last_color] = color_hist[j];
            }
}
printf("\nThere are %d colors.",last_color);
printf("\nStarting sort.");
sort(0,last_color);
printf("\nSort completed.");
printf("\nModifying extra colors [    ]");
for (i=0; i<256; i++)
        frequency[i] = i;
for (i=256; i<=last_color; i++)
    {
```

(handwritten note) Line # is first item in line

(handwritten note) mask out 1's bit of 6-bit data

(handwritten note) divide by 2 (now 5-bit)

(handwritten note) Form color number = triple of R, G, B

(handwritten note) His color_hist is only 1 byte per posn — Max value = 255

(handwritten note) Colors not among 256 most common must be modified to one of the 256 values

(handwritten note) what is the logic?

```
        gotoxy(25,7);
        printf("%5d",i);
        d1 = 32768;
        for (j=0; j<256; j++)
        {
                Color.Red = (hues[i] << 1) & 0x3E;
                Color.Green = (hues[i] >> 4) & 0x3E;
                Color.Blue = (hues[i] >> 9) & 0x3E;
                Color2.Red = (hues[j] << 1) & 0x3E;
                Color2.Green = (hues[j] >> 4) & 0x3E;
                Color2.Blue = (hues[j] >> 9) & 0x3E;
                temp_d = (Color.Red - Color2.Red)*(Color.Red -
                    Color2.Red) + (Color.Green -
                    Color2.Green)*(Color.Green -
                    Color2.Green) +
                    (Color.Blue - Color2.Blue)*(Color.Blue -
                    Color2.Blue);
                if (temp_d < d1)
                {
                    d1 = temp_d;
                    d2 = j;
                }
        }
        frequency[i] = d2;
    }
    for (j=0; j<256; j++)
    {
        Color.Red = (hues[j] << 1) & 0x3E;
        Color.Green = (hues[j] >> 4) & 0x3E;
        Color.Blue = (hues[j] >> 9) & 0x3E;
        Pal_Array[j][0] = Color.Red;
        Pal_Array[j][1] = Color.Green;
        Pal_Array[j][2] = Color.Blue;
    }
    setMode(0x13);
    setVGApalette(&Pal_Array[0][0]);
    for (j=0; j<32768; j++)
        color_hist[j] = 0;
    for (j=0; j<=last_color; j++)
        color_hist[hues[j]] = frequency[j];
    rewind(file_1);
    y1 = 0;
```

(handwritten margin note, left:) color modification

(handwritten margin note, lower left:) set VGA mode & palette

(handwritten margin note, lower left:) feed new freqgen

(handwritten margin note, right:) Store modifications

260

```
fread(&xres,sizeof(int),1,file_1);
fread(&yres,sizeof(int),1,file_1);
while (!feof(file_1))
{
        fread(&scanline,sizeof(int),1,file_1);
        if (scanline >= yres)
        {
                printf("Faulty data file.\n");
                exit(1);
        }
        fread(&r[0],sizeof(char),xres,file_1);
        fread(&g[0],sizeof(char),xres,file_1);
        fread(&b[0],sizeof(char),xres,file_1);
        for (index=0;index<xres;index++)
        {
                Color.Red   = (r[index] & 0x3e);
                Color.Green = (g[index] & 0x3e);
                Color.Blue  = (b[index] & 0x3e);
                color_no =  (Color.Red >> 1) | (Color.Green
                     << 4) | (Color.Blue << 9);
                plot(index,y1,color_hist[color_no]);
        }
        y1 += 1;
  }
  getch();
  setMode(3);
  fclose(file_1);
}



/*
      ┌─────────────────────────────────────────────┐
      │        setMode() = Sets Video Mode          │
      └─────────────────────────────────────────────┘                 /*

void setMode(int mode)
{
  reg.h.ah = 0;
  reg.h.al = mode;
  int86 (0x10,&reg,&reg);
}
```

[handwritten margin notes] Read (triplets) triples and display as spending modified colors

[handwritten note] Read ... get modified color.

```
*/
┌──────────────────────────────────────────────────────┐
│  ┌────────────────────────────────────────────────┐  │
│  │  plot() = Function to plot point to VGA 256 Color Screen │
│  └────────────────────────────────────────────────┘  │
└──────────────────────────────────────────────────────┘
                                                        */

void plot(int x, int y, int color)
{
  unsigned int offset;
  char far *address;
  offset = 320 * y + x;
  address = (char far *)(0xA0000000L + offset);
  *address = color;
}
```

(handwritten note:) 320 screen — should be parm

(handwritten note:) Very slow way to plot — Should use incremental addr calc —

```
/*
┌──────────────────────────────────────────────────────┐
│  ┌────────────────────────────────────────────────┐  │
│  │  setVGApalette() = Function to set all 256 color registers │
│  └────────────────────────────────────────────────┘  │
└──────────────────────────────────────────────────────┘
                                                        */

void setVGApalette(unsigned char *buffer)
{
  reg.x.ax = 0x1012;
  segread(&inreg);
  inreg.es = inreg.ds;
  reg.x.bx = 0;
  reg.x.cx = 256;
  reg.x.dx = (int)&buffer[0];
  int86x(0x10,&reg,&reg,&inreg);
}
/*
┌──────────────────────────────────────────────────────┐
│  ┌────────────────────────────────────────────────┐  │
│  │      sort() = Quicksort to sort colors by frequency │
│  └────────────────────────────────────────────────┘  │
└──────────────────────────────────────────────────────┘
                                                        */

void sort(unsigned int start, unsigned int end)
{
  unsigned int pivot,temp2;
  unsigned char temp;

  if (start < (end - 1))
  {
```

```
        i = start;
        j = end;
        pivot = (frequency[i] + frequency[j] +
                    frequency[(i+j)/2])/3;
        do
        {
                while (frequency[i] > pivot)
                            i++;
                while (frequency[j] < pivot)
                            j-;
                if (i < j)
                {
                            temp = frequency[i];
                            frequency[i] = frequency[j];
                            frequency[j] = temp;
                            temp2 = hues[i];
                            hues[i++] = hues[j];
                            hues[j-] = temp2;

                }
          }             while (i < j);
        if (j < end)
        {
                sort(start,j);
                sort(j+1,end);
        }
  }
  if (frequency[end] > frequency[start])
  {
  temp = frequency[start];
  frequency[start] = frequency[end];
  frequency[end] = temp;
  temp2 = hues[start];
  hues[start] = hues[end];
  hues[end] = temp2;
  }
}

void gotoxy(int x, int y)
{
  reg.h.ah = 2;
  reg.h.bh = 0;
  reg.h.dh = y-1;
```

```
  reg.h.dl = x-1;
  int86(0x10, &reg, &reg);
}
```

Figure 14-1. Program to Display Ray-tracing Data

Now, let's look at the program in detail. First, I should point out that to make the program independent of graphics routines that differ from one version of C to another, I have included functions that perform the graphics tasks needed to create the display. There are three and they are all fairly simple.

The function *setMode* makes use of the ROM BIOS video services to set the display mode. The function properly sets up the register contents and then generates the interrupt that calls the proper ROM BIOS service. We are really only interested in two display modes, mode 3 which is the normal text mode, and mode 19 (13H) which is the VGA graphics mode.

The second function is *plot,* which plots a pixel at the appropriate point on the display. The VGA memory board contains memory for four color planes. In many of the modes, color is determined by sending a single bit to the same address in each of the four memory planes. This requires some complicated manipulation of registers, since the memory planes cannot be addressed directly. Fortunately for mode 19, a full byte is used to describe the color of each pixel and each byte is at an adjacent memory address so that all we have to do is compute the address at which the pixel resides in memory and send the byte to it. (Actually, inside the VGA card, all sorts of funny things go on, with the bytes being rotated through the four memory planes so that any one memory plane only stores every fourth byte with the intervening memory locations being empty. This is totally invisible to us. From the outside world, it looks as if we were simply storing data in an ordinary memory array.)

The third function is *setVGApalette.* The VGA has 256 color registers that store the color shades to be used for the display. The ROM BIOS video service that is used in this function takes data from a buffer and stores it in all of these color registers in a single operation. To do this, we first set up the *a* register to access the appropriate video service. We then read in the current segment where the buffer is and assign it to register *es*. We put 0 in register *bx* and 256 in register *cx* to indicate the starting register number and the number of registers to be filled with data. We put the buffer address into register *dx*. Then we execute the interrupt to perform the operation.

The final function used by this program is *sort*. This is a standard Quicksort algorithm. Since it is described in many computer books including my book, *Graphics Programming in C*, I won't go into any detail. Suffice to say that it sorts the contents of the array in which the frequency of occurrence of each color is accumulated. It puts the indexes of this array (which represent the different shades of color) into a new array in the order of the number of occurrences, beginning with the most frequently occurring color.

The program starts by checking whether it was called with a file name specified. If not, a message is printed out (with the display in text mode), which indicates that a file name must be included to run the program. The program then exits. If a file name was specified, an attempt is made to open the specified file. If the file cannot be opened, the program prints out a message to this effect and then exits. If the file is successfully opened, the program next allocates memory for the array *color_hist,* which will be used to store the occurrences of colors. The array of information for the color registers, *Pal_Array,* and the *color_hist* array are then initialized to all zeroes. The first four bytes of the file, which are the integer values for *xres,* the number of display pixels in the *x* direction, and *yres*, the number of display pixels in the *y* direction, are then read. The heading and the resolution data are then displayed on the screen. Next, the program displays the line "Collecting color data [   ]" with a space for the line number. The program then starts a *while* loop which will continue until the end of the file is encountered.

The loop begins by reading the number of the scan line from the file. If it is greater than the maximum line that was defined, there is an error and the program displays, "Faulty data file" and exits. If the scan line is acceptable, it is displayed at the proper place on the screen. Next, the program reads first a line of red data, then a line of green data, and then a line of blue data from the file. These are stored in *r, g,* and *b* arrays. A *for* loop takes the red, green, and blue values for each pixel (not including the least significant bit, thereby accomplishing the division by two) then shifts and combines them into a unique color number. This value is used as an index for the *color_hist* array and the contents of that address is incremented.

Once the loop is complete, the program runs another *for* loop which scans the *color_hist* array and increments a variable, *last_color,* each time a color occurs at least once. The index for this color is placed in an array *hues* and the frequency with which it occurs in an array *frequency.* Each of these arrays is of size 8192, assuming that there will be no more than 8192 different colors in any particular picture. If there are more than 8192 colors, the program will probably bomb. The next thing that happens is that a line is displayed telling how many colors were in the picture, so if there are too many colors, you may get to see this before anything goes haywire. Assuming there weren't too many colors, the program displays "Starting sort," then runs the sort function, and then displays "Sort completed."

The frequency of occurrence data is no longer needed; instead we will fill the *frequency* array with a color number from 0 to 255 for each color. We begin by assigning the first 256 colors the numbers 0 to 255. Then the program displays "Modifying extra colors[   ]" with a space for the color number being processed. The program enters a *for* loop which it iterates for each of the additional colors from 256 to the *last_color* number. Within this loop, first the number of the color being worked on is displayed. Then another *for* loop is entered which is reiterated for each of the 256 initial colors. Within this loop, each color index for the current color being processed and the current one of the 256 initial colors is decomposed into the original red, green, and blue color data. The sum of the squares of the difference between red, green, and blue values is then computed. At each iteration, the smallest sum of squares is saved along with its color number. When the current color has been checked against all 256 initial colors, it is assigned the number of the color for which the sum of the squares of the differences was smallest.

When the two loops are complete, all of the colors beyond the first 256 have been assigned color numbers that correspond to the color for which the sum of the squares of the differences was smallest. The graphics mode is set for the 256 color display and *setVGApalette* is run to set the VGA color values for the first 256 colors. Then we refill the *color_hist* array with the number of the color associated with each index value or with a zero if that index has no color and we rewind the file. The file is then read all over again, beginning by reading the *xres* and *yres* values and then entering a *while* loop that reiterates until the end of file is encountered. For each iteration, the scan line number is read first followed by the red, green, and blue data for a complete line. Then a *for* loop is run for each pixel of the line. The color data for that pixel is combined into an index number in the same manner as was done above. The color number for that index is taken from the *color_hist* array and the pixel is plotted in that color at the appropriate point on the screen. When both loops are complete, the full picture is being displayed. The program waits for a character to be entered at the keyboard. When this occurs, the screen is reset to the text mode, the file is closed, and the program terminates.

Using High-Resolution VGA Cards

Many VGA cards currently being sold have high-resolution modes that produce much higher quality displays than envisioned when the first VGA specifications came out. Unfortunately, the methodology for doing this with each card seems to be different. It would be a great step forward if a standard for implementing enhanced displays could be agreed upon, but it's unlikely.

Here we are going to give a program for producing a high resolution display from ray tracing data using the Vega VGA1024i display card. This card supports a number of extended high-resolution modes. The one we are going to use is 800 by 600 pixels with 256 colors. First, go into a ray-tracing data file and change the XRES and YRES parameters to 800 and 600, respectively. Then run *render* with this file to generate a new raw data file at the improved resolution. (This is going to take longer than for a 320 by 200 display, since there are now 480,000 elements to process instead of 64,000.)

Run the program listed in Figure 14-2, to convert the raw data file to a display. The first thing to observe is that this program looks very similar to the *colproc* program given in Figure 14-1. In fact, everything is the same except the way the graphics mode is set up and the way to write to the screen. First, look at the *setMode* function, which is used to set the display mode. Note that this function now begins with an *if* statement. For modes less than 32H, the function is just the same as the one used with the regular display modes. However, for the extended graphics functions (modes beyond 32H), a different ROM BIOS call is used, placing the mode in a different register, and sending an initializing output to one of the VGA registers. Although this function uses the ROM BIOS, this part of the ROM BIOS is contained in the VGA board, so that for a different make of VGA board, the results could be completely different.

Let's look at the *plot* function. Before, we used the *x* and *y* pixel values to create an offset which was added to the basic video memory address to create the address where the pixel color was sent. Now we begin by creating the offset (which can be larger because we now have 640 pixels in a line instead of 320). However, this larger video memory is banked to be able to handle more memory within the memory space allotted to the VGA. Thus, if the offset is greater than 65536 (64k), we must divide it by 65536 to obtain the bank number. The remainder is the new value of offset. The function keeps a record of the number of the last active bank in global memory. If the desired bank is different from the currently active bank, the function selects the new bank. The new bank number is stored in *active_bank*. The function then provides outputs to several of the VGA registers to select this new bank.

The way this is done is not very straightforward, but should be self-evident from the program listing. Once the correct memory bank has been selected, the function creates a memory address from the offset and the base memory address, and sends the pixel color there. (If the correct bank is already selected, the function can skip all that bank selection stuff and simply create the address and send the pixel. Basically, these two functions are all that need to be changed to use the extended 640 pixel by 480 row by 256 color mode.

```
/*
      ┌─────────────────────────────────────────────────────────┐
      │                                                         │
      │  800proc = Program to Process 800x600 Color Data for VGA │
      │                                                         │        */
      └─────────────────────────────────────────────────────────┘

#include <dos.h>
#include <stdio.h>

void gotoxy(int x, int y);
void plot(int x, int y, int color);
void setMode(int mode);
void setVGApalette(unsigned char *buffer);
void sort(unsigned int start, unsigned int end);

typedef struct
{
  char Red;
  char Green;
  char Blue;
}
RGB;

enum { red=0,grn=1,blu=2 };

union REGS reg;
struct SREGS inreg;

#define   MAXXRES        800    /* set max horiz coord expected */

unsigned int Col_Array[256][2];
unsigned char Pal_Array[256][3];
RGB Color,Color2;

int i,k,xres, yres,
last_color,scanline,r1,r2,g1,g2,b1,b2,bank=0,active_bank=0;
```

```
unsigned char r[MAXXRES], g[MAXXRES], b[MAXXRES];
FILE *file_1;
unsigned char far *color_hist;
long int color_no;
unsigned int j;
unsigned char frequency[8192];
unsigned int hues[8192];

void main(argc,argv)
int argc;
char *argv[];

{
  int index;
  int rgbindex;
  int y1;
  unsigned int d1, temp_d;
  unsigned char d2;

  setMode(3);
  if (argc != 2)
  {
        printf("VGA Color Processor by Roger Stevens\n");
        printf("Usage: %s filename.RAW\n",argv[0]);
        exit(1);
  }
  if ((file_1 = fopen(argv[1],"rb"))==NULL)
  {
        printf("Couldn't open file %s\n",argv[1]);
        exit(1);
  }

  color_hist = farmalloc(32768);
  for (i=0;i<256;i++)
  {
  Pal_Array[i][red] = 0;
  Pal_Array[i][grn] = 0;
  Pal_Array[i][blu] = 0;
  }
  for (j=0; j<32768; j++)
        color_hist[j] = 0;
  xres = yres = 0;
```

```
fread(&xres,sizeof(int),1,file_1);
fread(&yres,sizeof(int),1,file_1);
printf("VGA color post-processor by Roger Stevens\n");
printf("Image file resolution is: %d  by  %d\n",xres,yres);
for (i=0;i<256;i++)
{
Pal_Array[i][red] = 0;
Pal_Array[i][grn] = 0;
Pal_Array[i][blu] = 0;
}
y1 = 0;
printf("Collecting color data [   ]");
while (!feof(file_1))
{
        fread(&scanline,sizeof(int),1,file_1);
                if (scanline >= yres)
                printf("Faulty data file.\n");
                exit(1);
                }
        gotoxy(24,3);
        printf("%d",scanline);
        fread(&r[0],sizeof(char),xres,file_1);
        fread(&g[0],sizeof(char),xres,file_1);
        fread(&b[0],sizeof(char),xres,file_1);
        for (index=0;index<xres;index++)
        {
                Color.Red   = (r[index] & 0x3e);
                Color.Green = (g[index] & 0x3e);
                Color.Blue  = (b[index] & 0x3e);
                color_no =  (Color.Red >> 1) | (Color.Green
                    << 4) | (Color.Blue << 9);
                if (color_hist[color_no] < 255)
                        color_hist[color_no]++;
        }
        y1 += 1;
}
last_color = -1;
for (j=0; j<32768; j++)
{
        if (color_hist[j] > 0)
        {
                last_color++;
```

```
                    hues[last_color] = j;
                    frequency[last_color] = color_hist[j];
        }
}
printf("\nThere are %d colors.",last_color);
printf("\nStarting sort.");
sort(0,last_color);
printf("\nSort completed.");
printf("\nModifying extra colors [     ]");
for (i=0; i<256; i++)
        frequency[i] = i;
for (i=256; i<=last_color; i++)
{
        gotoxy(25,7);
        printf("%5d",i);
        d1 = 32768;
        for (j=0; j<256; j++)
        {
                Color.Red = (hues[i] << 1) & 0x3E;
                Color.Green = (hues[i] >> 4) & 0x3E;
                Color.Blue = (hues[i] >> 9) & 0x3E;
                Color2.Red = (hues[j] << 1) & 0x3E;
                Color2.Green = (hues[j] >> 4) & 0x3E;
                Color2.Blue = (hues[j] >> 9) & 0x3E;
                temp_d = (Color.Red - Color2.Red)*(Color.Red-
                    Color2.Red) + (Color.Green -
                    Color2.Green)*(Color.Green - Color2.Green) +
                    (Color.Blue -Color2.Blue)*(Color.Blue -
                    Color2.Blue);
                if (temp_d < d1)
                {
                    d1 = temp_d;
                    d2 = j;
                }
        }
        frequency[i] = d2;
}
for (j=0; j<256; j++)
{
        Color.Red = (hues[j] << 1) & 0x3E;
        Color.Green = (hues[j] >> 4) & 0x3E;
        Color.Blue = (hues[j] >> 9) & 0x3E;
```

```
        Pal_Array[j][0] = Color.Red;
        Pal_Array[j][1] = Color.Green;
        Pal_Array[j][2] = Color.Blue;
}
setMode(0x67);
setVGApalette(&Pal_Array[0][0]);
for (j=0; j<32768; j++)
        color_hist[j] = 0;
for (j=0; j<=last_color; j++)
        color_hist[hues[j]] = frequency[j];
rewind(file_1);
y1 = 0;
fread(&xres,sizeof(int),1,file_1);
fread(&yres,sizeof(int),1,file_1);
for (y1; y1<480; y1++)
{
        fread(&scanline,sizeof(int),1,file_1);
        if (scanline >= yres)
        {
            printf("Faulty data file.\n");
            exit(1);
        }
        fread(&r[0],sizeof(char),xres,file_1);
        fread(&g[0],sizeof(char),xres,file_1);
        fread(&b[0],sizeof(char),xres,file_1);
        for (index=0;index<xres;index++)
        {
                Color.Red   = (r[index] & 0x3e);
                Color.Green = (g[index] & 0x3e);
                Color.Blue  = (b[index] & 0x3e);
                color_no =  (Color.Red >> 1) | (Color.Green
                    << 4) | (Color.Blue << 9);
                plot(index,y1,color_hist[color_no]);
        }
}
getch();
setMode(3);
fclose(file_1);
}
```

```
/*
       ┌────────────────────────────────────────────────┐
       │           setMode() = Sets Video Mode           │
       └────────────────────────────────────────────────┘
                                                            */
void setMode(int mode)
{
  if (mode > 0x32)
  {
        active_bank = 0;
        reg.x.ax = 0x6F05;
        reg.h.bl = mode;
        int86 (0x10,&reg,&reg);
        outpw(0x3C4,0xEA06);
  }
  else
  {
        reg.h.ah = 0;
        reg.h.al = mode;
        int86 (0x10,&reg,&reg);
  }
}


/*
       ┌────────────────────────────────────────────────┐
       │  plot() = Function to plot point to VGA 256 Color Screen │
       └────────────────────────────────────────────────┘
                                                            */

void plot(int x, int y, int color)
{
  long int offset;
  char far *address;
  int temp,temp2;

  offset = 640L * (long)y + (long)x;
  ank = offset/65536L;
  offset = offset % 65536L;
  if (bank != active_bank)
  {
        active_bank = bank;

        reg.h.ah = bank & 0x01;
        reg.h.al = 0xF9;
```

```
        outpw(0x3C4,reg.x.ax);
        temp = inpw(0x3CC);
        temp = temp & 0xDF;
        if ((bank & 0x02) != 0)
                    temp = temp | 0x20;
        outpw(0x3C2,temp);
        outp(0x3C4,0xF6);
        temp = inpw(0x3C5);
        temp = temp & 0xF0;
        temp2 = ((bank & 0x0C) >> 2) | (bank & 0x0C);
        temp = temp | temp2;
        outp(0x3C5,temp);
    }
  address = (char far *)(0xA0000000L + offset);
  *address = color;
}

/*
```

```
    setVGApalette() = Function to set all 256 color registers
```

```
                                                                */
```

```
void setVGApalette(unsigned char *buffer)
{
  reg.x.ax = 0x1012;
  segread(&inreg);
  inreg.es = inreg.ds;
  reg.x.bx = 0;
  reg.x.cx = 256;
  reg.x.dx = (int)&buffer[0];
  int86x(0x10,&reg,&reg,&inreg);
}
/*
```

```
            sort() = Quicksort to sort colors by frequency
```

```
                                                                */
```

```
void sort(unsigned int start, unsigned int end)
{
    unsigned int pivot,temp2;
    unsigned char temp;
```

```
    if (start < (end - 1))
    {
         i = start;
         j = end;
         pivot = (frequency[i] + frequency[j] +
             frequency[(i+j)/2])/3;
         do
         {
             while (frequency[i] > pivot)
                     i++;
             while (frequency[j] < pivot)
                      j-;
             if (i < j)
             {
                     temp = frequency[i];
                     frequency[i] = frequency[j];
                     frequency[j] = temp;
                     temp2 = hues[i];
                     hues[i++] = hues[j];
                     hues[j-] = temp2;
             }
    }    while (i < j);
    if (j < end)
    {
        sort(start,j);
        sort(j+1,end);
    }
}
if (frequency[end] > frequency[start])
{
    temp = frequency[start];
    frequency[start] = frequency[end];
    frequency[end] = temp;
    temp2 = hues[start];
    hues[start] = hues[end];
    hues[end] = temp2;
}
}
```

```
void gotoxy(int x, int y)
{
  reg.h.ah = 2;
  reg.h.bh = 0;
  reg.h.dh = y-1;
  reg.h.dl = x-1;
  int86(0x10, &reg, &reg);
}
```

Figure 14-2. Program to Generate 800 x 600 Display

Saving the Display in .PCX Format

The .PCX file format was created by ZSoft for use in PC Paintbrush. It has now become a recognized standard for storing graphics screens. The format for a .PCX file is given in Appendix B. The program described here takes the file of raw data from the ray tracer, and uses the same technique described above to determine the colors needed for the display on the VGA. However, instead of displaying the file, it converts the resulting information to the .PCX format and stores it in a .PCX file having the same name as the .RAW file. The program to do this is listed in Figure 14-3.

The program begins exactly like the preceding one, checking to see whether a file name is specified on the call line and if not, displaying an error message and exiting. Similarly, it then tries to open the file if one is specified, and if unsuccessful, displays an error message and quits. If the file is opened successfully, the program strips off that part of the file name preceding the dot and appends .PCX to it. It then opens this new file and sends the proper information for the .PCX format file header to it. Next, the program does exactly what the preceding program did to collect information on the occurrence of colors, assign the 256 color register values, and find the least squares fit for those colors not among the first 256. The program then rewinds the file, reads the *xres* and *yres* values, and enters a *while* loop that continues until the end of file is encountered.

At the beginning of each iteration of the loop, the program reads the scan line number from the file and, if it exceeds the allowable maximum value, displays an error message and exits. If the scan line value is OK, a line of red, green, and blue pixel data is read to the appropriate arrays. For each pixel in the line, the proper index is created from the color data and used to obtain the pixel color from the *col_hist* array. This data is then encoded in the .PCX format.

Essentially, this format simply outputs the byte to the file if it is a single occurrence and does not have the two most significant bits as ones. Otherwise two bytes are output. The first has its two most significant bits set to one and the remaining bits give a count (between 1 and 63) of the number of sequential occurrences of the same byte value.

```
/*

    pcxgen = Program to Process Color Data for VGA and
             save to a .PCX disk file.
             Includes 320x200 and 640x480 modes

             By Roger T. Stevens    5/5/90

                                                          */

#include <dos.h>
#include <stdio.h>
#include <stream.hpp>
#include <stdlib.h>
#include <string.h>

void gotoxy(int x, int y);
void plot(int x, int y, int color);
void setMode(int mode);
void setVGApalette(unsigned char *buffer);
void sort(unsigned int start, unsigned int end);

typedef struct rgb
{
    char Red;
    char Green;
    char Blue;
}
RGB;
```

```
#define red      0
#define grn      1
#define blu      2

union REGS reg;
struct SREGS inreg;

#define   MAXXRES      800    /* set max horiz coord expected */

unsigned int Col_Array[256][2];
unsigned char Pal_Array[256][3];
RGB Color,Color2;
int i,k,add1,add2,number,line_length,end,start_line,end_line,
      xres, yres, last_color,scanline,r1,r2,g1,g2,b1,b2;
unsigned char PALETTE[16] =
      {0,1,2,3,4,5,20,7,56,57,58,59,60,61,62,63};
unsigned char ch,ch1,old_ch,num_out,red_p,green_p,blue_p;
unsigned char r[MAXXRES], g[MAXXRES], b[MAXXRES];
FILE *file_1, *fsave;
unsigned char far *color_hist;
long int color_no,j;
unsigned char frequency[8192];
unsigned int hues[8192];
char filename[15];

main(argc,argv)

int argc;
char *argv[];

{
      int index,rgbindex,y1,length;
      unsigned int d1, temp_d;
      unsigned char d2;

      setMode(3);

      cout <<
```

```
    cout << "                                                       \n";

    cout << "                                                       \n";

    cout << "        Program to Process Color Data for VGA and      \n";

    cout << "                save to a .PCX disk file.              \n";

    cout << "           Includes 320x200 and 640x480 modes          \n";

    cout << "                                                       \n";

    cout <<

              "                 By Roger T. Stevens    5/5/90         \n";


    if (argc != 2)
    {
    cout <<
             "                                                       \n";
cout <<
             "                 Useage: pcxgen filename.RAW           \n";
    }
cout <<
             "                                                       \n";
cout <<
             "                                                       \n";
```

```
    if (argc != 2)
        exit(1);
    if ((file_1 = fopen(argv[1],"rb"))==NULL)
    {
        printf("Couldn't open file %s\n",argv[1]);
        exit(1);
    }
    for (i=0;i<256;i++)
    {
        Pal_Array[i][red] = 0;
        Pal_Array[i][grn] = 0;
```

```
      Pal_Array[i][blu] = 0;
}
color_hist = farmalloc(32768);
for (j=0; j<32768; j++)
      color_hist[j] = 0;
xres = yres = 0;
fread(&xres,sizeof(int),1,file_1);
fread(&yres,sizeof(int),1,file_1);
cout << "\n\nImage file resolution is: " << xres << " by " <<
      yres << "\n";
if (!((((xres == 320) && (yres == 200)) || ((xres == 640) &&
      (yres == 480)))))
{
      cout << "Does not support this resolution.\n";
      exit(0);
}
length = strcspn(argv[1],".");
strncpy(filename,argv[1],length);
strcat(filename,".pcx");
fsave = fopen(filename,"wb");
fputc(0x0A,fsave);
fputc(0x05,fsave);
fputc(0x01,fsave);
fputc(0x08,fsave);
fputc(0,fsave);
fputc(0,fsave);
fputc(0,fsave);
fputc(0,fsave);
xres--;
yres--;
fwrite(&xres,sizeof(int),1,fsave);
fwrite(&yres,sizeof(int),1,fsave);
xres++;
yres++;
fwrite(&xres,sizeof(int),1,fsave);
fwrite(&yres,sizeof(int),1,fsave);
ch = 0x00;
for (i=0; i<16; i++)
{
      red_p = (((PALETTE[i] & 0x20) >> 5) |
                  ((PALETTE[i] & 0x04) >> 1)) * 85;
      green_p = (((PALETTE[i] & 0x10) >> 4) |
```

```
                                    (PALETTE[i] & 0x02)) * 85;
            blue_p = (((PALETTE[i] & 0x08) >> 3) |
                        ((PALETTE[i] & 0x01) << 1)) * 85;
            fputc(red_p,fsave);
            fputc(green_p,fsave);
            fputc(blue_p,fsave);
    }
    fputc(0x00,fsave);
    fputc(0x01,fsave);
    fputc(0x40,fsave);
    fputc(0x01,fsave);
    line_length = xres;
    end = xres;
    for (i=68; i<128; i++)
            fputc(0x00,fsave);
    y1 = 0;
    printf("Collecting color data from scan line [   ]");
    while (!feof(file_1))
    {
            fread(&scanline,sizeof(int),1,file_1);
                    if (scanline >= yres)
                    {
                            printf("Faulty data file.\n");
                            exit(1);
                    }
            gotoxy(39,13);
            printf("%3d",scanline);
            fread(&r[0],sizeof(char),xres,file_1);
            fread(&g[0],sizeof(char),xres,file_1);
            fread(&b[0],sizeof(char),xres,file_1);
            for (index=0;index<xres;index++)
            {
                    Color.Red   = (r[index] & 0x3e);
                    Color.Green = (g[index] & 0x3e);
                    Color.Blue  = (b[index] & 0x3e);
                    color_no =  (Color.Red >> 1) | (Color.Green
                        << 4) |(Color.Blue << 9);
                    if (color_hist[color_no] < 255)
                        color_hist[color_no]++;
            }
            y1 += 1;
    }
```

```
last_color = -1;
for (j=0; j<32768; j++)
{
        if (color_hist[j] > 0)
        {
                last_color++;
                hues[last_color] = j;
                frequency[last_color] = color_hist[j];
        }
}
printf("\nThere are %d colors.",last_color);
printf("\nStarting sort.");
sort(0,last_color);
printf("\nSort completed.");
printf("\nModifying extra colors [      ]");
for (i=0; i<256; i++)
        frequency[i] = i;
for (i=256; i<=last_color; i++)
{
        gotoxy(25,17);
        printf("%5d",i);
        d1 = 32768;
        for (j-0; j<256; j++)
        {
                Color.Red = (hues[i] << 1) & 0x3E;
                Color.Green = (hues[i] >> 4) & 0x3E;
                Color.Blue = (hues[i] >> 9) & 0x3E;
                Color2.Red = (hues[j] << 1) & 0x3E;
                Color2.Green = (hues[j] >> 4) & 0x3E;
                Color2.Blue = (hues[j] >> 9) & 0x3E;
                temp_d = (Color.Red - Color2.Red)*(Color.Red -
                        Color2.Red) + (Color.Green -
                        Color2.Green)*(Color.Green -
                        Color2.Green) +
                        (Color.Blue - Color2.Blue)*(Color.Blue -
                        Color2.Blue);
                if (temp_d < d1)
                {
                        d1 = temp_d;
                        d2 = j;
                }
        }
```

```
            frequency[i] = d2;
    }
    for (j=0; j<256; j++)
    {
            Color.Red = (hues[j] << 1) & 0x3E;
            Color.Green = (hues[j] >> 4) & 0x3E;
            Color.Blue = (hues[j] >> 9) & 0x3E;
            Pal_Array[j][0] = Color.Red;
            Pal_Array[j][1] = Color.Green;
            Pal_Array[j][2] = Color.Blue;
    }
    for (j=0; j<32768; j++)
            color_hist[j] = 0;
    for (j=0; j<=last_color; j++)
            color_hist[hues[j]] = frequency[j];
    rewind(file_1);
    y1 = 0;
    fread(&xres,sizeof(int),1,file_1);
    fread(&yres,sizeof(int),1,file_1);
    while (!feof(file_1))
    {
            fread(&scanline,sizeof(int),1,file_1);
            if (scanline >= yres)
            {
                    printf("Faulty data file.\n");
                    exit(1);
            }
            fread(&r[0],sizeof(char),xres,file_1);
            fread(&g[0],sizeof(char),xres,file_1);
            fread(&b[0],sizeof(char),xres,file_1);
            Color.Red   = (r[0] & 0x3e);
            Color.Green = (g[0] & 0x3e);
            Color.Blue  = (b[0] & 0x3e);
            color_no =  (Color.Red >> 1) | (Color.Green << 4) |
                    (Color.Blue << 9);
            number = 1;
            old_ch = color_hist[color_no];
            for (index=1; index<=xres; index++)
            {
                    Color.Red   = (r[index] & 0x3e);
                    Color.Green = (g[index] & 0x3e);
                    Color.Blue  = (b[index] & 0x3e);
```

```
                    color_no =  (Color.Red >> 1) | (Color.Green
                          << 4) |(Color.Blue << 9);
                    if (index == xres)
                          ch = old_ch - 1;
                    else
                          ch = color_hist[color_no];
                    if ((ch == old_ch) && (number < 63))
                          number++;
                    else
                    {

                          num_out = ((unsigned char)number | 0xC0);
                          if (((old_ch & 0xC0) ==
                                0xC0) || (number > 1))
                          fputc(num_out,fsave);
                          fputc(old_ch,fsave);
                          old_ch = ch;
                          number = 1;

                    }
              }
              y1 += 1;
     }
     fputc(0x0C,fsave);
     for(i=0; i<256; i++)
           for (j=0; j<3; j++)
                      fputc(Pal_Array[i][j] ^ 4,fsave);
     fclose(fsave);
     fclose(file_1);
     cout << "File transformation complete.\n";
}


/*
     ┌──────────────────────────────────────────────────────┐
     │   sort() = Quicksort to sort colors by frequency       │
     └──────────────────────────────────────────────────────┘
                                                            */

void sort(unsigned int start, unsigned int end)
{
  unsigned int pivot,temp2;
  unsigned char temp;

  if (start < (end - 1))
  {
```

```
        i = start;
        j = end;
        pivot = (frequency[i] + frequency[j] +
                    frequency[(i+j)/2])/3;
        do
        {
                while (frequency[i] > pivot)
                    i++;
                while (frequency[j] < pivot)
                    j-;
                if (i < j)
                {
                        temp = frequency[i];
                        frequency[i] = frequency[j];
                        frequency[j] = temp;
                        temp2 = hues[i];
                        hues[i++] = hues[j];
                        hues[j-] = temp2;
                }
        }       while (i < j);
        if (j < end)
        {
                sort(start,j);
                sort(j+1,end);
        }
    }
    if (frequency[end] > frequency[start])
    {
        temp = frequency[start];
        frequency[start] = frequency[end];
        frequency[end] = temp;
        temp2 = hues[start];
        hues[start] = hues[end];
        hues[end] = temp2;
    }
}

void gotoxy(int x, int y)
{
  reg.h.ah = 2;
  reg.h.bh = 0;
  reg.h.dh = y-1;
```

```
    reg.h.dl = x-1;
    int86(0x10, &reg, &reg);
}
```

```
/*
        ┌─────────────────────────────────────────────────────┐
        │              setMode( ) = Sets Video Mode            │
        └─────────────────────────────────────────────────────┘
                                                                  */
void setMode(int mode)
{
    reg.h.ah = 0;
    reg.h.al = mode;
    int86 (0x10,&reg,&reg);
}
```

Figure 14-3. Program to Convert Ray-Tracing Data to a .PCX File

The second byte is the value of the recurring byte. The program does this by storing the previous byte value and comparing it with the current one. When they agree and the number is within bounds, the number counter is incremented. When they disagree, the information for the count and the previous byte is sent to the file and the counter reset. When all of the input data is processed, the information for setting the colors of the color registers is appended to the end of the .PCX file in the proper format, both files are closed, and the program terminates. The program works equally well with the standard 320 by 200 resolution or the extended 640 by 480 resolution. We have set things up so that if anything other than these two specified resolutions is read in from the data file, the program displays an error message and terminates.

Viewing the .PCX File

There are a number of programs available for viewing .PCX files, but as the number of types of display adapters and display modes increases, it becomes increasingly likely that not every program will work with every type of display. The program listed here will display any .PCX file created by PCXGEN. It is a

287

simple barebones program, but if you can create the display with this program, you know that the basic information is there in .PCX format, so it should work with any other program that is truly .PCX compatible. The program is listed in Figure 14-4.

```
/*
```

```
     zs256 = Program to read .pcx file and display as
             VGA mode 13H (320 x 200 x 256colors)or
             extended mode 67H (640 x 480 x 256
             colors) screen.

             By Roger T. Stevens    5/5/90
```

```
                                                        */
```

```c
#include <dos.h>
#include <stdio.h>
#include <stream.hpp>
#include <stdlib.h>

int restore_screen(char file_name[]);
void gotoxy(int x, int y);
void plot(int x, int y, int color);
void setMode(int mode);
void setVGApalette(unsigned char *buffer);

union REGS reg;
struct SREGS inreg;

unsigned char Pal_Array[256][3];
int xres, yres, active_bank, bank;

main(argc,argv)
int argc;
char *argv[];
```

```
{
  setMode(3);
  if (argc != 2)
  {

        cout << "Display 256 Color VGA Mode 13H or 67H" <<
            " Screen from .PCX File\n";
        cout << "              By Roger T. Stevens\n";
        cout << "Usage: zs256 filename.pcx\n";
        exit(1);
  }
  restore_screen(argv[1]);
  getch();
  setMode(3);
}

int restore_screen(char file_name[])
{
  #include <dos.h>
  #include <stdio.h>

  FILE *f1;
  unsigned char ch,ch1,red,green,blue,color,line_length,end;
  int line_end,i,j,k,m,pass,x1,y1,x2,y2;

  if ((f1 = fopen(file_name,"rb")) == NULL)
  {
        printf("\nCan't find %s.\n",file_name);
        return(1);
  }
  else
  {
        ch = fgetc(f1);
        if (ch != 0x0A)
        {
                cout << "\n" << file_name <<
                    " is not a valid ZSoft file.\n";
                fclose(f1);
                return(1);
        }
```

```
    }
    fseek(f1,-769L,SEEK_END);
    ch = fgetc(f1);
    if (ch != 0x0C)
    {
            cout << "\n" << file_name << " is not a Mode 19 file.\n";
            fclose(f1);
            return(1);
    }
    for (i=0; i<256; i++)
            for (j=0; j<3; j++)
            {
                Pal_Array[i][j] = fgetc(f1);
                Pal_Array[i][j] = Pal_Array[i][j] / 4;
            }
    fseek(f1,12L,SEEK_SET);
    fread(&xres,sizeof(int),1,f1);
    fread(&yres,sizeof(int),1,f1);
    if ((xres == 320) && (yres == 200))
            setMode(0x13);
    else
    {
            if ((xres == 640) && (yres == 480))
                setMode(0x67);
            else
            {
                cout << "\n" << file_name <<
                        " is not a Mode 13H or Mode 67H file.\n";
                fclose(f1);
                return(1);
            }
    }

    setVGApalette(&Pal_Array[0][0]);
    fseek(f1,128L,SEEK_SET);
    for (k=0; k<yres; k++)
    {
            for (i=0; i<xres; i++)
            {
                        ch1 = fgetc(f1);
                        if ((ch1 & 0xC0) != 0xC0)
                        {
```

```
                              plot (i, k, ch1);
                    }
                    else
                    {
                         ch1 &= 0x3F;
                         pass = ch1;
                         ch = fgetc(f1);
                         for (m=0; m<pass; m++)
                         {
                                plot(i++, k, ch);
                         }
                         i-;
                    }
          }
     }
  fclose(f1);
  return(0);
}



/*
       ┌─────────────────────────────────────────────────────────┐
       │  setVGApalette() = Function to set all 256 color registers │
       └─────────────────────────────────────────────────────────┘
                                                                   */

void setVGApalette(unsigned char *buffer)
{
  reg.x.ax = 0x1012;
  segread(&inreg);
  inreg.es = inreg.ds;
  reg.x.bx = 0;
  reg.x.cx = 256;
  reg.x.dx = (int)&buffer[0];
  int86x(0x10,&reg,&reg,&inreg);
}

void gotoxy(int x, int y)
{
  reg.h.ah = 2;
  reg.h.bh = 0;
  reg.h.dh = y-1;
  reg.h.dl = x-1;
  int86(0x10, &reg, &reg);
```

```
}

/*
┌─────────────────────────────────────────────────────────┐
│                                                           │
│            setMode() = Sets Video Mode                    │
│                                                           │
└─────────────────────────────────────────────────────────┘
                                                         */
void setMode(int mode)
{
  if (mode > 0x32)
  {
        active_bank = 0;
        reg.x.ax = 0x6F05;
        reg.h.bl = mode;
        int86 (0x10,&reg,&reg);
        outpw(0x3C4,0xEA06);
  }
  else
  {
        reg.h.ah = 0;
        reg.h.al = mode;
        int86 (0x10,&reg,&reg);
  }
}

/*
┌─────────────────────────────────────────────────────────┐
│                                                           │
│    plot() = Function to plot point to VGA 256 Color Screen│
│                                                           │
└─────────────────────────────────────────────────────────┘
                                                         */

void plot(int x, int y, int color)
{
  long int offset;
  char far *address;
  int temp,temp2;

  offset = (long)xres * (long)y + (long)x;
  bank = offset/65536L;
  offset = offset % 65536L;
  if (bank != active_bank)
  {
        active_bank = bank;
```

```
            reg.h.ah = bank & 0x01;
            reg.h.al = 0xF9;
            outpw(0x3C4,reg.x.ax);
            temp = inpw(0x3CC);
            temp = temp & 0xDF;
            if ((bank & 0x02) != 0)
                temp = temp | 0x20;
            outpw(0x3C2,temp);
            outp(0x3C4,0xF6);
            temp = inpw(0x3C5);
            temp = temp & 0xF0;
            temp2 = ((bank & 0x0C) >> 2) | (bank & 0x0C);
            temp = temp | temp2;
            outp(0x3C5,temp);
    }
    address = (char far *)(0xA0000000L + offset);
    *address = color;
}
```

Figure 14-4. Program for Displaying .PCX Files

CHAPTER 15

Rendering Fractal Scenes

If you have been carefully observing the programs so far, you have probably noticed a few references to fractals and wondered why nothing was said about them in the description. Fractals are treated differently from other objects, and introduce a number of unique problems. We have waited until this chapter to cover all of their aspects in a single place.

The Midpoint-Displacement Technique

The method used to generate our fractal scenery is known as the midpoint-displacement method. It was originally described by A. Fournier, D. Fussell, and L. Carpenter in "Computer Rendering of Stochastic Models"*Communications of the ACM*, in June 1982. Essentially, the technique is as follows. We begin with a single triangle and find the midpoint of each side of the triangle, randomly displacing it in height. The displacement has a mean which is:

$$u = (y_1 + y_2) \qquad \text{(Equation 15-1)}$$

where y_1 and y_2 are the heights of the two ends of the side. (In other words, the mean of the random distribution is actually the mean altitude of the side.) The variance of the random distribution is:

$$v = (L/2)^{2H} \qquad \text{(Equation 15-2)}$$

where L is the length of the side and H is the fractal dimension. After we have performed this operation for all three triangle sides, we connect each vertex of the triangle with the displayed midpoints of its adjacent sides, creating a set of four new triangles. This procedure is then repeated with each of the four new triangles. The process is repeated as many times as desired. The result is a fairly realistic representation of a mountain.

In July 1983, James T. Kajiya published a paper, "New Techniques for Ray Tracing Procedurally Defined Objects" in *Computer Graphics*. Kajiya pointed out that any fractal object generated by the midpoint displacement method in ray tracing would have so many individual facets that attempting to check the intersection of every ray with every facet would take an impossibly large amount of computer time. Kajiya's solution to this dilemma was to begin only with the initiating triangle. Around this, he placed what he called a "cheesecake" extent, which was a triangular faced solid having a height such that it would include any displacements that might occur in succeeding triangles generated by midpoint displacement. (Actually, since a random process was involved, the extent dimensions were set up to include all cases with better than 99 percent probability; it was impossible to assure that every case would be within the extent.) Now, if a ray being traced did not intersect this extent, it also wouldn't intersect the fractal, so the ray tracing task was done. If there was an intersection with the extent, Kajiya generated the next four midpoint displacement triangles, placed extents around each of them, and checked for intersections with each extent. He continued with this process, generating only those lower levels of the fractal that were needed to check for actual intersections with the ray being traced. This substantially reduced the number of intersection checks that needed to be performed, and thus reduced the computer time to a reasonable amount. Since then, other articles have appeared, using basically thesame technique, but suggesting more efficient extents which could reduce the computer time even further.

Actually, this technique slightly misses the mark. The cause of much wasted computer time is the attempt to intersect each facet directly with the ray. It is solved by placing extents around larger and larger subsets of the fractal. Generating pieces of the fractal on demand doesn't really contribute to the situation; since many facets will have to be generated more than once, the actual fractal generation time will be larger than if all facets were generated initially.

With computer memory continually decreasing in cost, the storage requirements for an entire fractal is no longer prohibitive.

Handling a Fractal with Our Ray-Tracing Program

We can begin to see that these strange procedures have counterparts that are already set up in our ray-tracing program. Let's start with a triangle and perform the midpoint displacement procedure to create more and more triangles down to a predetermined level. We can consider all of these primitive facets to be objects of class *Triangle* and list them as we would any other objects. Suppose that at each step in the midpoint displacement procedure, we specify a bounding box around the four triangles at the next level down. We now have a hierarchy of bounding boxes that are very similar to Kajiya's cheesecake extents in their function (although our boxes are rectangles and thus not as efficient as Kajiya's cheesecakes). We can then use the techniques that we have already set up to ray-trace the fractal. The amount of time is not too excessive — even for a lowly PC.

Before we proceed to do this, a few things need to be said. We are treating each fractal as an object, which means that it carries with it the whole baggage of the basic object class, which uses up several hundred bytes of memory. This tends to limit us to a level of four, which results in a fractal with 1024 facets before we run out of memory and the program bombs. We could define the facets for the special fractal case in a more efficient manner and have ample space. This would require quite a bit of reprogramming, and would tend to obscure the relationship between the fractal facets and ordinary objects. If you're really into ray-tracing fractals, however, you may want to try this. I would suggest that you take everything out of the base class except what is needed for a fractal facet, and then add in other things to the derived classes as they are required.

Implementing Fractal Processing

We're ready to begin developing our procedures for handling fractals in the ray-tracing program. Let's start by looking at the definition of the world structure in Figure 5-1. There are three variables that are used in treating fractals. They are *fractal_dim, fractal_scalar,* and *limit.* The first is actually twice the fractal dimension as given in Equation 15-1. It has been set at 0.9. You can adjust it to change the "ruggedness" of the terrain, but be ready for some surprises in the scenes that you generate. The second is a scalar that is necessary to make sure that the fractal mountain is the right size to fit into the picture. It has been initialized to 0.002. Be careful when you change these two parameters; it is easy to get a mountain that takes up almost the whole picture, which may require 10 to 12 hours to ray-trace the scene, even when using a 386 machine with a math coprocessor. The final parameter level cannot be any larger than 4 unless you rework the program to allow more facets, without using up all of the memory.

Next turn to the *input.cpp* file. In the *Get_Object* function, you'll see that there is a case for getting a fractal object, which calls the function *GetFractal.* Note that this function returns *newobj* which is of class *Triangle* so that once we leave this function, there will never be any difference between this and an ordinary triangle. (However, it gets a lot more complicated than this as we shall see.) The next part of the function is just the same as that for a triangle, getting the same parameters and performing the same checking to assure that all necessary parameters have been read in.

Now we come to the first major difference when the function *Fractal_comp* is called. This is part of the file *fractal.cpp,* which is listed in Figure 15-1. This function does the same calculations that were performed for the triangle at the end of the *GetTriangle* function and also calculates the variance to be used for each midpoint displacement. These three variances are stored in the three components of the vector *vect3.* Next *GetFractal* calls *Make_fractal_triangles,* passing it the data on the three vertices of the triangle; the variances, the address of the current object, and the level. This function begins by creating four new triangles, the color data for them, and a bounding box. If this is the top level, the current object address is set up as the bounding box's next object address, and the address of the bounding box is stored to be returned when the function terminates. If we are at some lower level, the bounding box's next object address is set to NULL. The function then sets up the location vector for each of the first three new triangles and computes the three bisectors of the sides of the original triangle. Next, the altitude displacement for each bisector is computed. A seed is generated for each side for the random number generator. This makes the random number generator a little less than random. However, it is needed because some of the triangle sides are common to two triangles. If different values of altitude displacement were calculated for the two uses of the same side, there would be objectionable discontinuities in the figure. The seed is based upon the three coordinates of the bisect point in such a way that it is unique to a particular position but will be the same each time that position occurs, so that the same random number is produced. After the seed is generated, *gauss* is called to generate the altitude displacement, which is multiplied by the variance and added to the bisector altitude value. To avoid underground mountains, the new altitude of the bisector is never allowed to fall below zero. Next, each of the three new triangles has its color data set to the default color data. The remaining vectors for the three new triangles and the information for the fourth triangle (which is the connection of the three bisectors) are then computed. Then the function *Fractal_comp* for all four new triangles is run to do the remaining computations, including the variances for the next level bisectors. If the level has not reached zero, we decrease the level by one and then call *Make_fractal_triangles* recursively for each of the four new triangles to make four more new triangles at the next lower level. The four next higher-level triangles are then deleted. If we have reached the lowest (zero) level, we don't generate any more triangles, but place the address of the four low level ones in the list of objects, increase the object count by four and, return. The lowest level triangles are in the list, with bounding boxes surrounding every set of four, and a bounding box surrounding each set of four of these bounding boxes, and so forth, so that at the top is only a single bounding box encompassing the entire fractal. The ray-tracing program then treats these just as it would any other objects.

Figure 15-1. The *fractal.cpp* File

```
/*
        ┌─────────────────────────────────────────────────────────┐
        │                                                         │
        │        fractal.cpp = Functions to treat fractals        │
        │                                                         │
        │           By Roger T. Stevens - 5/12/90                 │
        │                                                         │
        └─────────────────────────────────────────────────────────┘
*/

#include <ctype.h>
#include <string.h>
#include <stdio.h>
#include <math.h>
#include <dos.h>
#include "render.hpp"

/*
      ┌─────────────────────────────────────────────────────────┐
      │                                                           │
      │    gauss() = Function to generate Gaussian random variable│
      │                                                           │
      └─────────────────────────────────────────────────────────┘
*/

float gauss(unsigned int seed)
{
  float x=0;
  int i;

  if (seed != 0)
        srand(seed);
  for (i=0; i<12; i++)
        x += (float)(rand())/32768.0;
  x -= 6.0;
  return(x);
}

/*
      ┌─────────────────────────────────────────────────────────┐
      │                                                           │
      │    Make_fractal_triangles() = Create four new fractal     │
      │                               triangles from a triangle   │
      │                                                           │
      └─────────────────────────────────────────────────────────┘
                                                                    /*
```

```
Object *Make_fractal_triangles(Vector loc, Vector vect1, Vector
      vect2, Vector vect3, Object *queue, int level)
{
  Vector bisect1, bisect2, bisect3, temp;
  unsigned int seed;
  float temp1, temp2, temp3, mu, max_ht;
  Triangle *newtri0, *newtri1, *newtri2, *newtri3;

  BBox *newobj;
  col_max = Vector(63,63,63);
  newtri0 = new Triangle;
  newtri1 = new Triangle;
  newtri2 = new Triangle;
  newtri3 = new Triangle;
  newtri0->col_data = new color_data;
  newtri1->col_data = new color_data;
  newtri2->col_data = new color_data;
  newtri3->col_data = new color_data;
  newobj = new BBox;

  newobj->type = BBOX;
  if (level == WORLD.level)
  {
        newobj->nextobj = queue;
        queue = newobj;
  }
  else
        newobj->nextobj = NULL;
  newtri0->loc = loc;
  newtri1->loc = loc + vect1;
  newtri2->loc = loc + vect2;
  bisect1 = loc + vect1 / 2;
  bisect2 = loc + vect2 / 2;
  bisect3 = newtri1->loc + (vect2 - vect1) / 2;
  seed = ((unsigned int)(bisect3.x * 10000 + bisect3.y * 100 +
        bisect3.z))%32767 + 2;
  bisect3.y += gauss(seed) * vect3.z;
  bisect3.y = MAX(bisect3.y, 0);
```

```
seed = ((unsigned int)(bisect1.x * 10000 + bisect1.y * 100 +
        bisect1.z))%32767 + 2;
bisect1.y += gauss(seed) * vect3.x;
bisect1.y = MAX(bisect1.y, 0);
seed = ((unsigned int)(bisect2.x * 10000 + bisect2.y * 100 +
        bisect2.z))%32767 + 2;
bisect2.y += gauss(seed) * vect3.y;
bisect2.y = MAX(bisect2.y, 0);
*newtri0->col_data = def.col_data;
*newtri1->col_data = def.col_data;
*newtri2->col_data = def.col_data;
*newtri3->col_data = def.col_data;
newtri0->vect1 = bisect1 - newtri0->loc;
newtri0->vect2 = bisect2 - newtri0->loc;
newtri1->vect1 = bisect3 - newtri1->loc;
newtri1->vect2 = bisect1 - newtri1->loc;
newtri2->vect1 = bisect2 - newtri2->loc;
newtri2->vect2 = bisect3 - newtri2->loc;
newtri3->loc = bisect1;
newtri3->vect1 = bisect3 - newtri3->loc;
newtri3->vect2 = bisect2 - newtri3->loc;
Fractal_comp(newtri0);
Fractal_comp(newtri1);
Fractal_comp(newtri2);
Fractal_comp(newtri3);
if (level > 0)
{
        level-;
        newobj->child = Make_fractal_triangles(newtri3->loc,
                newtri3->vect1, newtri3->vect2,
                newtri3->vect3, queue,level);
        newobj->child->nextobj = Make_fractal_triangles
                (newtri2->loc, newtri2->vect1,
                newtri2->vect2, newtri2->vect3, queue,level);
        newobj->child->nextobj->nextobj =
                Make_fractal_triangles(newtri1->loc,
                newtri1->vect1, newtri1->vect2,
                newtri1- >vect3, queue, level);
        newobj->child->nextobj->nextobj->nextobj =
```

```
                    Make_fractal_triangles(newtri0->loc,
                    newtri0->vect1, newtri0->vect2,
                    newtri0->vect3, queue,level);
        newobj->child->nextobj->nextobj->nextobj->nextobj = NULL;
        delete newtri0;
        delete newtri1;
        delete newtri2;
        delete newtri3;
}
else
{
        newtri0->nextobj = NULL;
        newtri1->nextobj = newtri0;
        newtri2->nextobj = newtri1;
        newtri3->nextobj = newtri2;
        newobj->nextobj = NULL;
        newobj->child = newtri3;
        WORLD.objcount += 4;
}

        if (level == WORLD.level)
                    return(queue);
        return(newobj);
}


/*

    ┌────────────────────────────────────────────────┐
    │ ┌──────────────────────────────────────────────┐│
    │ │  Fractal_comp() = Computes fractal parameters ││
    │ └──────────────────────────────────────────────┘│
    └────────────────────────────────────────────────┘

*/

void Fractal_comp(Triangle *newobj)
{
  Vector temp;
  temp = newobj->vect2 - newobj->vect1;
  newobj->vect3.z = temp % temp;
  newobj->vect3.z = pow(newobj->vect3.z/4,WORLD.fractal_dim) *
        WORLD.fractal_scalar;
  newobj->vect3.x = newobj->vect1 % newobj->vect1;
  newobj->vect3.x = pow(newobj->vect3.x/4,WORLD.fractal_dim) *
        WORLD.fractal_scalar;
  newobj->vect3.y = newobj->vect2 % newobj->vect2;
```

```
    newobj->vect3.y = pow(newobj->vect3.y/4,WORLD.fractal_dim) *
        WORLD.fractal_scalar;
    newobj->norm = newobj->vect1 ^ newobj->vect2;
    newobj->norm = ~ newobj->norm;
    newobj->n1 = newobj->norm % newobj->loc;
    newobj->len1 = newobj->vect1 % newobj->vect1;
    newobj->len2 = newobj->vect2 % newobj->vect2;
}
```

CHAPTER 16

Quaternions and Their Mathematics

History and Definition of Quaternions

The discovery of quaternions by Sir William Hamilton in 1843 marked the revival of mathematics through Great Britain which provided the foundation for important discoveries in both mathematics and physics throughout the next century. Quaternions have many similarities to numbers (both real and complex) but differ in having the surprising characteristic that their multiplication does not follow the commutative law. By this we mean the following. We normally accept as true for numbers that:

$$a \times b = b \times a \qquad \text{(Equation 16-1)}$$

The order in which the numbers are multiplied doesn't matter; we get the same result no matter what order is used. For quaternions, this is not true. In fact, we find that if a and b are quaternions then:

$$a \times b = - (b \times a) \qquad \text{(Equation 16-2)}$$

So just what is a quaternion, anyway? We may define a quaternion as consisting of a scalar q_0, and a three-dimensional vector having components q_1, q_2, and q_3, directed along the mutually orthogonal axes identified by the unit vectors i, j, and k. These vectors follow the rules for vector cross products in a right-hand coordinate system, namely:

$$ij = k \qquad\qquad ji = -k$$

$$jk = i \qquad\qquad kj = -i$$

$$ki = j \qquad\qquad ik = -j \qquad \text{(Equation 16-3)}$$

and

$$ijk = i^2 = j^2 = k^2 = -1 \qquad \text{(Equation 16-4)}$$

We can write the quaternion as:

$$Q = q_0 + iq_1 + jq_2 + kq_3 \qquad \text{(Equation 16-5)}$$

or alternately as:

$$Q = q_0 + \underline{q} \qquad \text{(Equation 16-6)}$$

where the underlining means that the variable is a three-dimensional vector, or:

$$\underline{q} = iq_1 + jq_2 + kq_3 \qquad \text{(Equation 16-7)}$$

Probably you're wondering just what quaternions are for, besides being an interesting mathematical exercise. One important use is in the dynamics of flight. Suppose we represent the position of an aircraft by an ordinary three-dimensional coordinate system. In following the aircraft through complex maneuvers, we often want to keep track of some quantities in a coordinate system centered at and oriented to the aircraft and of other quantities in a ground-based coordinate system. This involves a lot of coordinate transformations and for certain rotations, singularities occur. These don't bother an observer; when the aircraft angle is such that one coordinate system needs to be rotated 90 degrees to get to another, we observe that particular angular relationship without comment. But computers get confused when they try to handle division by zero or find tangents that go to infinity. Thus with the usual matrix transformations of one three-dimensional coordinate system to another, computer programs have to be written with code devoted to handling singular points. Unfortunately, if you miss only one singular point, your program may work just fine, for a long time before the aircraft gets to the proper angle to expose the problem.

Happily there is a technique for using quaternions to perform the rotations required to transform from one coordinate system to another. Using quaternions, singularities never occur, and there is no problem dealing with exceptional points. The transformations involved when an aircraft is in all sorts of strange positions and performing all kinds of strange maneuvers can be handled simply, without exceptions, making the program robust.

In this book, we aren't concerned with aircraft flight, although if you have occasion to get into that field, you'll be glad to get a grounding in quaternion mathematics. What we are going to do is apply quaternions to Julia and dragon sets. It turns out that the same kinds of iterated equations that make use of complex numbers to generate two-dimensional Julia and dragon sets, can be used with quaternions to create four-dimensional Julia and dragon sets. We'll get into the details of this later; first we have to become familiar with how the mathematics of quaternions works.

Quaternion Mathematics

Quaternion addition and subtraction can be done on a component-by-component basis just like vectors are added and subtracted. Quaternion multiplication gets a little more complicated. Suppose we have two quaternions, *P* and *Q*. The product is:

$$PQ = (p_0q_0 + p_0\underline{q} + q_0\underline{p} + i^2p_1q_1 + j^2p_2q_2 + k^2p_3q_3 +$$

$$ip_1(jq_2 + kq_3) + jp_2(iq_1 + kq_3) + kp_3(iq_1 + jq_2)$$

$$= p_0q_0 + p_0\underline{q} + q_0\underline{p} - (\underline{p}.\underline{q}) + \underline{p} \times \underline{q}$$ (Equation 16-8)

where $\underline{p}.\underline{q}$ and $\underline{p} \times \underline{q}$ are the vector dot product and vector cross product respectively as defined in any text on vector analysis. This expression has two scalar terms (which added give one scalar) and three three-dimensional vector terms (which added give one three-dimensional vector). The result consists of a scalar and a three-dimensional vector (which is a quaternion) so that the product of two quaternions is a quaternion. Note that since one of these terms is not commutative ($\underline{p} \times \underline{q} = - \underline{q} \times \underline{p}$), the quaternion multiplication is also not commutative. Next, we define the conjugate of a quaternion, Q^*. The conjugate of the quaternion $Q = q_0 + q$ is defined as $Q^* = q_0 - q$. Applying the rule for quaternion multiplication, we find that:

$$QQ^* = (q_0 + \underline{q})(q_0 - \underline{q}) = q_0{}^2 + q_0\underline{q} - q_0\underline{q} - (\underline{q} . -\underline{q}) + (\underline{q} \times \underline{q})$$

$$= \sum_{i=0}^{3} q^2{}_i$$

(Equation 16-9)

(Observe that $\underline{q} \times \underline{q} = 0$.) The product Q^*Q is a degenerate form of the general multiplication case, in which the vector portion disappears and the result is a scalar only. This product is called the *norm* of the quaternion. The *norm* can take on any positive real value and, in many cases, it is useful to have it equal to one. This is accomplished by imposing the condition on every quaternion that:

$$\sum_{i=0}^{3} q^2{}_i = 1$$

(Equation 16-10)

When this condition is imposed, the four component elements of the quaternion are no longer independent, since the specification of any three components determines the value of the fourth.

Next, we want to consider the product of a quaternion and a vector. Given a quaternion Q and a vector $\underline{r}$, we impose the multiplication rule and obtain:

$$Q\underline{r} = (q_0 + iq_1 + jq_2 + kq_3)(ir_1 + jr_2 + kr_3)$$

$$= q_0\underline{r} - (\underline{q} \cdot \underline{r}) + (\underline{q} \times \underline{r}) \qquad \text{(Equation 16-11)}$$

Similarly,

$$\underline{r}Q = q_0\underline{r} - (\underline{r} \cdot \underline{q}) + (\underline{r} \times \underline{q}) \qquad \text{(Equation 16-12)}$$

Now that we understand how to multiply a vector and a quaternion, consider the geometric effects of such multiplications. Begin with the operation $\underline{r}Q$. As a matter of convenience, we are going to consider $\underline{r}$ to be composed of two vectors, $\underline{s}$ and $\underline{t}$. The portion $\underline{s}$ is perpendicular to the vector portion ($\underline{q}$) of the quaternion Q, and the portion $\underline{t}$ is aligned with $\underline{q}$ (parallel to $\underline{q}$ and either in the same or the exactly opposite direction). Perform the multiplication of the $\underline{s}$ portion. The result is:

$$\underline{s}Q = q_0\underline{s} + (\underline{s} \times \underline{q}) \qquad \text{(Equation 16-13)}$$

Note that the dot product ordinarily produced by the multiplication drops out, since our definition states that $\underline{s}$ is perpendicular to $\underline{q}$, making the dot product of the pair zero. Since the result of our multiplication therefore does not have a constant term, it is a vector, rather than a quaternion. The magnitude of $\underline{s}Q$ is:

$$|\underline{s}Q| = |\underline{s}|(\sqrt{(q_0{}^2 + |q|)}) \qquad \text{(Equation 16-14)}$$

However, we have already specified that the norm of Q is 1, which means that:

$$q_0{}^2 + |q|^2 = 1 \qquad \text{(Equation 16-15)}$$

Thus the portion of Equation 16-14 that is under the square root sign drops out, which means that the magnitude of $\underline{s}$ is unchanged. Let's look at Figure 16-1 to see what the multiplication means geometrically. Suppose that $\underline{s}$ is in the plane of the paper and that $\underline{q}$ is directed inward, perpendicular to the plane of the paper. Since the cross product is perpendicular to both vectors, $\underline{s} \times \underline{q}$ is also in the plane of the paper. The resultant, $\underline{s}Q$ is thus a rotation of s about the axis that is defined by $\underline{q}$. Since the magnitude of $\underline{s}$ remains the same; it is a rotation only, with no scaling. The amount of this rotation is $\tan^{-1} |\underline{q}|/q_0$. The direction of rotation is that of a left-handed screw in the direction $\underline{q}$. (Incidentally, if we perform the multiplication $Q\underline{s}$ instead of $\underline{s}Q$, the only difference is that the rotation is in the opposite direction.)

We still have to consider the effect of multiplication of the other vector component, $\underline{t}$, and the quaternion. Performing the multiplication, we have:

$$\underline{t}Q = Q\underline{t} = q_0\underline{t} - (\underline{q} \cdot \underline{t}) \qquad \text{(Equation 16-16)}$$

The order is unimportant in the dot product, since it is commutative, the trouble is that the result is a quaternion, which doesn't help us too much if we are looking for a method whereby quaternions may be used to transform (rotate) coordinate systems. Suppose, however, that we take the result of this multiplication and multiply it by Q^*. We obtain the following equation:

$$Q^*\underline{t}Q = q_0^2\underline{t} + \underline{q}(\underline{q} \cdot \underline{t}) \qquad \text{(Equation 16-17)}$$

However, since $\underline{q}$ and $\underline{t}$ are aligned,

$$\underline{q}(\underline{q} \cdot \underline{t}) = |\underline{q}|\underline{t} \qquad \text{(Equation 16-18)}$$

which reduces Equation 16-17 to:

$$Q^*\underline{t}Q = \underline{t} \qquad \text{(Equation 16-19)}$$

Thus, this operation leaves $\underline{t}$ unchanged, resolving our worries about that component of vector. Now we have to make sure that this operation does nothing drastic to the $\underline{s}$ component. It turns out that pre-multiplication by $Q*$ is exactly the same as post-multiplication by Q, which means that the total effect is to rotate $\underline{s}$ around $\underline{q}$ by twice the angle $\tan^{-1} |\underline{q}|/q_0$. So the operation $Q*\underline{r}Q$ can be used to perform the rotation from one coordinate system to another without any singularities occurring. An advantage is that the components of $\underline{q}$ are the same in either coordinate system, so that the expression of the components of $\underline{q}$ is independent of the coordinate system selected.

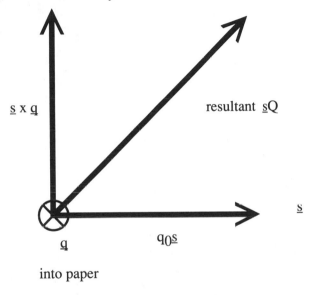

Figure 16-1. Geometry of Quaternion-Vector Multiplication

This is a brief introduction to some of the mathematical uses and manipulations of quaternions. In the next chapter, we shall develop the C++ class *Quaternion* and set up its mathematical operations.

CHAPTER 17

Quaternion Mathematics with C++

In this chapter, we'll look in some detail at using C++ to define the class *Quaternion* of quaternions—those mathematical curiosities described theoretically in the previous chapter. All of the information that is needed to define quaternions for use in the ray-tracing of Julia sets and dragons is included in two files. The first of these, *qmath.hpp* is a header file which contains the definition of the class. It is listed in Figure 17-1. The second file, *qmath.cpp,* contains the detailed definitions of all of the functions that are contained within the class. It is listed in Figure 17-2. For the quaternion programs, the vector mathematics has also been included in the two quaternion mathematics files, so as to make it simpler to compile, link and execute these files. Since vector mathematics has already been described in Chapter 4, it will not be described here.

First, look at Figure 17-1. The class of quaternions contains four floating-point variables, one for the real term and one for each of three coordinates of a Cartesian coordinate system. The keyword *public* appears at the beginning of the class definition, so all members of the class are available to external functions. There are three constructors: one for use when no parameters are passed at initialization, another for use when four floating-point variables are passed, and a third for use when another quaternion is passed. Thus we can have the statement:

q = Quaternion(6,7,8,9)

where *q* is a quaternion which takes on the real value of 6 and the *i, j,* and *k* values of 7, 8, and 9, respectively, and we can also have:

q = Quaternion()

where *q* is a quaternion that takes on the real *i, j,* and *k* values of 0, 0, and 0.

Figure 17-1. Quaternion Mathematics Header File

```
/*

    qmath.hpp = Header File for Quaternion Mathematics

*/

#include <stream.hpp>
#include <math.h>
class Vector {
    public:
    float x, y, z;

    Vector();
    Vector(float x1, float y1, float z1);
    Vector(Vector &);
    Vector operator+(Vector &);
    Vector operator-(Vector &);
    Vector operator-();
    Vector operator=(Vector &);
    Vector operator*(Vector &);
    Vector operator*(float );
    Vector operator/(float );
    float operator%(Vector &); // Dot product
    Vector operator^(Vector &);// Cross product
    Vector operator~();              // Normalize vector
    Vector min(Vector &);
    Vector max(Vector &);
    Vector Rotate(float cos1, float sin1, float cos2, float sin2);
    Vector Rev_Rotate(float cos1, float sin1, float cos2, float
        sin2);
    friend ostream &operator<<(ostream&,Vector&);
```

314

```
};

class Quaternion
{
    public:
    float real, i, j, k;
    Quaternion();
    Quaternion (float real1, float i1, float j1, float k1);
    Quaternion (Quaternion &);
    Quaternion operator+(Quaternion &);
    Quaternion operator-(Quaternion &);
    Quaternion operator-();
    Quaternion operator=(Quaternion &);
    Quaternion operator*(Quaternion &);
    Quaternion operator*(float);
    Quaternion operator/(float);
    Quaternion operator/(Quaternion &);
    Quaternion operator~();                    // Normalize quaternion
    Quaternion sqr();
    friend ostream &operator<<(ostream&,Quaternion&);
    friend float mag(Quaternion&);
    friend float mag_sq(Quaternion&);
};
```

Overloading of Quaternion Operators

First, we are going to look at the details of the operator overloading for the Quaternion class (refer to Figure 17-2 for the listings) wherein the first two operations, addition (+) and subtraction (-) of two quaternions, are very simple. For the first, the values of each pair of like coordinates are added together; for the second, the value of each coordinate for the second quaternion is subtracted from the value of the like coordinate for the first quaternion. Now look at the next function, which is overloading of - for a single quaternion only. This occurs in expressions like:

c = -a;

where both *c* and *a* are quaternions. This will only work because the - operator is already defined in C++ as being applicable to a single variable as well as the difference between two variables. Note that if we decided to use the operator / as the operator for subtraction, we could only use it to define subtraction between two quaternions, since there is no single variable variation of /.

Now, let's look at multiplication (*). You can trace through the code in the previous chapter and see how the components of each variable in the quaternion are calculated. Remember that quaternion multiplication is not commutative, which you can check for yourself by tracing through the code.

The code for overloading of the division operator (/) is a little misleading if you don't examine it carefully. There are two temporary quaternions, *temp1* and *temp2*. Consider the denominator to be of the form $a + b$, where a is the real part of the quaternion and b is the imaginary part. We begin by setting *temp1* to equal $a - b$, then we set *temp2* to be the product of the numerator and *temp1*. We then recompute *temp1* so that it is the product $(a + b)(a - b)$ or $a^2 - b^2$. Because of the non-commutative nature of quaternion multiplication, it turns out that all of the $i, j,$ and k terms drop out of this result, so that, although it is a quaternion, it has only a real part. This is the denominator of a fraction which is identical to the old one, since we have multiplied numerator and denominator by the same thing. We now get the final form of the numerator by dividing each term of *temp2* by the real part of *temp1* (which is the only part there is). This is a typical technique for performing a division in complex numbers and then transforming so that there is no complex part in the denominator. The thing that makes this unusual is that one would think that when the non-real part of the denominator had several orthogonal terms, the technique would fail. Fortunately, everything that is not real cancels out in the denominator.

Next, look at the operator used to normalize a quaternion. In this case, we want an operator that accepts only one input parameter. The ~ normally gives the user the complement of an integer. Normalization simply divides all components of the vector by its magnitude so that the resulting vector has a magnitude of one.

Other Quaternion Functions

There are functions that don't make use of overloading of the quaternion class operators. The *print* function is an overload of the << operator of the *ostream* class to make it possible to use *cout* (for example) with quaternions as well as other types of data. The form in which the quaternion is output is a starting parenthesis, followed by the four floating-point coordinates (separated by commas), followed by a close parenthesis (refer to Chapter 3).

We now come to a *sqr* function. This function simply squares a quaternion. There appear to be several missing terms. If you work out the multiplication for yourself, you will see that a number of pairs of terms cancel out, so that what is given in the function is correct.

The function *mag_sq* is a specialized magnitude function used in determining threshold values for Julia sets and dragon curves. It is actually the square of the magnitude of the first two terms of the quaternion, with the remaining two terms ignored. The function *getQuaternion* is used to read a quaternion from the input data file.

Figure 17-2. Quaternion Mathematics Function File

```
/*
       qmath.cpp = Functions for Quaternion Mathematics

*/

#include <stream.hpp>
#include "qrender.hpp"

/*
                    Quaternion Constructors

*/
```

```
Quaternion::Quaternion()
{
    real = 0;
    i = 0;
    j = 0;
    k = 0;
}
Quaternion::Quaternion(float real1, float i1, float j1, float k1)
{
    real = real1;
    i = i1;
    j = j1;
    k = k1;
}
Quaternion::Quaternion(Quaternion & arg)
{
    real = arg.real;
    i = arg.i;
    j = arg.j;
    k = arg.k;
}


/*
┌──────────────────────────────────────────────────────────┐
│                                                            │
│             Quaternion Overload of + Operator              │
│                                                            │
└──────────────────────────────────────────────────────────┘
*/

Quaternion Quaternion::operator+(Quaternion & arg)
{
    Quaternion result;
    result.real = real + arg.real;
    result.i = i + arg.i;
    result.j = j + arg.j;
    result.k = k + arg.k;
    return result;
}

/*
┌──────────────────────────────────────────────────────────┐
│                                                            │
│          Quaternion Overload of - Operator (a - b)         │
│                                                            │
└──────────────────────────────────────────────────────────┘
*/
```

```
Quaternion Quaternion::operator-(Quaternion & arg)
{
    Quaternion result;
    result.real = real - arg.real;   result.i = i - arg.i;
    result.j = j - arg.j;
    result.k = k - arg.k;
    return result;
}
```

```
/*
  ┌─────────────────────────────────────────────────────┐
  │         Quaternion Overload of - Operator (-a)        │
  └─────────────────────────────────────────────────────┘
/*
```

```
Quaternion Quaternion::operator-()
{
    Quaternion result;
    result.real = -real;
    result.i = - i;
    result.j = - j;
    result.k = - k;
    return result;
}
```

```
/*
  ┌─────────────────────────────────────────────────────┐
  │             Quaternion Overload of * Operator         │
  │               (Quaternion X a Quaternion)             │
  └─────────────────────────────────────────────────────┘
/*
```

```
Quaternion Quaternion::operator*(Quaternion & arg)
{
    Quaternion result;
    result.real = real * arg.real - i * arg.i - j * arg.j - k *
      arg.k;
    result.i = real * arg.i + i * arg.real + j * arg.k - k * arg.j;
    result.j = real * arg.j + j * arg.real + k * arg.i - i * arg.k;
    result.k = real * arg.k + k * arg.real + i * arg.j - j * arg.i;
    return result;
}
```

```
/*
  ┌─────────────────────────────────────────────────────┐
  │   Quaternion Overload of * Operator (Quaternion X a float)  │
  └─────────────────────────────────────────────────────┘
/*
```

319

```
Quaternion Quaternion::operator*(float arg)
{
    Quaternion result;
    result.real = real * arg;
    result.i = i * arg;
    result.j = j * arg;
    result.k = k * arg;
    return result;
}
```

```
/*
    ┌─────────────────────────────────────────────┐
    │                                               │
    │         Quaternion Overload of / Operator     │
    │        (Quaternion Divided by a Quaternion)   │
    │                                               │
    └─────────────────────────────────────────────┘
*/
```

```
Quaternion Quaternion::operator/(Quaternion &arg)
{
    Quaternion temp1, temp2, result;
    temp1 = Quaternion(arg.real, -arg.i, -arg.j, -arg.k);
    cout << "Numerator: " << *this << "\n";
    cout << "Denominator: " << arg << "\n";
    cout << "Multiplier: " << temp1 << "\n";
    temp2 = *this * temp1;
    cout << "Numerator product: " << temp2 << "\n";
    temp1 = arg * temp1;
    cout << "Denominator product: " << temp1 << "\n";
    result.real = temp2.real / temp1.real;
    result.i = temp2.i / temp1.real;
    result.j = temp2.j / temp1.real;
    result.k = temp2.k / temp1.real;
    return result;
}
```

```
/*
    ┌─────────────────────────────────────────────┐
    │                                               │
    │         Quaternion Overload of = Operator     │
    │                                               │
    └─────────────────────────────────────────────┘
*/
```

```
Quaternion Quaternion::operator=(Quaternion & rvalue)
{
    real = rvalue.real;
```

```
    i = rvalue.i;
    j = rvalue.j;
    k = rvalue.k;
    return *this;
}


/*
    ┌────────────────────────────────────────────────────────────┐
    │  Quaternion Overload of ~ Operator (Normalize a Quaternion)  │
    └────────────────────────────────────────────────────────────┘
*/

Quaternion Quaternion:: operator~()
{
    Quaternion result;
    float length;
    length = real*real + i*i + j*j + j*j;
    length = sqrt(length);
    result.real = real/length;
    result.i = i/length;
    result.j = j/length;
    result.k = k/length;
    return result;
}


/*
    ┌────────────────────────────────────────────────────────────┐
    │                 Print Out Quaternion Contents                │
    │                                                              │
    └────────────────────────────────────────────────────────────┘
*/

ostream &operator<<(ostream& s,Quaternion& arg)
{
    s << "(" << arg.real << "," << arg.i <<"," << arg.j << "," <<
            arg.k << ")";
    return s;
}
```

```
/*
┌─────────────────────────────────────────────────────┐
│              Function to square a Quaternion          │
└─────────────────────────────────────────────────────┘
*/

Quaternion Quaternion:: sqr()
{
    Quaternion result;
    float temp;
    temp = 2 * real;
    result.real = real * real - i * i - j * j - k * k;
    result.i = temp * i;
    result.j = temp * j;
    result.k = temp * k;
    return (result);
}


/*
┌─────────────────────────────────────────────────────┐
│              Function to find the square of the       │
│                 magnitude of a Quaternion             │
└─────────────────────────────────────────────────────┘
*/

float mag_sq(Quaternion& arg)
{
    float result;
    result = arg.real*arg.real + arg.i*arg.i;
    return result;
}


/*
┌─────────────────────────────────────────────────────┐
│        Function to find the magnitude of a Quaternion │
└─────────────────────────────────────────────────────┘
*/

float mag(Quaternion& arg)
{
    float result;
    result = arg.real*arg.real + arg.i*arg.i + arg.j*arg.j +
        arg.k*arg.k;
    return sqrt(result);
}
```

```
/* ┌─────────────────────────────────────────────┐
   │              Vector Constructors              │
*/ └─────────────────────────────────────────────┘

Vector::Vector()
{
    x = 0;
    y = 0;
    z = 0;
}

Vector::Vector(float x1, float y1, float z1)
{
    x = x1;
    y = y1;
    z = z1;
}

Vector::Vector(Vector & otherVector)
{
    x = otherVector.x;
    y = otherVector.y;
    z = otherVector.z;
}


/* ┌─────────────────────────────────────────────┐
   │           Vector Overload of + Operator       │
*/ └─────────────────────────────────────────────┘

Vector Vector::operator+(Vector & arg)
{
    Vector result;
    result.x = x + arg.x;
    result.y = y + arg.y;
    result.z = z + arg.z;
    return result;
}
```

```
/*
        Vector Overload of - Operator (a - b)

*/

Vector Vector::operator-(Vector & arg)
{
   Vector result;
   result.x = x - arg.x;
   result.y = y - arg.y;
   result.z = z - arg.z;
   return result;
}

/*
            Vector Overload of - Operator (-a)

*/

Vector Vector::operator-()
{
   Vector result;
   result.x = - x;
   result.y = - y;
   result.z = - z;
   return result;
}

/*
     Vector Overload of * Operator (Vector Times a Vector)

*/

Vector Vector::operator*(Vector & arg)
{
   Vector result;
   result.x = x * arg.x;
   result.y = y * arg.y;
```

```
   result.z = z * arg.z;
   return result;
}

/*
   ┌─────────────────────────────────────────────────────────────┐
   │                                                               │
   │   Vector Overload of * Operator (Vector Times a Float)        │
   │                                                               │
   └─────────────────────────────────────────────────────────────┘
*/

Vector Vector::operator*(float arg)
{
   Vector result;
   result.x = x * arg;
   result.y = y * arg;
   result.z = z * arg;
   return result;
}

/*
   ┌─────────────────────────────────────────────────────────────┐
   │   Vector Overload of / Operator (Vector Divided by a Float)   │
   │                                                               │
   └─────────────────────────────────────────────────────────────┘
*/

Vector Vector::operator/(float arg)
{
   Vector result;
   result.x = x / arg;
   result.y = y / arg;
   result.z = z / arg;
   return result;
}

/*
   ┌─────────────────────────────────────────────────────────────┐
   │             Vector Overload of = Operator                     │
   │                                                               │
   └─────────────────────────────────────────────────────────────┘
*/
```

```cpp
Vector Vector::operator=(Vector & rvalue)
{
   x = rvalue.x;
   y = rvalue.y;
   z = rvalue.z;
   return *this;
}

/*

     ┌─────────────────────────────────────────────────────────┐
     │  Vector Overload of % Operator (Dot Product of Two Vectors) │
     └─────────────────────────────────────────────────────────┘

*/

float Vector::operator%(Vector & arg)
{
   float result;
   result = x*arg.x + y*arg.y + z*arg.z;
   return result;
}

/*

     ┌─────────────────────────────────────────────────────────┐
     │       Vector Overload of ^ Operator (Cross Product       │
     │                    of Two Vectors)                       │
     └─────────────────────────────────────────────────────────┘

*/

Vector Vector::operator^(Vector & arg)
{
   Vector result;
   result.x = y*arg.z - z*arg.y;
   result.y = z*arg.x - x*arg.z;
   result.z = x*arg.y - y*arg.x;
   return result;
}

/*

     ┌─────────────────────────────────────────────────────────┐
     │   Vector Overload of ~ Operator (Normalize a Vector)     │
     └─────────────────────────────────────────────────────────┘

*/
```

```
Vector Vector::operator~()
{
   Vector result;
   float l;
   l = *this % *this;
   l = sqrt(l);
   result.x = x/l;
   result.y = y/l;
   result.z = z/l;
   return result;
}
```

```
/*
   ┌──────────────────────────────────────────────────┐
   │         max = Return the maximum of two vectors    │
   └──────────────────────────────────────────────────┘
*/
```

```
Vector Vector::max(Vector & arg)
{
   Vector result;
   result.x = MAX(x,arg.x);
   result.y = MAX(y,arg.y);
   result.z = MAX(z,arg.z);
   return result;
}
```

```
/*
   ┌──────────────────────────────────────────────────┐
   │         min = Return the minimum of two vectors    │
   └──────────────────────────────────────────────────┘
*/
```

```
Vector Vector::min(Vector & arg)
{
   Vector result;
   result.x = MIN(x,arg.x);
   result.y = MIN(y,arg.y);
   result.z = MIN(z,arg.z);
   return result;
}
```

```
/*
┌─────────────────────────────────────────────────────┐
│                                                       │
│                Print Out Vector Contents              │
│                                                       │
└─────────────────────────────────────────────────────┘
*/
ostream &operator<<(ostream& s,Vector& arg)
{
    s << "(" << arg.x << "," << arg.y <<"," << arg.z << ")";
    return s;
}
```

328

CHAPTER 18

Julia Sets and Dragons in Quaternions

Julia sets are derived from the iterated equation:

$$z_{n+1} = z_n^2 + c \qquad \text{(Equation 18-1)}$$

and dragon curves are derived from the iterated equation:

$$z_{n+1} = cz_n^2 \qquad \text{(Equation 18-2)}$$

where both z and c are complex numbers in both equations. The results can be plotted in the complex plane to give two-dimensional displays of unusual beauty and interest. Similar equations can be used to produce curves in four-dimensions, using quaternions. The corresponding equation for a quaternion Julia set is:

$$q_{n+1} = q_n^2 + c \qquad \text{(Equation 18-3)}$$

and dragon curves are derived from the iterated equation:

$$q_{n+1} = cq_n^2 \qquad \text{(Equation 18-4)}$$

where c and z are quaternions. The best we can do in plotting these curves is to take a three-dimensional slice and project it onto our two-dimensional display. We now have many more possibilities, since rotating the basic curve in four dimensional space gives innumerable possible displays on the computer screen.

In the last chapter, we developed the mathematics for quaternion operations using C++ and a *Quaternion* class. That makes the computations easy, although lengthy. We are going to make use of a simplified ray-tracing method using a z-buffer. The z-buffer is a matrix of x and y points, with each pair of points having a z height assigned to it. Later we'll explain how all this works. Three separate programs will be used. The first program is *quater.cpp*. This program performs the quaternion calculations and stores them in the z-buffer on a disk file. The second program, *qrender.cpp*, does the simplified ray tracing and stores the results in a file similar to that used by the ray-tracing program described in earlier chapters. The third program, *quatproc.cpp*, processes the color data from the previous file and generates the color display. Now for the details.

The Header File

The file *qrender.hpp* is the header file for both the *quater.cpp* and *qrender.cpp* files. It is listed in Figure 18-1. This file contains the *#define* statements, which are used to make switch statements throughout the programs easier to understand, along with prototypes for various functions, and a couple of miscellaneous math functions.

Input for the Quaternion Program

The first two programs require different inputs to describe the curve to be generated. The *quater.cpp* program requires limits of the display in three dimensions, the parameters of the quaternion, the maximum number of iterations, and the divergence boundary value. The *qrender.cpp* program requires color data, position of the light source, and position of the viewer. Rather than having to have two separate data files to describe each curve to be generated, all data for a curve is kept in a single file. The technique to read this file is very similar to that used in the ray tracing program described previously. The same input program is used for either generating quaternions, or ray tracing them. It is stored in the file *qin.cpp* and can be linked to the desired file at the appropriate time. This file is listed in Figure 18-2. In looking at the programs that follow, you need to remember that the *quater.cpp* and *qrender.cpp* programs each use only part of the data included in the *qin.cpp* file, but each must have dummy variables to store all of the data, even data which it doesn't use.

The same parser, *get_string,* that was used for the ray tracing program is used here. Refer to Chapter 8 for a description of how the parser works. Although the parser is the same, the list of allowable inputs is quite different. The function *qin()* processes the inputs from the data file, looping until the end of the file is encountered. You will observe from the listing that the processing for each input is rather simple. At the beginning of each loop through the function, the function gets a string from the data file which identifies the type of input. The function then enters a long *switch* routine and immediately goes to the section for the particular input being processed. The actual processing is very simple, usually involving getting one or more numbers in string form, converting them to integer or floating point format, as needed, and storing the result in the appropriate variable. The permissible input variable names and their functions are described in the following sections.

```
/*

        Header File for Quaternion Ray Tracing Program
                By Roger T. Stevens - 7/10/90


*/

#include <dos.h>
#include <stream.hpp>
#include <stdio.h>
#include <math.h>
#include <string.h>
#include <conio.h>
#include <stdlib.h>
#include <ctype.h>
#include "qmath.hpp"

#define BACKGROUND       0
#define AMB              1
#define DIFF             2
#define SREFLECT         3
#define REFLECT          4
#define FILE_NAME        5
#define FLIP             6
```

```
#define LIGHT_PHI        7
#define LIGHT_THETA      8
#define VIEW_PHI         9
#define XRES            10
#define YRES            11
#define XMAX            12
#define XMIN            13
#define YMAX            14
#define YMIN            15
#define ZMAX            16
#define ZMIN            17
#define QUATERNION      18
#define MAX_SIZE        19
#define MAX_ITERATIONS  20
#define JULIA           21
#define DRAGON          22
#define Null            23
#define last_no         24

void compute_color(char FileName[32]);
Vector Intensity(int i, int j);
int get_string(char string_buf[]);
int qin(void);

/*
```

```
                      Math Definitions
```

```
*/

#define MIN(x,y) ((x)<(y) ? (x) : (y))
#define MAX(x,y) ((x)>(y) ? (x) : (y))
#define Max(x,y,z)  (x>y && x>z ? x : (y>z ? y : z))
#define Min(x,y,z)  (x<y && x<z ? x : (y<z ? y : z))
```

Figure 18-1 Header File for Quaternion Ray Tracing Program

Background

This denotes a vector that represents the red, green, and blue components of the background color of the picture. The program is set up so that when the height of any pixel is equal to zero, that pixel is painted in the background color.

It must be followed by one or more non-string type characters, which must be followed by three numbers (separated by one or more non-string type characters), that are between zero and one.

```
/*
```

```
         qin() = Function to process input data
                  Roger T. Stevens 7-16-90
```

```
*/

#include "qrender.hpp"

Vector get_vector(void) ;
Quaternion get_quaternion(void) ;

extern Vector background,ambient,diffuse,specular;
extern int b,Flip,divergence_boundary,max_iterations,Xres,
                                              Yres,flag;
extern float LightPhi,LightTheta,ViewPhi,Xmax,Xmin,Ymax,
                                         Ymin,Zmax,Zmin;
extern Quaternion c;
extern char ObjectFile[32];
extern char file_in[32];
char string_buf[32];
char string_types[128][32] = {"BACKGROUND","AMB","DIFF",
    "SREFLECT","REFLECT","FILE_NAME","FLIP","LIGHT_PHI",
    "LIGHT_THETA","VIEW_PHI","XRES","YRES","XMAX",
    "XMIN","YMAX","YMIN","ZMAX","ZMIN","QUATERNION",
    "MAX_SIZE","MAX_ITERATIONS","JULIA","DRAGON",NULL};
FILE *fget;

int qin(void)
{
    int Type;

    fget = fopen(file_in,"rb");
    while (!feof(fget))
    {
```

```
Type = get_string(string_buf);
        switch(Type)
        {
            case BACKGROUND:
                background = vector();
                break;
            case AMB:
                ambient = get_vector();
                break;

            case DIFF:
                diffuse = get_vector();
                break;
            case SREFLECT:
                get_string(string_buf);
                b = atoi(string_buf);
                break;
            case REFLECT:
                specular = get_vector();
                                    break;
            case FILE_NAME:
                get_string(string_buf);
                strcpy(ObjectFile,string_buf);
                break;
            case FLIP:
                get_string(string_buf);
                Flip = atoi(string_buf);
                break;
            case LIGHT_PHI:
                get_string(string_buf);
                LightPhi = atof(string_buf);
                LightPhi *= 0.017453925;
                break;
            case LIGHT_THETA:
                get_string(string_buf);
                LightTheta = atof(string_buf);
                LightTheta *= 0.017453925;
                break;
            case VIEW_PHI:
                get_string(string_buf);
                ViewPhi = atof(string_buf);
                ViewPhi *= 0.017453925;
```

```
            break;
    case XRES:
            get_string(string_buf);
            Xres = atoi(string_buf);
            break;
    case YRES:
            get_string(string_buf);
            Yres = atoi(string_buf);
            break;

    case XMAX:
            get_string(string_buf);
            Xmax = atof(string_buf);
            break;
    case XMIN:
            get_string(string_buf);
            Xmin = atof(string_buf);
            break;
    case YMAX:
            get_string(string_buf);
            Ymax = atof(string_buf);
            break;
    case YMIN:
            get_string(string_buf);
            Ymin = atof(string_buf);
            break;
    case ZMAX:
            get_string(string_buf);
            Zmax = atof(string_buf);
            break;
    case ZMIN:
            get_string(string_buf);
            Zmin = atof(string_buf);
            break;
    case QUATERNION:
            c = get_quaternion();
            break;
    case MAX_SIZE:
            get_string(string_buf);
            divergence_boundary = atof(string_buf);
            break;
    case MAX_ITERATIONS:
```

```
                    get_string(string_buf);
                    max_iterations = atoi(string_buf);
                    break;
                case JULIA:
                    flag = 0;
                    break;
                case DRAGON:
                    flag = 1;
                    break;
                case Null:
                    break;
                default:
                    cout << "Illegal input parameter type "
                        << Type << " buffer: '"
                        << string_buf << "'.\n";
                    exit(0);
            }
    }
    fclose(fget);
}

/*
```

```
        get_string() = Reads a string of data from file
```

```
*/

int get_string(char string_buf[])
{
    char ch;
    int flag = 0,i,result,test;
    string_buf[0] = NULL;
    result = last_no;
    while (!feof(fget))
    {
            ch = toupper(fgetc(fget));
            if (flag == 0)
            {
                if ((isalnum(ch)) || (ch == '.') || (ch == '-')
                    || (ch == ')'))
                {
```

```
                string_buf[0] = ch;
                break;
            }
            else
            {
                if (ch == '{')
                        flag = 1;
            }
        }
        else
            if (ch == '}')
                flag = 0;
    }
    for (i=1; i<32; i++)
    {
        if (ch == ')')
        {
            string_buf[1] = NULL;
            break;
        }
        ch = toupper(fgetc(fget));
        if ((isalnum(ch)) || (ch == '_') || (ch == '.'))
            string_buf[i] = ch;
        else
        {
            string_buf[i] = NULL;
            break;
        }
    }
    for (i=0; i<last_no; i++)
    {
        if (strcmp(string_buf,string_types[i]) == 0)
        {
            result = i;
            break;
        }
    }
        cout << "String buffer contains: " << string_buf <<
            " which is type " << result << "\n";
    return(result);
}
/*
```

```
        get_vector() = Get vector from the file
```

```
*/

Vector get_vector(void)
{
        Vector result;
        get_string(string_buf);
        result.x = atof(string_buf);      get_string(string_buf);
        result.y = atof(string_buf);
        get_string(string_buf);
        result.z = atof(string_buf);
        return(result);
}

/*
        get_quaternion ( ) = Get Quaternion from the file
```

```
*/

Quaternion get_quaternion(void)
{
        Quaternion result;
        get_string(string_buf);
        result.real = atof(string_buf);
        get_string(string_buf);
        result.i = atof(string_buf);
        get_string(string_buf);
        result.j = atof(string_buf);
        get_string(string_buf);
        result.k = atof(string_buf);
        return(result);
}
```

Figure 18-2. Program for Inputting Quaternion Data

AMB

This denotes a vector that represents the color of ambient light which strikes the quaternion object. This is the color that will appear on parts of the object that are entirely shielded from the light source. It must be followed by one or more non-string type characters, and be followed by three numbers (separated by one or more non-string type characters) which are between zero and one.

DIFF

This denotes a vector that is the diffuse color of the object. This is the inherent color of the object, which is sent to the observer when a light source strikes the object. It must be followed by one or more non-string type characters followed by three numbers (separated by one or more non-string type characters) which are between zero and one.

SREFLECT

This denotes an integer that is the power used in computing Phong shading of a curved object. It must be followed by one or more non-string type characters, followed by an integer.

REFLECT

This denotes a vector that represents the color of reflected light from the quaternion object when the Phong shading is computed. It must be followed by one or more non-string type characters followed by three numbers (separated by one or more non-string type characters) which are between zero and one.

FILE_NAME

This denotes a string that is the name of the file (without extension) which is used for storage of intermediate results. The *quater.cpp* program generates a z-buffer file which it stores in *filename.zbf*, where *filename* is the name you assigned using this command. The *qrender.cpp* file stores the color data in a file named *filename.raw*. It must be followed by one or more non-string type characters, followed by a string of no more than eight characters selected from those characters which are acceptable as part of a DOS file name.

FLIP

This denotes an integer that determines if the display will be flipped over in the vertical direction. It must be followed by one or more non-string type characters, followed by either a zero if the display is not to be flipped, or a one if the display is to be flipped.

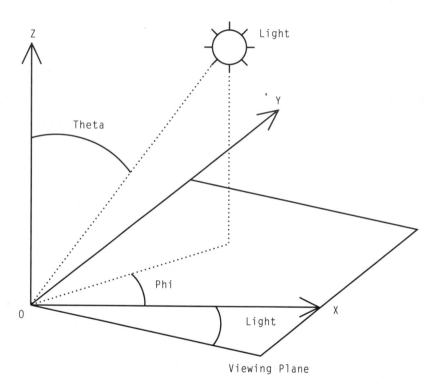

Figure 18-3. Ray Tracing Geometry for Z-Buffer System

LIGHT_PHI

This denotes an integer that represents the angle in degrees of the light source around the z (height) axis. The geometry of the situation is shown in Figure 18-3. It must be followed by one or more non-string type characters, followed by an integer.

LIGHT_THETA

This denotes an integer that represents the angle in degrees of the light source off the z (height) axis. The geometry of the situation is shown in Figure 18-3. It must be followed by one or more non-string type characters, followed by an integer.

VIEW_PHI

This denotes an integer which represents the angle in degrees of the x-y plane with respect to the viewing plane. It must be followed by one or more non-string type characters, followed by an integer.

XRES

This denotes an integer which represents the resolution of the display in pixels in the horizontal direction. In the quaternion programs, this should be the number of the maximum column in the x direction. As there is also a zero pixel, the number is one less than the number of screen columns. It must be followed by one or more non-string type characters, followed by an integer.

YRES

This denotes an integer which represents the resolution of the display in rows in the vertical direction. In the quaternion programs, it represents the number of the last row. Since there is also a zero row, the number is one less than the actual row resolution of the screen. It must be followed by one or more non-string type characters, followed by an integer.

XMAX

This denotes a floating point number which represents the maximum value of the real part of the quaternion for which computations are to be made. It must be followed by one or more non-string type characters, followed by a floating-point number.

XMIN

This denotes a floating-point number which represents the minimum value of the real part of the quaternion for which computations are to be made. It must be followed by one or more non-string type characters, which must be followed by a floating-point number.

YMAX

This denotes a floating-point number which represents the maximum value of the *i* part of the quaternion for which computations are to be made. It must be followed by one or more non-string type characters, followed by a floating point number.

YMIN

This denotes a floating-point number which represents the minimum value of the *i* part of the quaternion for which computations are to be made. It must be followed by one or more non-string type characters, followed by a floating-point number.

ZMAX

This denotes a floating-point number which represents the maximum value of the *j* part of the quaternion for which computations are to be made. It must be followed by one or more non-string type characters, followed by a floating point number.

ZMIN

This denotes a floating-point number which represents the minimum value of the *j* part of the quaternion for which computations are to be made. It must be followed by one or more non-string type characters, followed by a floating-point number.

QUATERNION

This denotes the constant quaternion which is used in the iterated calculations. It must be followed by one or more non-string type characters, followed by four numbers (separated by one or more non-string type characters).

MAX_SIZE

This denotes the floating-point number which is the size of the specialized square of the iterated quaternion which is considered to be the divergence boundary. When the quaternion reaches this value, it is considered to have diverged and no further iterations are performed. It must be followed by one or more non-string type characters, followed by a floating-point number.

MAX_ITERATIONS

This denotes an integer which represents the maximum number of iterations of the iterated equation which are to take place. If the quaternion has not exceeded the divergence boundary after this many iterations, the process terminates and the quaternion is considered not to have diverged. It must be followed by one or more non-string type characters, which must be followed by an integer.

JULIA

This indicates that a quaternion Julia Set is to be computed.

DRAGON

This indicates that a quaternion dragon curve is to be computed.

```
/*

            C++ Quaternion Fractal Generator
            Julia Sets =  f(q) = q * q + c
            Dragon Curves =  f(q) = c * q * (q - 1)
            By Roger T. Stevens  7-11-90

*/

#include <dos.h>
#include <stream.hpp>
#include <stdio.h>
#include <math.h>
#include <stdlib.h>
```

```
#include "qrender.hpp"

void julia(void);
void dragon(void);

Vector background,ambient,diffuse,specular;
int Xres, Yres, Zres;
int Height[800];
int scale_factor, divergence_boundary, max_iterations, i, k, row
                                                            col,
       no_of_iterations, b, Flip, flag, Type;
float Xmax, Xmin, Ymin, Ymax, Zmin, Zmax, dx, dy, dz, x, y, z,
                                                       deltaZ,
zval,ZFactor,LightPhi,LightTheta,ViewPhi;
FILE *fsave;
char ObjectFile[32];
Quaternion q,c,q_sq;
char file_in[32];

/*
┌─────────────────────────────────────────────────────────┐
│                      Main Program                         │
└─────────────────────────────────────────────────────────┘
*/
main(int argc, char *argv[])
{
     strcpy(file_in, argv[1]);
     qin();
     printf("Xres: %d    Yres: %d\n",Xres,Yres);
     printf("XMax: %f    XMin: %f\n",Xmax,Xmin);
     printf("YMax: %f    YMin: %f\n",Ymax,Ymin);
     printf("ZMax: %f    ZMin: %f\n",Zmax,Zmin);
     strcat(ObjectFile,".zbf");
     Zres = 256;
     q = Quaternion(0,0,0,0);
     scale_factor = 32767 / Zres;
     ZFactor = (float)scale_factor / (2*(Zmax - Zmin));
     fsave = fopen(ObjectFile,"wb");
     fwrite(&Xres,1,2,fsave);
     fwrite(&Yres,1,2,fsave);
     fwrite(&scale_factor,1,2,fsave);
```

```
dx = (float)(Xmin - Xmax) / Xres;
dy = (float)(Ymin - Ymax) / Yres;
dz = (float)(Zmax - Zmin) / Zres;
for (col=0; col<=Xres; col++)
{
        x = Xmax + col * dx;
        for (row=0; row<=Yres; row++)
        {
                y = Ymax + row * dy;
                deltaZ = 0.5*(Zmax - Zmin);
                z = Zmin;
                if (flag == 0)
                        julia();
                else
                        dragon();
                if (no_of_iterations < max_iterations)
                        Height[row] = Zmin * ZFactor;
                else
                {
                        z =Zmax;
                        if (flag == 0)
                                julia();
                        else
                                dragon();
                        if (no_of_iterations ==
                                        max_iterations)
                            Height[row] = Zmax * ZFactor;
                         else
                         {
                            z -= deltaZ;
                            for (k=0; k<7; k++)
                            {
                                deltaZ *= 0.5;
                                if (flag == 0)
                                        julia();
                                else
                                        dragon();
                                if (no_of_iterations <
                                    max_iterations)
                                {
                                        zval = z;
                                        z -= deltaZ;
```

```
                                               }
                                        else
                                               z += deltaZ;
                                 }
                                 Height[row] = zval * ZFactor;
                          }
                   }
            }
            fwrite(&Height,2,Yres+1,fsave);
            cout << "\nProcessing column # " << col;
      }
   cout <<                                                  \n
                                                            \n"
         <<                                                 \n"
         < "          Processing Complete.                  \n";
   printf("            Data in File: %12s                   \n",ObjectFile);
   cout << "                                                \n"
         << "                                               \n";
   fclose(fsave);
}
/*
   ┌─────────────────────────────────────────────────────┐
   │        julia() = Function to generate Julia Set       │
   └─────────────────────────────────────────────────────┘

*/

void julia(void)
{
      no_of_iterations = 0;
      q = Quaternion(x, y, z, 0);
      while ((no_of_iterations < max_iterations) &&
              (mag_sq(q) < divergence_boundary))
      {
              q = q.sqr();
              q = q + c;
              no_of_iterations++;
      }
}


/*
```

```
                 dragon ( ) = Function to generate dragon curves
*/
void dragon (void)
{
    no_of_iterations = 0;
    q = Quaternion(x, y, z, 0);
    while ((no_of_iterations < max_iterations) &&
             (mag_sq(q) < divergence_boundary))
    {
             q_sq = q.sqr();
             q = q - q_sq;
             q = c * q;
             no_of_iterations++;
    }
}
```

Figure 18-4. Listing of Quaternion Fractal Generator

Computing the Quaternions

Figure 18-4 lists the quaternion fractal generator. The main program is called with a command line argument which is the name (including extension) asthe file containing data on the curve to be generated. The program begins by transferring this file name to *file_in*. It then calls *qin* to read the data from the file. Next it displays various parameters, which the user can check to assure that the correct data file is being processed. Next, the program appends the extension *.zbf* to the output file name that was read from the data file. It then assigns a value of 256 for the resolution in the *z* direction. (The *x* and *y* resolutions are read from the data file.) The initial value of the quaternion *q* is set to zero to begin the iteration process. The program then computes the scale factor. The scale factor is a height multiplier used to multiply heights that are a fraction of one, by as large a number as possible without the maximum height exceeding the largest possible signed integer. The output file is then opened and the *x* and *y* resolutions and the scale factor are written out to it. Next, the incremental change (*dx, dy,* and *dz*) in *x, y,* and *z* for one pixel movement in the *x* or *y* direction or one resolution element in the z direction are computed. The program enters a pair of nested *for* loops to enable it to determine a height value for each pixel in the xy plane. If we were going to take the simple approach, we'd just make another loop, this time through z, starting with the lowest value. At the first increment where the iterated equation blew up, we'd stop and record this value of z in our height matrix. Unfortunately, this takes too long, so we're going to make use of a binary searching technique. We first perform the iterations for the minimum value of z. If this doesn't blow up, we try again for the maximum value. If this doesn't blow up either, our search is over and we set the height to the maximum value. If the maximum value causes blow up, we try again for a value half way between the two extremes. If this blows up, we work our way down in an increment half the size of the previous one; if it doesn't blow up, we move upward by the same increment. In this way, we can move through 256 levels of height with only eight steps. There is one thing we need to be careful about. After we have performed the eight sets of iterations, the last attempt either does or does not cause blow up. If it doesn't, then it is the proper value for the height matrix, but if it does, then the previous value of z is the one that should be used. Therefore, we always save the previous value, so that it will be available if we need to load it into the matrix.

The functions *julia* and *dragon* perform the quaternion iterations. A flag is set by the input from the data program to determine which function is used. You can easily determine that these functions iterate the equations shown above. After a full line of the matrix has been filled with height values, this line is written to the output file. When the program ends, it displays a message which includes the name of the output file. The output file is then closed and the program terminates.

Ray Tracing the Object

We now have a file full of height data, so we need to process it to obtain color values for a display. The program *qrender.cpp,* listed in Figure 18-5, performs this function. As with the quaternion program, this program passes an argument on the command line which is the name of the data file. The program begins by transferring this file name to the variable *file_in*. Next it displays a title and then zeroes the height buffer. Then *qin* is called to read the input data. The program opens a file having the file name and the extension *.zbf* as the file from which to read the height data, and another file having the file name and the extension *.raw* as the output file for the color data. The names of these files are displayed. Next, the values for *SinViewPhi* and *CosViewPhi* are computed for the angle which came from the input data file. These are then used to define the *view* vector. The value of the *light* vector is also determined. The program then reads the values of *Xres* and *Yres* from the height file and displays them on the screen. It then displays, "Hit any key to continue..." and waits for a keystroke.

The purpose of this program is to generate a file of pixel color data which can be processed to render a 256 color-shaded display. However, for quick observation of what is going on, the functions *setMode* and *plot* have been included and the program thereby plots a pixel each time that it is saving the pixel color data to a file. The data is plotted in EGA 16 color mode, which makes interesting, if not realistic, displays, and also permits you to see something if you don't have a VGA display. The next thing that the program does is to set the display to a graphics mode using *setMode*. It then continues by reading the *Scaling* factor from the height file and writing it and the resolution parameters to the color output file. Next, the program reads the first row of height data from the height file. (The height buffer contains room for two rows of data, which are needed in determining the normal surface vector. Modulus arithmetic is used to define the height array addresses from here on, so that as each row is completed, a new row of height data is read into the buffer, overwriting the one that is no longer needed.) The program now enters a pair of nested *for* loops, which, for each column, scan an entire row, performing the necessary processing. At the beginning of each pass through the column loop, the program reads another row of height data.

The next thing that the program does is to compute the first point. It does this by taking the first height value together with its *x* and *y* coordinates and, making use of the viewing angle, projecting it onto the viewing plane. The resulting *y* value is also set as the horizon. Before proceeding further, the program sets all of the values of the red, green, and blue column arrays to the background color. Next, the program loops through the column, from bottom to top; at each pass through the loop, the appropriate height value is projected onto the viewing plane. If it is above the horizon, the intensity of the color at that point is obtained and, if the height is greater than zero, the color is stored in the color arrays for the projected row value. At the same time, the function *Pixel* plots two adjacent columns with the color which is the green color value divided by three. If you aren't interested in the instantaneous EGA plot, you can remove this and the next call to Pixel, and the program will then only generate the color data file. The program then finds the intensity of the color of the next value in the column that is to be plotted. Since this is projected onto the viewing plane, the next value may not be the adjacent pixel of the screen display. If this is the case, the program interpolates between the colors of the two pixels to fill in the pixels that were skipped due to projection. Each new pixel value is saved to the output file and displayed on the instantaneous display. When the end of the row loop is reached, the column number is written out to the color data file, followed by the whole column of red data, the column of green data, and the column of blue data. The program then loops through the next column. After all columns have been processed, an output message is displayed which includes the name of the color output data file. Both input and output files are then closed and the program terminates.

```
/*

    ┌──────────────────────────────────────────────────┐
    │                                                    │
    │            Z-Buffer Rendering Program              │
    │                                                    │
    │            Roger T. Stevens 7-24-90                │
    │                                                    │
    └──────────────────────────────────────────────────┘

*/

#include "qrender.hpp"

void cls(int color);
void plot(int x, int y, int color);
void setMode(int mode);
```

```
void Pixel(int x, int y, int color);

char ObjectFile[32];
char file_in[32];
int Xres, Yres, Zres=255;
int Height[2][800];
int Scaling,max_color=63,max_iterations,flag;
Vector view;     // global view vector
Vector light;    // global light vector
float ViewPhi, ViewTheta,SinViewPhi, CosViewPhi, LightPhi,
                                                LightTheta,
     Xmax,Xmin,Ymax,Ymin,Zmax,Zmin,divergence_boundary;
FILE *fget, *fsave;
int m,i, j, k, p, p0, p1, horizon;
Vector Pix, newPix, oldPix;
float h,temp;
char FileNameOut[32];
int Tilt,Flip;
Vector ambient;  // percentage of ambient light
Vector diffuse;  // percentage of diffuse light from reflection   -
grainular
Vector specular;  // percentage of specular light from reflection-
Euclidian }
Vector background;
int b  = 2;     // shininess
int Type, type, integer;
char red[800],green[800], blue[800];
Quaternion c;
```

```
/*
   ┌─────────────────────────────────────────────────┐
   │                                                   │
   │                  Main Program                     │
   │                                                   │
   └─────────────────────────────────────────────────┘

*/
main(int argc, char *argv[])
{
     strcpy(file_in, argv[1]);
     printf("Z-Buffer Rendering Program\n\n");
     for(i=0; i<2; i++)
        for(j=0; j<=Yres; j++)
                Height[i][j] = 0;
```

```
qin();
strcpy(FileNameOut,ObjectFile);
strcat(ObjectFile, ".zbf");
strcat(FileNameOut, ".raw");
cout << "\nSaving " << FileNameOut << "\n";
fsave = fopen(FileNameOut,"wb");
cout << "\nLoading " << ObjectFile << "\n";
fget = fopen(ObjectFile,"rb");
SinViewPhi = sin(ViewPhi);
CosViewPhi = cos(ViewPhi);
view = Vector(0, -CosViewPhi, SinViewPhi);
light = Vector(sin(LightTheta) * cos(LightPhi),
                                   sin(LightTheta) *
       sin(LightPhi), cos(LightTheta));
fget = fopen(ObjectFile,"rb");
fread(&Xres,2,1,fget);
fread(&Yres,2,1,fget);
cout << "Resolution is " << Xres << " pixels by " << Yres << "
     rows.\n";
cout << "Hit any key to continue...\n";
setMode(0x0E);
fread(&Scaling,2,1,fget);
fwrite(&Xres,2,1,fsave);
fwrite(&Yres,2,1,fsave);
fwrite(&Scaling,2,1,fsave);
fread(&Height[0][0],2,Yres+1,fget);
for (i=0; i<(Xres-1); i++)
{
    fread(&Height[(i+1)%2][0],2,Yres+1,fget);
    p0 =  (float)Zres * ((Height[i % 2][0] / (float)Scaling) *
          CosViewPhi);
    horizon = p0;
    for (j=0; j<Yres; j++)
    {
        red[j] = background.x*max_color;
        green[j] = background.y*max_color;
        blue[j] = background.z*max_color;
    }
    for (j=1; j<Yres; j++)
    {
        p1 = (float)Zres * ((j / ((float)Zres)) * SinViewPhi +
            (Height[i % 2][j] / (float)Scaling) *
```

```
        CosViewPhi);
if (p1 > horizon)
{
    oldPix = Intensity(i, j);
    Pixel(i, p1, oldPix.y/3);
    if (Height[i % 2][j] !=0)
    {
        red[p1] = oldPix.x;
        green[p1] = oldPix.y;
        blue[p1] = oldPix.z;
     }
    else
    {
        red[p1] = background.x*max_color;
        green[p1] = background.y*max_color;
        blue[p1] = background.z*max_color;
    }
    p = p1 - 1;
    newPix = Intensity(i, j-1);
    while (p > horizon)
    {
        h = (float)(p - p0) / (float)(p1 - p0);
        Pix = ((oldPix * h) + (newPix * (1 -
            h)))/max_color;
        Pixel(i, p, Pix.y/3);
        if (Height[i % 2][j] !=0)
        {
            red[p] = Pix.x;
            green[p] = Pix.y;
            blue[p] = Pix.z;
         }
        else
        {
            red[p] = background.x*max_color;
            green[p] = background.y*max_color;
            blue[p] = background.z*max_color;
        }
        p-;
     }
    horizon = p1;
}
  p0 = p1;
```

```
        }
        fwrite(&i,2,1,fsave);
        fwrite(&red[0],1,Yres+1,fsave);
        fwrite(&green[0],1,Yres+1,fsave);
        fwrite(&blue[0],1,Yres+1,fsave);
    }
    getch();
    cout << \n                              \n"
        << "                                 \n"
        << "        Processing Complete.     \n";
      printf("      Data in File: %12s       \n",FileNameOut);
   cout << "                                 \n"
        << "                                 \n";
      fclose(fget);
      fclose(fsave);
}
/*
```

```
    plot ( ) =Plots a point at (x,y) in color
    for Enhanced Graphics Adapter, using Turbo C port
    output functions
```

```
*/

void plot(int x, int y, int color)
{
    #define dataOut(reg, value)    {outp(0x3CE, reg);\
                                     outp(0x3CF, value);}
     #define EGAaddress 0xA0000000L

     unsigned char mask, dummy;
     char far *color_address;
     color_address = (char far *) (EGAaddress +
          ((long)y * 80L + ((long)x / 8L)));
     mask = 0x80 >> (x % 8);
     dummy = *color_address;
     dataOut(0,color);
     dataOut(1,0x0F);
     dataOut(3,0);
     dataOut(8,mask);
     *color_address &= 0xFF;
     dataOut(0,0);
```

```
        dataOut(1,0);
        dataOut(3,0);
        dataOut(8,0xFF);
}


/*
        ┌────────────────────────────────────────────────┐
        │            setMode() = Sets Video Mode           │
        └────────────────────────────────────────────────┘

*/

union REGS reg;

void setMode(int mode)
{
        reg.h.ah = 0;
        reg.h.al = mode;
        int86 (0x10,&reg,&reg);
}


/*
        ┌────────────────────────────────────────────────┐
        │        Pixel() = plots two adjacent pixels on screen  │
        └────────────────────────────────────────────────┘

*/

void Pixel(int x, int y, int color)
{
    plot(2*x, Yres-y, color);
    plot(2*x+1, Yres-y, color);
}


/*
        ┌────────────────────────────────────────────────┐
        │        Intensity() = Finds light intensity at a point │
        └────────────────────────────────────────────────┘

*/
Vector Intensity(int i, int j)
{
        Vector n1, n2, difference, normal, reflected,temp;
        float CosTheta,   CosAlpha;
```

```
n1 = Vector((Xmax-Xmin)/(Xres+1), 0, (float)(
                                Height[(i+1)%2][j] -
      Height[i%2][j]));
n2 = Vector(0, (Ymax-Ymin)/(Yres+1),
                                (float)(Height[i%2][j+1] -
      Height[i%2][j]));
normal = n1 ^ n2;
normal = ~normal;
CosTheta = normal % light;
if (CosTheta < 0)
      return(ambient * max_color);
else
{
      reflected = (normal - light) * (2.0*CosTheta);
      CosAlpha = view % reflected;
      temp = specular * pow(CosAlpha, b) + ambient +
                                (diffuse *
                  CosTheta);
      temp = temp * max_color;
      return(temp);     }
}
}
```

Figure 18-5. Program to Ray Trace a Quaternion

Determining the Color of a Pixel

The intensity of a color is determined by the part of the above program that makes up a function called *Intensity*. It begins by finding a vector normal to the quaternion surface at a designated point in the height matrix. First, a vector is defined which begins at the designated point and height and proceeds to the point represented by the next x, the same y, and the next height. Next, another vector is defined which goes from the designated point and height to the same x, the next y, and the next height. We end up then with two orthogonal vectors on the surface. We then take the cross product of these, which is a vector normal to the surface. This is then normalized to be a unit vector. We next find the cosine of an angle *theta*, which is the angle between the light source vector and the normal vector. This is found by taking the dot product between the two vectors.

If this angle is less than zero, we return the ambient light value. This is the light from the object surface when it is not directly illuminated by the light source. If the angle is greater than zero, the color of the pixel is made up of the sum of three components. The first is the ambient color, the second is the diffused color multiplied by the cosine of the angle *theta,* and the third is the specular reflection. To find this, first find the reflected vector, which is the vector which is the difference between the light vector and the normal vector multiplied by twice the cosine of *theta.* Then take the cosine of the angle between the reflected vector and the viewing vector and raise it to a power that is specified in the input data file. This is the Phong shading model. You may select the power (SREFLECT in the input data file) to give the kind of highlights that you desire. The result of this operation multiplied by the specified reflected color gives you the third component of pixel color.

Producing the Color Picture

We now have a color data file and a color picture whose colors are more abstract than actual. To produce the shaded picture, use the program *quatproc.c.* This program is listed in Figure 18-6. It is like the *colproc* program that was described in Chapter 14, except that it scans columns rather than rows. (The column scanning is necessary with the Z- buffer, since some of the projected values may overlap, and if they do, we want the highest altitude to override the others.)

```
/*
            quadproc = Program to Process VGA Color Data for
                       Quaternions

*/
#include <dos.h>
#include <stdio.h>

void gotoxy(int x, int y);
void plot(int x, int y, int color);
void setMode(int mode);
void setVGApalette(unsigned char *buffer);
```

```
void sort(unsigned int start, unsigned int end);

typedef struct
{
      char Red;
      char Green;
      char Blue;
}
RGB;

enum { red=0,grn=1,blu=2 };

union REGS reg;
struct SREGS inreg;

#define   MAXXRES        800      /* set max horiz coord expected
                                                              */
unsigned int Col_Array[256][2];
unsigned char Pal_Array[256][3];
RGB Color,Color2;

int i,k,xres, yres, last_color,scanline,r1,r2,g1,g2,b1,b2;
unsigned char r[MAXXRES], g[MAXXRES], b[MAXXRES];
FILE *file_1;
unsigned char far *color_hist;
long int color_no;
unsigned int j;
unsigned char frequency[8192];
unsigned int hues[8192];

void main(argc,argv)

int argc;
char *argv[];

{
    int index;
    int rgbindex;
    int x1;
    unsigned int d1, temp_d;
    unsigned char d2;
```

```
    setMode(3);
    if (argc != 2)
    {
        printf("VGA Color Processor for Quaternions by"
               " Roger Stevens\n");
        printf("Usage: %s filename.RAW\n",argv[0]);
        exit(1);
    }
    if ((file_1 = fopen(argv[1],"rb"))==NULL)
    {
        printf("Couldn't open file %s\n",argv[1]);
        exit(1);
    }
    color_hist = farmalloc(32768);
    for (i=0;i<256;i++)
    {
        Pal_Array[i][red] = 0;
        Pal_Array[i][grn] = 0;
        Pal_Array[i][blu] = 0;
}
    for (j=0; j<32768; j++)
            color_hist[j] = 0;
    xres = yres = 0;
    fread(&xres,sizeof(int),1,file_1);
    fread(&yres,sizeof(int),1,file_1);
    printf("VGA color post-processor for Quaternions by"
           " Roger Stevens\n");
    printf("Image file resolution is: %d  by  %d\n",xres,yres);
    for (i=0;i<256;i++)
    {
        Pal_Array[i][red] = 0;
        Pal_Array[i][grn] = 0;
        Pal_Array[i][blu] = 0;
}
    x1 = 0;
    printf("Collecting color data [   ]");
    while (!feof(file_1))
    {
        fread(&scanline,sizeof(int),1,file_1);
            if (scanline >= xres)
            {
                    printf("Faulty data file.\n");
```

```
                    exit(1);
                }
        gotoxy(24,3);
        printf("%d",scanline);
        fread(&r[0],sizeof(char),yres+1,file_1);
        fread(&g[0],sizeof(char),yres+1,file_1);
        fread(&b[0],sizeof(char),yres+1,file_1);
        for (index=0;index<=yres;index++)
        {
                Color.Red   = (r[index] & 0x3e);
                Color.Green = (g[index] & 0x3e);
                Color.Blue  = (b[index] & 0x3e);
                color_no =  (Color.Red >> 1) | (Color.Green <<
                                                    4) |
                    (Color.Blue << 9);
                 if (color_hist[color_no] < 255)
                        color_hist[color_no]++;
        }
        x1 += 1;
}
last_color = -1;
for (j=0; j<32768; j++)
{
        if (color_hist[j] > 0)
        {
                last_color++;
                hues[last_color] = j;
                frequency[last_color] = color_hist[j];
        }
}
printf("\nThere are %d colors.",last_color);
printf("\nStarting sort.");
sort(0,last_color);
printf("\nSort completed.");
printf("\nModifying extra colors [     ]");
for (i=0; i<256; i++)
        frequency[i] = i;
for (i=256; i<=last_color; i++)
{
        gotoxy(25,7);
        printf("%5d",i);
          d1 = 32768;
```

```
        for (j=0; j<256; j++)
        {
            Color.Red = (hues[i] << 1) & 0x3E;
            Color.Green = (hues[i] >> 4) & 0x3E;
            Color.Blue = (hues[i] >> 9) & 0x3E;
            Color2.Red = (hues[j] << 1) & 0x3E;
            Color2.Green = (hues[j] >> 4) & 0x3E;
            Color2.Blue = (hues[j] >> 9) & 0x3E;
            temp_d = (Color.Red - Color2.Red)*(Color.Red -
                Color2.Red) + (Color.Green -
                Color2.Green)*(Color.Green - Color2.Green) +
                (Color.Blue - Color2.Blue)*(Color.Blue -
                Color2.Blue);
            if (temp_d < d1)
            {
                d1 = temp_d;
                d2 = j;
                    }
            }
        frequency[1] = d2;
}
for (j=0; j<256; j++)
{
    Color.Red = (hues[j] << 1) & 0x3E;
    Color Green = (hues[j] >> 4) & 0x3E;
    Color.Blue = (hues[j] >> 9) & 0x3E;
    Pal_Array[j][0] = Color.Red;
    Pal_Array[j][1] = Color.Green;
    Pal_Array[j][2] = Color.Blue;
}
setMode(0x13);
setVGApalette(&Pal_Array[0][0]);
for (j=0; j<32768; j++)
    color_hist[j] = 0;
for (j=0; j<=last_color; j++)
        color_hist[hues[j]] = frequency[j];
rewind(file_1);
x1 = 0;
fread(&xres,sizeof(int),1,file_1);
fread(&yres,sizeof(int),1,file_1);
while (!feof(file_1))
{
```

```
                fread(&scanline,sizeof(int),1,file_1);
                    if (scanline >= xres)
                    {
                            printf("Faulty data file.\n");
                            exit(1);
                    }
                fread(&r[0],sizeof(char),yres+1,file_1);
                fread(&g[0],sizeof(char),yres+1,file_1);
                fread(&b[0],sizeof(char),yres+1,file_1);
                for (index=0;index<=yres;index++)
                {
                    Color.Red   = (r[index] & 0x3e);
                    Color.Green = (g[index] & 0x3e);
                    Color.Blue  = (b[index] & 0x3e);
                    color_no =  (Color.Red >> 1) | (Color.Green <<
                                                                4) |
                    (Color.Blue << 9);
                    plot(x1,yres-index,color_hist[color_no]);
                }
                x1 += 1;
        }
    getch();
    setMode(3);
    fclose(file_1);
}



/*
        ┌─────────────────────────────────────────────────┐
        │            setMode() = Sets Video Mode           │
        │                                                  │
        └─────────────────────────────────────────────────┘
*/
void setMode(int mode)
{
    reg.h.ah = 0;
    reg.h.al = mode;
    int86 (0x10,&reg,&reg);
}


/*
        ┌─────────────────────────────────────────────────┐
        │  plot() = Function to plot point to VGA 256 Color Screen │
        └─────────────────────────────────────────────────┘
                                                                */
```

```
void plot(int x, int y, int color)
{
    unsigned int offset;
    char far *address;
    offset = 320 * y + x;
    address = (char far *)(0xA0000000L + offset);
    *address = color;
}

/*
    ┌─────────────────────────────────────────────────────────┐
    │ setVGApalette() = Function to set all 256 color registers │
    └─────────────────────────────────────────────────────────┘
*/
void setVGApalette(unsigned char *buffer)
{
    reg.x.ax = 0x1012;
    segread(&inreg);
    inreg.es = inreg.ds;
    reg.x.bx = 0;
    reg.x.cx - 256;
    reg.x.dx = (int)&buffer[0];
    int86x(0x10,&reg,&reg,&inreg);
}
/*
    ┌─────────────────────────────────────────────────────────┐
    │ sort ( ) = Quicksort to sort colors by frequency          │
    └─────────────────────────────────────────────────────────┘
*/
void sort(unsigned int start, unsigned int end)
{
    unsigned int pivot,temp2;
    unsigned char temp;

    if (start < (end - 1))
    {
        i = start;
        j = end;
        pivot = (frequency[i] + frequency[j] +
                frequency[(i+j)/2])/3;
```

```
        do
        {
            while (frequency[i] > pivot)
                i++;
            while (frequency[j] < pivot)
                j-;
            if (i < j)
            {
                temp = frequency[i];
                frequency[i] = frequency[j];
                frequency[j] = temp;
                temp2 = hues[i];
                hues[i++] = hues[j];
                hues[j-] = temp2;
            }
        }       while (i < j);
                if (j < end)
                {
                    sort(start,j);
                    sort(j+1,end);
                }
    }
    if (frequency[end] > frequency[start])
    {
        temp = frequency[start];
        frequency[start] = frequency[end];
        frequency[end] = temp;
        temp2 = hues[start];
        hues[start] = hues[end];
        hues[end] = temp2;
    }
}
void gotoxy(int x, int y)
{
    reg.h.ah = 2;
    reg.h.bh = 0;
    reg.h.dh = y-1;
    reg.h.dl = x-1;
    int86(0x10, &reg, &reg);
}
```

Figure 18-6. Program to Display Quaternion Data

Appendix A:
Data Files for Ray Tracing

Plates 4 through 12 were generated with the ray-tracing program. The data files for these plates have the extension .ray. Plates 13 through 16 were generated with the quaternion program. The data files for these plates have the extension .qat. The data files are listed below so that you can duplicate the color plates. After that, you're on your own. It sometimes takes a number of tries to determine exactly where to position each element of a picture and how large to make it.

```
{
```

```
                        Plate 04.ray

            Picture of spheres and a brick wall

            By Roger T. Stevens - 12/31/89
```

```
                                                                }
```

```
FILE_NAME = WSphere.RAW

{   PATTERNS USED}

PATTERN ( x_size = 60,                  { CHECKERED GROUND }
          y_size = 60,
          name   = CHECK,
```

```
        RECTANGLE (
          start_x = 0,
          start_y = 0,
          end_x   = 40,
          end_y   = 40,
          diff    = (.1,1.0,.4),
          dither  = 0,
        )
        RECTANGLE (
          start_x = 40,
          start_y = 40,
          end_x   = 80,
          end_y   = 80,
          diff    = (.1,1.0,.1),
          dither  = 0,
        )
      )
PATTERN ( x_size = 80,              { PATTERN FOR BRICKS }
          y_size = 50,
          name   = BRICK,
          RECTANGLE (
          start_x = 0, start_y = 2,
            end_x   = 18, end_y   = 23,
            diff    = (1.00, .20, .20);
            dither  = 0,
          )
          RECTANGLE (
            start_x = 62, start_y = 2,
            end_x   = 80, end_y    = 23,
            diff    = (1.00, .24, .20);
            dither  = 2,
          )
          RECTANGLE (
            start_x = 22, start_y = 2,
            end_x   = 58, end_y    = 23,
            diff    = (.80, .20, .20);
            dither  = 0,
          )
          RECTANGLE (
            start_x = 2, start_y = 27,
            end_x   = 38, end_y    = 48,
            diff    = (.85, .35, .10);
```

```
              dither  = 0,
          )
          RECTANGLE (                              { brick 4 }
            start_x = 42, start_y = 27,
            end_x   = 78, end_y    = 48,
            diff    = (.70, .25, .20);
            dither  = 0,
          )
      )

PARALLELOGRAM ( loc  = (  -10000, 0,  -10000),
                v1   = (20000, 0,    0),
                v2   = (  0, 0, 20000),
                diff = (  .8, .8, 0),
                dither  = 0,
                pattern = CHECK
                xmult = 2
                ymult = 2
              )
BEGIN_BBOX
    BEGIN_BBOX
        SPHERE ( loc = (210, 55, -80),
                 radius = 40,
                 diff = (.5, .3, .5),
                 xmult   = 1.5,
                 ymult   = 1.5
                 mirror = (.9, .9, .9)
               )
        QUADRATIC ( loc = (210, 0, -80),
                    a     = 1,
                    b     = 0,
                    c     = 1,
                    d     = 150,
                    xmin = -13,
                    xmax = 13,
                    ymin = 0,
                    ymax = 50,
                    zmin = -13,
                    zmax = 13,
                    diff = (.1, .1, .1),
                    mirror = (.8, .8, .8)
                  )
        )
```

```
        END_BBOX
        BEGIN_BBOX
             SPHERE ( loc      = (200, 90, 70),
                         radius   = 35,
                         diff     = (.3, .5, .9),
                         amb      = (.32, .32, .32),
                         reflect  = .60
                         sreflect = 20
                         xmult    = 1.0,
                         ymult    = 1.0
                      )
             QUADRATIC ( loc = (200, 0, 70),
                         a    = 1,
                         b    = 0,
                         c    = 1,
                         d    = 150,
                         xmin = -13,
                         xmax = 13,
                         ymin = 0,
                         ymax = 90,
                         zmin = -13,
                         zmax = 13,
                         diff = (.1, .1, .1),
                         mirror = (.8, .8, .8)
                      )
        END_BBOX
END_BBOX

BEGIN_BBOX
        PARALLELOGRAM ( loc = (150, 00, -15),
                         v1  = (0, 0, 30),
                         v2  = (0, 60, 0)
                         diff = (1, 1, 1),
                         pattern = BRICK
                         xmult = .5,
                         ymult = .5
                      )
        PARALLELOGRAM ( loc = (150, 00, -15),
                         v1  = (150, 0, 0),
                         v2  = (0, 60, 0)
                         diff = (1, 1, 1),
                         pattern = BRICK
```

```
                           xmult = .5,
                           ymult = .5
                        )
     PARALLELOGRAM ( loc = (150, 00, 15),
                     v1  = (150, 0, 0),
                     v2  = (0, 60, 0)
                     diff = (1, 1, 1),
                     pattern = BRICK
                     xmult = .5,
                     ymult = .5
                        )
     PARALLELOGRAM ( loc = (150, 60, -15),
                     v1  = (0, 0, 30),
                     v2  = (150, 0, 0)
                     diff = (1, 1, 1),
                     pattern = BRICK
                     xmult = .5,
                     ymult = .5
                        )
END_BBOX

BEGIN_BBOX

     PARALLELOGRAM ( loc = (200, 60, -15),
                     v1  = (0, 0, 30),
                     v2  = (0, 60, 0)
                     diff = (1, 1, 1),
                     pattern = BRICK
                     xmult = .5,
                     ymult = .5
                        )
     PARALLELOGRAM ( loc = (200, 60, -15),
                     v1  = (50, 0, 0),
                     v2  = (0, 60, 0)
                     diff = (1, 1, 1),
                     pattern = BRICK
                     xmult = .5,
                     ymult = .5
                        )
     PARALLELOGRAM ( loc = (200, 60, 15),
                     v1  = (50, 0, 0),
                     v2  = (0, 60, 0)
```

```
                           diff = (1, 1, 1),
                           pattern = BRICK
                           xmult = .5,
                           ymult = .5
                       )
END_BBOX
OBSERVER ( loc   = (-20 , 70, -40),
            lookat = (200, 50, 0)
          )
LAMP ( loc = (120, 120, -50),
       radius = 5,
       dist = 80
     )
LAMP ( loc = (120, 150, 80),
       radius = 5,
       dist = 70
     )
SKY  ( horiz  = (0, .4, .6),
       zenith = (0, .4, .6),
       dither = 1
     )
XRES = 320
YRES = 200

FOC_LENGTH = 80

{
```

```
┌────────────────────────────────────────────────┐
│                                                  │
│                  Plate 05.ray                    │
│                                                  │
│        Picture of three cones and spheres        │
│                                                  │
│         By Roger T. Stevens - 12/31/89           │
│                                                  │
└────────────────────────────────────────────────┘
```

```
                                                         }
```

```
FILE_NAME = CONE5.RAW
{  PATTERNS USED}

PATTERN ( x_size = 80,                  { CHECKERED GROUND }
          y_size = 80,
```

```
        name    = CHECK,
        RECTANGLE (
          start_x = 0,
          start_y = 0,
          end_x   = 40,
          end_y   = 40,
          diff    = (.75, .25, .75),
          dither  = 0,
        )
        RECTANGLE (
          start_x = 40,
          start_y = 40,
          end_x   = 80,
          end_y   = 80,
          diff    = (.75, .25, .75),
          dither  = 0,
        )
     )
PARALLELOGRAM ( loc  = (  -10000, 0,  -10000),
                v1   = (20000, 0,     0),
                v2   = (  0, 0, 20000),
                diff = (  1, 1, .75),
                dither  = 0,
                pattern = CHECK
                xmult = 2
                ymult = 2
             )
BEGIN_BBOX
        SPHERE ( loc = (230, 90, -70),
                 radius = 30,
                 diff = (.7, .7, .7),
                 xmult   = 1
                 ymult   = 1
                 mirror = (.9, .9, .9)
                 )
     CONE         (loc = (230, 60, -70),
                    radius = 35
                    height = 60
                    diff = (1, 0, 0),
                    )
END_BBOX
```

```
BEGIN_BBOX
        SPHERE ( loc        = (220, 90, 50),
                 radius     = 30,
                 diff       = (.7, .7, .7),
                 mirror     = (.9, .9, .9)
                 xmult      = 1.0,
                 ymult      = 1.0
               )
    CONE          (loc = (220, 60, 50),
                   radius = 30
                   height = 60
                   diff = (0, 1, 0.6),
                   )
END_BBOX

BEGIN_BBOX
        SPHERE ( loc = (350, 90, 0),
                 radius = 30,
                 diff = (.7, .7, .7),
                 xmult   = 1
                 ymult   = 1
                 mirror = (.9, .9, .9)
               )
          CONE        (loc = (350, 60, 0),
                       radius = 35
                       height = 60
                       diff = (0, 0, 1),
                       )
END_BBOX
OBSERVER ( loc     = (-20 , 70, -40),
           lookat = (200, 50, -15)
          )
LAMP ( loc = (120, 400, -50),
      radius = 5,
      dist = 250
     )
LAMP ( loc = (-200, 450, 140)
      radius = 5,
      dist = 220
     )
SKY  ( horiz  = (0, .4, .8),
       zenith = (0, .4, .9),
```

```
        dither = 1
    )
XRES = 320
YRES = 200
FOC_LENGTH = 65
{
```

```
┌─────────────────────────────────────────────────────────┐
│ ┌───────────────────────────────────────────────────────┐ │
│ │                                                         │ │
│ │                     Plate 06.ray                        │ │
│ │                                                         │ │
│ │   New York World's Fair 1939 - Trylon and Perisphere    │ │
│ │                                                         │ │
│ │            By Roger T. Stevens - 2/18-90                │ │
│ │                                                         │ │
│ └───────────────────────────────────────────────────────┘ │
└─────────────────────────────────────────────────────────┘
```

```
}

FILE_NAME = NYWF39.RAW

{  PATTERNS USED}

PATTERN ( x_size = 60,                    { CHECKERED GROUND }
          y_size = 60,
          name   = CHECK,
          RECTANGLE (
            start_x = 0,
            start_y = 0,
            end_x   = 30,
            end_y   = 30,
            diff    = (.1,1.0,.4),
            dither  = 0,
          )
          RECTANGLE (
            start_x = 30,
            start_y = 30,
            end_x   = 60,
            end_y   = 60,
            diff    = (.1,1.0,.1),
            dither  = 0,
          )
      )
```

```
PARALLELOGRAM ( loc  = (  -10000, 0,  -10000),
                v1   = (20000, 0,    0),
                v2   = (  0, 0, 20000),
                diff = (  .8, .8, 0),
                dither  = 0,
                pattern = CHECK
                xmult = 1
                ymult = 1
              )
SPHERE ( loc = (350, 30, -40),
         radius = 30,
         diff = (1.0,1.0,1.0),
       )
BEGIN_BBOX
      TRIANGLE (
      loc = (380,0,20),
      v1 = (60,0,0),
      v2 = (30,150,17),
      diff = (1.0,1.0,1.0),
      xmult = 1.5,
      ymult = 1.5,
      )
      TRIANGLE (
      loc = (380,0,20),
      v1 = (30,0,52),
      v2 = (30,150,17),
      diff = (1.0,1.0,1.0),
      xmult = 1.5,
      ymult = 1.5,
      )
END_BBOX
OBSERVER ( loc   = (-80 , 70, -40),
           lookat = (200, 70, 0)
         )
{ ** A lamp ** }
LAMP ( loc = (0, 150, 120),
       radius = 5,
       dist = 200
     )
SKY  ( horiz  = (0, .2, .9),
       zenith = (0, .2, .9),
       dither = 1
```

```
     )
XRES = 320

YRES = 200

FOC_LENGTH = 120
{
```

```
                    Plate 07.ray

            Picture of Pyramids in the Desert

                By Roger T. Stevens - 4/22-90
```

```
}

FILE_NAME = Pyramid.RAW

BEGIN_INSTANCES
      name = PYRAMID

BEGIN_BBOX
                TRIANGLE (loc 0, 0, 0)
                                v1 = (52, 0, 30)
                                v2 = (34.3, 30, 0)
                                diff = (.72, .41, .14)
                )
                TRIANGLE (loc 0, 0, 0)
                                v1 = (52, 0, -30)
                                v2 = (34.3, 30, 0)
                                diff = (.72, .41, .14)
                )
                TRIANGLE (loc 52, 0, -30)
                                v1 = (0, 0, 60)
                                v2 = (-17.7, 30, 30)
                                diff = (.72, .41, .14)
                )
END_BBOX
END_INSTANCES
```

```
PARALLELOGRAM ( loc  = (  -10000, 0,  -10000),
                v1   = (20000, 0,    0),
                v2   = (  0, 0, 20000),
                amb = (.48, .32, .40)
                diff = (  1.0, .8, .4),
                dither  = 0,
              )
INSTANCE_OF name = PYRAMID
                    loc = (200, 0, -40)
                    scale = (1.3, 1.3, 1.3)
        )
INSTANCE_OF name = PYRAMID
                  loc = (170, 0, 80)
                  scale = (1.2, 1.2, 1.2)
        )
INSTANCE_OF name = PYRAMID
                  loc = (225, 0, 20)
        )
INSTANCE_OF name = PYRAMID
                  loc = (350, 0, -70)
        )
INSTANCE_OF name = PYRAMID
                  loc = (400, 0, 120)
                  scale (1.25, 1.25, 1.25)
        )
INSTANCE_OF name = PYRAMID
                  loc = (500, 0, -60)
        )
INSTANCE_OF name = PYRAMID
                  loc = (700, 0, -100)
                  scale (1.25, 1.25, 1.25)
        )
INSTANCE_OF name = PYRAMID
                  loc = (750, 0, 140)
        )
INSTANCE_OF name = PYRAMID
                  loc = (900, 0, -80)
                  scale (1.25, 1.25, 1.25)
        )
INSTANCE_OF name = PYRAMID
                  loc = (950, 0, 300)
        )
```

```
INSTANCE_OF name = PYRAMID
                loc = (1050, 0, 0)
      )

OBSERVER ( loc    = (-20 , 70, -40),
           lookat = (200, 50, 0)
         )
LAMP ( loc = (120, 180,  80),
       radius = 5,
       dist = 70
     )
LAMP ( loc = (-20, 350, -400),
       radius = 5,
       dist = 1500
     )
SKY  ( horiz  = (0, .4, .7),
       zenith = (0, .4, .7),
       dither = 1
     )
XRES = 320
YRES = 200
FOC_LENGTH = 75

{
```

```
Plate 08.ray

Indian Story Teller

By Roger T. Stevens - 4/22-90
```

```
}

FILE_NAME = MSPHERE4.RAW

     OBSERVER
         (loc = (2.100000, 1.000000, 1.700000),
          lookat = (0.000000, 0.8000000, 0.000000)
         )
```

```
XRES = 320
YRES = 200

SKY
    (horiz = (0.078000, 0.361000, 0.753000)
     zenith = (0.078000, 0.361000, 0.753000)
     dither = 0
     )
LAMP
    (loc = (4.000000, 3.000000, 2.000000)
     radius = 5
     dist = 5
     )
LAMP
    (loc = (1.000000, -4.000000, 4.000000)
     radius = 5
     dist = 5
     )
LAMP
    (loc = (-3.000000, 1.000000, 5.000000)
     radius = 5
     dist = 0
     )
        PARALLELOGRAM
    (loc = (-1000,0,-1000)
         v1 = (0,0,20000)
         v2 = (20000,0,0)
         diff = (1.000000, 0.750000, 0.330000),
     reflect = 0.000000,
     sreflect = 0.000000,
     trans = (0.000000, 0.000000, 0.000000),
     index = 0.000000,
     )
        BEGIN_BBOX
SPHERE
    (loc = (0.000000, 0.500000, 0.000000),
     radius = 0.500000,
     diff = (0.00000, 0.0000, 0.850000),
     reflect = 0.500000,
     sreflect = 3.000000,
     trans = (0.000000, 0.000000, 0.000000),
     index = 0.000000,
```

```
    )
SPHERE
    (loc = (0.272166, 0.772166, 0.544331),
     radius = 0.166667,
     diff = (1.00000, 0.0000, 0.0000),
     reflect = 0.500000,
     sreflect = 3.000000,
     trans = (0.000000, 0.000000, 0.000000),
     index = 0.000000,
    )
SPHERE
    (loc = (0.420314, 0.920314, 0.618405),
     radius = 0.055556,
     diff = (0.00000, 0.450000, 0.0000),
     reflect = 0.500000,
     sreflect = 3.000000,
     trans = (0.000000, 0.000000, 0.000000),
     index = 0.000000,
    )
SPHERE
    (loc = (0.461844, 0.804709, 0.433220),
     radius = 0.055556,
     diff = (0.00000, 0.450000, 0.0000),
     reflect = 0.500000,
     sreflect = 3.000000,
     trans = (0.000000, 0.000000, 0.000000),
     index = 0.000000,
    )
SPHERE
    (loc = (0.304709, 0.961844, 0.433220),
     radius = 0.055556,
     diff = (0.00000, 0.450000, 0.0000),
     reflect = 0.500000,
     sreflect = 3.000000,
     trans = (0.000000, 0.000000, 0.000000),
     index = 0.000000,
    )
SPHERE
    (loc = (0.230635, 0.887770, 0.729516),
     radius = 0.055556,
     diff = (0.00000, 0.450000, 0.0000),
     reflect = 0.500000,
```

```
        sreflect = 3.000000,
        trans = (0.000000, 0.000000, 0.000000),
        index = 0.000000,
        )
    SPHERE
        (loc = (0.115031, 0.929300, 0.544331),
         radius = 0.055556,
        diff = (0.00000, 0.450000, 0.0000),
        reflect = 0.500000,
        sreflect = 3.000000,
        trans = (0.000000, 0.000000, 0.000000),
        index = 0.000000,
        )
    SPHERE
        (loc = (0.082487, 0.739622, 0.655442),
         radius = 0.055556,
        diff = (0.00000, 0.450000, 0.0000),
        reflect = 0.500000,
        sreflect = 3.000000,
        trans = (0.000000, 0.000000, 0.000000),
        index = 0.000000,
        )
    SPHERE
        (loc = (0.387770, 0.730635, 0.729516),
         radius = 0.055556,
        diff = (0.00000, 0.450000, 0.0000),
        reflect = 0.500000,
        sreflect = 3.000000,
        trans = (0.000000, 0.000000, 0.000000),
        index = 0.000000,
        )
    SPHERE
        (loc = (0.239622, 0.582487, 0.655442),
         radius = 0.055556,
        diff = (0.00000, 0.450000, 0.0000),
        reflect = 0.500000,
        sreflect = 3.000000,
        trans = (0.000000, 0.000000, 0.000000),
        index = 0.000000,
        )
    SPHERE
        (loc = (0.429300, 0.615031, 0.544331),
```

```
     radius = 0.055556,
    diff = (0.00000, 0.450000, 0.0000),
    reflect = 0.500000,
    sreflect = 3.000000,
    trans = (0.000000, 0.000000, 0.000000),
    index = 0.000000,
    )
SPHERE
    (loc = (0.643951, 0.672546, 0.000000),
     radius = 0.166667,
    diff = (0.50000, 0.0000, 0.0000),
    reflect = 0.500000,
    sreflect = 3.000000,
    trans = (0.000000, 0.000000, 0.000000),
    index = 0.000000,
    )
SPHERE
    (loc = (0.802608, 0.881471, -0.111111),
     radius = 0.055556,
    diff = (0.00000, 0.450000, 0.0000),
    reflect = 0.500000,
    sreflect = 3.000000,
    trans = (0.000000, 0.000000, 0.000000),
    index = 0.000000,
    )
SPHERE
    (loc = (0.643951, 0.672546, -0.222222),
     radius = 0.055556,
    diff = (0.00000, 0.450000, 0.0000),
    reflect = 0.500000,
    sreflect = 3.000000,
    trans = (0.000000, 0.000000, 0.000000),
    index = 0.000000,
    )
SPHERE
    (loc = (0.594141, 0.858439, -0.111111),
     radius = 0.055556,
    diff = (0.00000, 0.450000, 0.0000),
    reflect = 0.500000,
    sreflect = 3.000000,
    trans = (0.000000, 0.000000, 0.000000),
    index = 0.000000,
```

```
        )
    SPHERE
        (loc = (0.802608, 0.781471, 0.111111),
         radius = 0.055556,
         diff = (0.00000, 0.450000, 0.350000),
         reflect = 0.500000,
         sreflect = 3.000000,
         trans = (0.000000, 0.000000, 0.000000),
         index = 0.000000,
        )
    SPHERE
        (loc = (0.594141, 0.858439, 0.111111),
         radius = 0.055556,
         diff = (0.00000, 0.450000, 0.350000),
         reflect = 0.500000,
         sreflect = 3.000000,
         trans = (0.000000, 0.000000, 0.000000),
         index = 0.000000,
        )
    SPHERE
        (loc = (0.643951, 0.672546, 0.222222),
         radius = 0.055556,
         diff = (0.00000, 0.450000, 0.350000),
         reflect = 0.500000,
         sreflect = 3.000000,
         trans = (0.000000, 0.000000, 0.000000),
         index = 0.000000,
        )
    SPHERE
        (loc = (0.852418, 0.595579, 0.000000),
         radius = 0.055556,
         diff = (0.00000, 0.450000, 0.350000),
         reflect = 0.500000,
         sreflect = 3.000000,
         trans = (0.000000, 0.000000, 0.000000),
         index = 0.000000,
        )
    SPHERE
        (loc = (0.693760, 0.486654, 0.111111),
         radius = 0.055556,
         diff = (0.00000, 0.450000, 0.350000),
         reflect = 0.500000,
```

```
        sreflect = 3.000000,
        trans = (0.000000, 0.000000, 0.000000),
        index = 0.000000,
        )
SPHERE
        (loc = (0.693760, 0.486654, -0.111111),
         radius = 0.055556,
        diff = (0.00000, 0.450000, 0.00000),
        reflect = 0.500000,
        sreflect = 3.000000,
        trans = (0.000000, 0.000000, 0.000000),
        index = 0.000000,
        )
SPHERE
        (loc = (0.172546, 1.143951, 0.000000),
         radius = 0.166667,
        diff = (0.800000, 0.0000, 0.00000),
        reflect = 0.500000,
        sreflect - 3.000000,
        trans = (0.000000, 0.000000, 0.000000),
        index = 0.000000,
        )
SPHERE
        (loc = (0.281471, 1.302608, -0.111111),
         radius - 0.055556,
        diff = (0.00000, 0.450000, 0.00000),
        reflect = 0.500000,
        sreflect = 3.000000,
        trans = (0.000000, 0.000000, 0.000000),
        index = 0.000000,
        )
SPHERE
        (loc = (0.358439, 1.094141, -0.111111),
         radius = 0.055556,
        diff = (0.00000, 0.450000, 0.00000),
        reflect = 0.500000,
        sreflect = 3.000000,
        trans = (0.000000, 0.000000, 0.000000),
        index = 0.000000,
        )
SPHERE
        (loc = (0.172546, 1.143951, -0.222222),
```

```
     radius = 0.055556,
     diff = (0.00000, 0.450000, 0.00000),
     reflect = 0.500000,
     sreflect = 3.000000,
     trans = (0.000000, 0.000000, 0.000000),
     index = 0.000000,
     )
SPHERE
     (loc = (0.095579, 1.352418, -0.000000),
      radius = 0.055556,
     diff = (0.00000, 0.450000, 0.00000),
     reflect = 0.500000,
     sreflect = 3.000000,
     trans = (0.000000, 0.000000, 0.000000),
     index = 0.000000,
     )
SPHERE
     (loc = (-0.013346, 1.193760, -0.111111),
      radius = 0.055556,
     diff = (0.00000, 0.450000, 0.00000),
     reflect = 0.500000,
     sreflect = 3.000000,
     trans = (0.000000, 0.000000, 0.000000),
     index = 0.000000,
     )
SPHERE
     (loc = (-0.013346, 1.193760, 0.111111),
      radius = 0.055556,
     diff = (0.00000, 0.450000, 0.00000),
     reflect = 0.500000,
     sreflect = 3.000000,
     trans = (0.000000, 0.000000, 0.000000),
     index = 0.000000,
     )
SPHERE
     (loc = (0.281471, 1.302608, 0.111111),
      radius = 0.055556,
     diff = (0.00000, 0.450000, 0.00000),
     reflect = 0.500000,
     sreflect = 3.000000,
     trans = (0.000000, 0.000000, 0.000000),
     index = 0.000000,
```

```
    )
SPHERE
    (loc = (0.172546, 1.143951, 0.222222),
     radius = 0.055556,
     diff = (0.00000, 0.450000, 0.00000),
     reflect = 0.500000,
     sreflect = 3.000000,
     trans = (0.000000, 0.000000, 0.000000),
     index = 0.000000,
    )
SPHERE
    (loc = (0.358439, 1.194141, 0.111111),
     radius = 0.055556,
     diff = (0.00000, 0.450000, 0.00000),
     reflect = 0.500000,
     sreflect = 3.000000,
     trans = (0.000000, 0.000000, 0.000000),
     index = 0.000000,
    )
SPHERE
    (loc = (-0.371785, 0.599619, 0.544331),
     radius = 0.166667,
     diff = (0.800000, 0.0000, 0.00000),
     reflect = 0.500000,
     sreflect = 3.000000,
     trans = (0.000000, 0.000000, 0.000000),
     index = 0.000000,
    )
SPHERE
    (loc = (-0.393621, 0.720501, 0.729516),
     radius = 0.055556,
     diff = (0.00000, 0.450000, 0.00000),
     reflect = 0.500000,
     sreflect = 3.000000,
     trans = (0.000000, 0.000000, 0.000000),
     index = 0.000000,
    )
SPHERE
    (loc = (-0.191247, 0.666275, 0.655442),
     radius = 0.055556,
     diff = (0.00000, 0.450000, 0.00000),
     reflect = 0.500000,
```

```
    sreflect = 3.000000,
    trans = (0.000000, 0.000000, 0.000000),
    index = 0.000000,
      )
SPHERE
      (loc = (-0.314270, 0.814270, 0.544331),
       radius = 0.055556,
      diff = (0.00000, 0.450000, 0.00000),
      reflect = 0.500000,
      sreflect = 3.000000,
      trans = (0.000000, 0.000000, 0.000000),
      index = 0.000000,
       )
SPHERE
      (loc = (-0.574159, 0.653845, 0.618405),
       radius = 0.055556,
      diff = (0.00000, 0.450000, 0.00000),
      reflect = 0.500000,
      sreflect = 3.000000,
      trans = (0.000000, 0.000000, 0.000000),
      index = 0.000000,
       )
SPHERE
      (loc = (-0.494808, 0.747614, 0.433220),
       radius = 0.055556,
      diff = (0.00000, 0.450000, 0.00000),
      reflect = 0.500000,
      sreflect = 3.000000,
      trans = (0.000000, 0.000000, 0.000000),
      index = 0.000000,
       )
SPHERE
      (loc = (-0.552323, 0.532964, 0.433220),
       radius = 0.055556,
      diff = (0.00000, 0.450000, 0.00000),
      reflect = 0.500000,
      sreflect = 3.000000,
      trans = (0.000000, 0.000000, 0.000000),
      index = 0.000000,
       )
SPHERE
      (loc = (-0.451136, 0.505851, 0.729516),
```

```
    radius = 0.055556,
    diff = (0.00000, 0.450000, 0.00000),
    reflect = 0.500000,
    sreflect = 3.000000,
    trans = (0.000000, 0.000000, 0.000000),
    index = 0.000000,
    )
SPHERE
    (loc = (-0.429300, 0.384969, 0.544331),
    radius = 0.055556,
    diff = (0.00000, 0.450000, 0.00000),
    reflect = 0.500000,
    sreflect = 3.000000,
    trans = (0.000000, 0.000000, 0.000000),
    index = 0.000000,
    )
SPHERE
    (loc = (-0.248762, 0.451625, 0.655442),
    radius = 0.055556,
    diff = (0.00000, 0.450000, 0.00000),
    reflect = 0.500000,
    sreflect = 3.000000,
    trans = (0.000000, 0.000000, 0.000000),
    index = 0.000000,
    )
SPHERE
    (loc = (-0.471405, 0.971405, 0.000000),
    radius = 0.166667,
    diff = (0.800000, 0.0000, 0.00000),
    reflect = 0.500000,
    sreflect = 3.000000,
    trans = (0.000000, 0.000000, 0.000000),
    index = 0.000000,
    )
SPHERE
    (loc = (-0.508983, 1.190426, -0.000000),
    radius = 0.055556,
    diff = (0.00000, 0.450000, 0.00000),
    reflect = 0.500000,
    sreflect = 3.000000,
    trans = (0.000000, 0.000000, 0.000000),
    index = 0.000000,
```

```
        )
    SPHERE
        (loc = (-0.335322, 1.107487, 0.111111),
         radius = 0.055556,
         diff = (0.00000, 0.450000, 0.00000),
         reflect = 0.500000,
         sreflect = 3.000000,
         trans = (0.000000, 0.000000, 0.000000),
         index = 0.000000,
        )
    SPHERE
        (loc = (-0.335322, 1.107487, -0.111111),
         radius = 0.055556,
         diff = (0.00000, 0.450000, 0.00000),
         reflect = 0.500000,
         sreflect = 3.000000,
         trans = (0.000000, 0.000000, 0.000000),
         index = 0.000000,
        )
    SPHERE
        (loc = (-0.645066, 1.054344, -0.111111),
         radius = 0.055556,
         diff = (0.00000, 0.450000, 0.00000),
         reflect = 0.500000,
         sreflect = 3.000000,
         trans = (0.000000, 0.000000, 0.000000),
         index = 0.000000,
        )
    SPHERE
        (loc = (-0.471405, 0.971405, -0.222222),
         radius = 0.055556,
         diff = (0.00000, 0.450000, 0.00000),
         reflect = 0.500000,
         sreflect = 3.000000,
         trans = (0.000000, 0.000000, 0.000000),
         index = 0.000000,
        )
    SPHERE
        (loc = (-0.607487, 0.835322, -0.111111),
         radius = 0.055556,
         diff = (0.00000, 0.450000, 0.00000),
         reflect = 0.500000,
```

```
        sreflect = 3.000000,
        trans = (0.000000, 0.000000, 0.000000),
        index = 0.000000,
        )
SPHERE
        (loc = (-0.645066, 1.154344, 0.111111),
         radius = 0.055556,
        diff = (0.00000, 0.450000, 0.00000),
        reflect = 0.500000,
        sreflect = 3.000000,
        trans = (0.000000, 0.000000, 0.000000),
        index = 0.000000,
        )
SPHERE
        (loc = (-0.607487, 0.835322, 0.111111),
         radius = 0.055556,
        diff = (0.00000, 0.450000, 0.00000),
        reflect = 0.500000,
        sreflect = 3.000000,
        trans = (0.000000, 0.000000, 0.000000),
        index = 0.000000,
        )
SPHERE
        (loc = (-0.471405, 0.971405, 0.222222),
         radius = 0.055556,
        diff = (0.00000, 0.450000, 0.00000),
        reflect = 0.500000,
        sreflect = 3.000000,
        trans = (0.000000, 0.000000, 0.000000),
        index = 0.000000,
        )
SPHERE
        (loc = (-0.643951, 0.327454, 0.000000),
         radius = 0.166667,
        diff = (0.500000, 0.0000, 0.00000),
        reflect = 0.500000,
        sreflect = 3.000000,
        trans = (0.000000, 0.000000, 0.000000),
        index = 0.000000,
        )
SPHERE
        (loc = (-0.835815, 0.342357, 0.111111),
```

```
        radius = 0.055556,
        diff = (0.00000, 0.450000, 0.00000),
        reflect = 0.500000,
        sreflect = 3.000000,
        trans = (0.000000, 0.000000, 0.000000),
        index = 0.000000,
      )
  SPHERE
      (loc = (-0.643951, 0.327454, 0.222222),
        radius = 0.055556,
        diff = (0.00000, 0.450000, 0.00000),
        reflect = 0.500000,
        sreflect = 3.000000,
        trans = (0.000000, 0.000000, 0.000000),
        index = 0.000000,
      )
  SPHERE
      (loc = (-0.693760, 0.513346, 0.111111),
        radius = 0.055556,
        diff = (0.00000, 0.450000, 0.00000),
        reflect = 0.500000,
        sreflect = 3.000000,
        trans = (0.000000, 0.000000, 0.000000),
        index = 0.000000,
      )
  SPHERE
      (loc = (-0.835815, 0.342457, -0.111111),
        radius = 0.055556,
        diff = (0.00000, 0.450000, 0.00000),
        reflect = 0.500000,
        sreflect = 3.000000,
        trans = (0.000000, 0.000000, 0.000000),
        index = 0.000000,
      )
  SPHERE
      (loc = (-0.693760, 0.513346, -0.111111),
        radius = 0.055556,
        diff = (0.00000, 0.450000, 0.00000),
        reflect = 0.500000,
        sreflect = 3.000000,
        trans = (0.000000, 0.000000, 0.000000),
        index = 0.000000,
```

```
    )
SPHERE
    (loc = (-0.643951, 0.327454, -0.222222),
     radius = 0.055556,
     diff = (0.00000, 0.450000, 0.00000),
     reflect = 0.500000,
     sreflect = 3.000000,
     trans = (0.000000, 0.000000, 0.000000),
     index = 0.000000,
    )
SPHERE
    (loc = (-0.786005, 0.156565, -0.000000),
     radius = 0.055556,
     diff = (0.00000, 0.450000, 0.00000),
     reflect = 0.500000,
     sreflect = 3.000000,
     trans = (0.000000, 0.000000, 0.000000),
     index = 0.000000,
    )
SPHERE
    (loc = (-0.594141, 0.141561, -0.111111),
     radius = 0.055556,
     diff = (0.00000, 0.450000, 0.00000),
     reflect = 0.500000,
     sreflect = 3.000000,
     trans = (0.000000, 0.000000, 0.000000),
     index = 0.000000,
    )
SPHERE
    (loc = (-0.594141, 0.151561, 0.111111),
     radius = 0.055556,
     diff = (0.00000, 0.450000, 0.00000),
     reflect = 0.500000,
     sreflect = 3.000000,
     trans = (0.000000, 0.000000, 0.000000),
     index = 0.000000,
    )
SPHERE
    (loc = (0.099619, 0.128215, 0.544331),
     radius = 0.166667,
     diff = (0.800000, 0.0000, 0.00000),
     reflect = 0.500000,
```

```
      sreflect = 3.000000,
      trans = (0.000000, 0.000000, 0.000000),
      index = 0.000000,
      )
  SPHERE
      (loc = (0.220501, 0.106479, 0.729516),
       radius = 0.055556,
      diff = (0.00000, 0.450000, 0.00000),
      reflect = 0.500000,
      sreflect = 3.000000,
      trans = (0.000000, 0.000000, 0.000000),
      index = 0.000000,
      )
  SPHERE
      (loc = (0.314270, 0.185730, 0.544331),
       radius = 0.055556,
      diff = (0.00000, 0.450000, 0.00000),
      reflect = 0.500000,
      sreflect = 3.000000,
      trans = (0.000000, 0.000000, 0.000000),
      index = 0.000000,
      )
  SPHERE
      (loc = (0.166275, 0.308753, 0.655442),
       radius = 0.055556,
      diff = (0.00000, 0.450000, 0.00000),
      reflect = 0.500000,
      sreflect = 3.000000,
      trans = (0.000000, 0.000000, 0.000000),
      index = 0.000000,
      )
  SPHERE
      (loc = (0.005851, 0.048861, 0.729516),
       radius = 0.055556,
      diff = (0.00000, 0.450000, 0.00000),
      reflect = 0.500000,
      sreflect = 3.000000,
      trans = (0.000000, 0.000000, 0.000000),
      index = 0.000000,
      )
  SPHERE
      (loc = (-0.048375, 0.251238, 0.655442),
```

```
      radius = 0.055556,
     diff = (0.00000, 0.450000, 0.00000),
     reflect = 0.500000,
     sreflect = 3.000000,
     trans = (0.000000, 0.000000, 0.000000),
     index = 0.000000,
     )
SPHERE
     (loc = (-0.115031, 0.070700, 0.544331),
      radius = 0.055556,
     diff = (0.00000, 0.450000, 0.00000),
     reflect = 0.500000,
     sreflect = 3.000000,
     trans = (0.000000, 0.000000, 0.000000),
     index = 0.000000,
     )
SPHERE
     (loc = (0.153845, -0.074159, 0.618405),
      radius = 0.055556,
     diff = (0.00000, 0.450000, 0.00000),
     reflect = 0.500000,
     sreflect = 3.000000,
     trans = (0.000000, 0.000000, 0.000000),
     index = 0.000000,
     )
SPHERE
     (loc = (0.032964, -0.052323, 0.433220),
      radius = 0.055556,
     diff = (0.00000, 0.450000, 0.00000),
     reflect = 0.500000,
     sreflect = 3.000000,
     trans = (0.000000, 0.000000, 0.000000),
     index = 0.000000,
     )
SPHERE
     (loc = (0.247614, 0.005192, 0.433220),
      radius = 0.055556,
     diff = (0.00000, 0.450000, 0.00000),
     reflect = 0.500000,
     sreflect = 3.000000,
     trans = (0.000000, 0.000000, 0.000000),
     index = 0.000000,
```

```
        )
    SPHERE
        (loc = (-0.172546, -0.143951, 0.000000),
         radius = 0.166667,
         diff = (0.800000, 0.0000, 0.00000),
         reflect = 0.500000,
         sreflect = 3.000000,
         trans = (0.000000, 0.000000, 0.000000),
         index = 0.000000,
        )
    SPHERE
        (loc = (-0.157543, -0.335815, 0.111111),
         radius = 0.055556,
         diff = (0.00000, 0.450000, 0.00000),
         reflect = 0.500000,
         sreflect = 3.000000,
         trans = (0.000000, 0.000000, 0.000000),
         index = 0.000000,
        )
    SPHERE
        (loc = (0.013346, -0.193760, 0.111111),
         radius = 0.055556,
         diff = (0.00000, 0.450000, 0.00000),
         reflect = 0.500000,
         sreflect = 3.000000,
         trans = (0.000000, 0.000000, 0.000000),
         index = 0.000000,
        )
    SPHERE
        (loc = (-0.172546, -0.143951, 0.222222),
         radius = 0.055556,
         diff = (0.00000, 0.450000, 0.00000),
         reflect = 0.500000,
         sreflect = 3.000000,
         trans = (0.000000, 0.000000, 0.000000),
         index = 0.000000,
        )
    SPHERE
        (loc = (-0.343435, -0.286005, -0.000000),
         radius = 0.055556,
         diff = (0.00000, 0.450000, 0.00000),
         reflect = 0.500000,
```

```
        sreflect = 3.000000,
        trans = (0.000000, 0.000000, 0.000000),
        index = 0.000000,
      )
SPHERE
    (loc = (-0.358439, -0.094141, 0.111111),
     radius = 0.055556,
    diff = (0.00000, 0.450000, 0.00000),
    reflect = 0.500000,
    sreflect = 3.000000,
    trans = (0.000000, 0.000000, 0.000000),
    index = 0.000000,
      )
SPHERE
    (loc = (-0.358439, -0.094141, -0.111111),
     radius = 0.055556,
    diff = (0.00000, 0.450000, 0.00000),
    reflect = 0.500000,
    sreflect = 3.000000,
    trans = (0.000000, 0.000000, 0.000000),
    index = 0.000000,
      )
SPHERE
    (loc = (-0.157543, -0.335815, -0.111111),
     radius = 0.055556,
    diff = (0.00000, 0.450000, 0.00000),
    reflect = 0.500000,
    sreflect = 3.000000,
    trans = (0.000000, 0.000000, 0.000000),
    index = 0.000000,
      )
SPHERE
    (loc = (-0.172546, -0.143951, -0.222222),
     radius = 0.055556,
    diff = (0.00000, 0.450000, 0.00000),
    reflect = 0.500000,
    sreflect = 3.000000,
    trans = (0.000000, 0.000000, 0.000000),
    index = 0.000000,
      )
SPHERE
    (loc = (0.013346, -0.193760, -0.111111),
```

```
       radius = 0.055556,
      diff = (0.00000, 0.450000, 0.00000),
      reflect = 0.500000,
      sreflect = 3.000000,
      trans = (0.000000, 0.000000, 0.000000),
      index = 0.000000,
      )
   SPHERE
      (loc = (0.471405, 0.028515, 0.000000),
       radius = 0.166667,
      diff = (0.800000, 0.0000, 0.00000),
      reflect = 0.500000,
      sreflect = 3.000000,
      trans = (0.000000, 0.000000, 0.000000),
      index = 0.000000,
      )
   SPHERE
      (loc = (0.690426, -0.008983, 0.000000),
       radius = 0.055556,
      diff = (0.00000, 0.450000, 0.00000),
      reflect = 0.500000,
      sreflect = 3.000000,
      trans = (0.000000, 0.000000, 0.000000),
      index = 0.000000,
      )
   SPHERE
      (loc = (0.607487, 0.164678, -0.111111),
       radius = 0.055556,
      diff = (0.00000, 0.450000, 0.00000),
      reflect = 0.500000,
      sreflect = 3.000000,
      trans = (0.000000, 0.000000, 0.000000),
      index = 0.000000,
      )
   SPHERE
      (loc = (0.607487, 0.164678, 0.111111),
       radius = 0.055556,
      diff = (0.00000, 0.450000, 0.00000),
      reflect = 0.500000,
      sreflect = 3.000000,
      trans = (0.000000, 0.000000, 0.000000),
      index = 0.000000,
```

```
   )
SPHERE
   (loc = (0.554344, -0.145066, 0.111111),
    radius = 0.055556,
    diff = (0.00000, 0.450000, 0.00000),
    reflect = 0.500000,
    sreflect = 3.000000,
    trans = (0.000000, 0.000000, 0.000000),
    index = 0.000000,
   )
SPHERE
   (loc = (0.471405, 0.028595, 0.222222),
    radius = 0.055556,
    diff = (0.00000, 0.450000, 0.00000),
    reflect = 0.500000,
    sreflect = 3.000000,
    trans = (0.000000, 0.000000, 0.000000),
    index = 0.000000,
   )
SPHERE
   (loc = (0.335322, -0.107487, 0.111111),
    radius = 0.055556,
    diff = (0.00000, 0.450000, 0.00000),
    reflect = 0.500000,
    sreflect = 3.000000,
    trans = (0.000000, 0.000000, 0.000000),
    index = 0.000000,
   )
SPHERE
   (loc = (0.554344, -0.145066, -0.111111),
    radius = 0.055556,
    diff = (0.00000, 0.450000, 0.00000),
    reflect = 0.500000,
    sreflect = 3.000000,
    trans = (0.000000, 0.000000, 0.000000),
    index = 0.000000,
   )
SPHERE
   (loc = (0.335322, -0.107487, -0.111111),
    radius = 0.055556,
    diff = (0.00000, 0.450000, 0.00000),
    reflect = 0.500000,
```

```
            sreflect = 3.000000,
            trans = (0.000000, 0.000000, 0.000000),
            index = 0.000000,
            )
        SPHERE
            (loc = (0.471405, 0.028595, -0.222222),
             radius = 0.055556,
            diff = (0.00000, 0.450000, 0.00000),
            reflect = 0.500000,
            sreflect = 3.000000,
            trans = (0.000000, 0.000000, 0.000000),
            index = 0.000000,
            )
            END_BBOX
FILE_NAME = MSPHERE4.RAW
        OBSERVER
            (loc = (2.100000, 1.000000, 1.700000),
             lookat = (0.000000, 0.8000000, 0.000000)
            )
        XRES = 320
        YRES = 200

        SKY
            (horiz = (0.078000, 0.361000, 0.753000)
             zenith = (0.078000, 0.361000, 0.753000)
             dither = 0
            )
        LAMP
            (loc = (4.000000, 3.000000, 2.000000)
             radius = 5
             dist = 5
            )
        LAMP
            (loc = (1.000000, -4.000000, 4.000000)
             radius = 5
             dist = 5
            )
        LAMP
            (loc = (-3.000000, 1.000000, 5.000000)
             radius = 5
             dist = 0
            )
```

```
    PARALLELOGRAM
    (loc = (-1000,0,-1000)
          v1 = (0,0,20000)
          v2 = (20000,0,0)
          diff = (1.000000, 0.750000, 0.330000),
     reflect = 0.000000,
     sreflect = 0.000000,
     trans = (0.000000, 0.000000, 0.000000),
     index = 0.000000,
     )
    BEGIN_BBOX
SPHERE
    (loc = (0.000000, 0.500000, 0.000000),
     radius = 0.500000,
     diff = (0.00000, 0.0000, 0.850000),
     reflect = 0.500000,
     sreflect = 3.000000,
     trans = (0.000000, 0.000000, 0.000000),
     index = 0.000000,
     )
SPHERE
    (loc = (0.272166, 0.772166, 0.544331),
     radius = 0.166667,
     diff = (1.00000, 0.0000, 0.0000),
     reflect = 0.500000,
     sreflect = 3.000000,
     trans = (0.000000, 0.000000, 0.000000),
     index = 0.000000,
     )
SPHERE
    (loc = (0.420314, 0.920314, 0.618405),
     radius = 0.055556,
     diff = (0.00000, 0.450000, 0.0000),
     reflect = 0.500000,
     sreflect = 3.000000,
     trans = (0.000000, 0.000000, 0.000000),
     index = 0.000000,
     )
SPHERE
    (loc = (0.461844, 0.804709, 0.433220),
     radius = 0.055556,
     diff = (0.00000, 0.450000, 0.0000),
```

```
        reflect = 0.500000,
        sreflect = 3.000000,
        trans = (0.000000, 0.000000, 0.000000),
        index = 0.000000,
        )
   SPHERE
        (loc = (0.304709, 0.961844, 0.433220),
         radius = 0.055556,
        diff = (0.00000, 0.450000, 0.0000),
        reflect = 0.500000,
        sreflect = 3.000000,
        trans = (0.000000, 0.000000, 0.000000),
        index = 0.000000,
        )
   SPHERE
        (loc = (0.230635, 0.887770, 0.729516),
         radius = 0.055556,
        diff = (0.00000, 0.450000, 0.0000),
        reflect = 0.500000,
        sreflect = 3.000000,
        trans = (0.000000, 0.000000, 0.000000),
        index = 0.000000,
        )
   SPHERE
        (loc = (0.115031, 0.929300, 0.544331),
         radius = 0.055556,
        diff = (0.00000, 0.450000, 0.0000),
        reflect = 0.500000,
        sreflect = 3.000000,
        trans = (0.000000, 0.000000, 0.000000),
        index = 0.000000,
        )
   SPHERE
        (loc = (0.082487, 0.739622, 0.655442),
         radius = 0.055556,
        diff = (0.00000, 0.450000, 0.0000),
        reflect = 0.500000,
        sreflect = 3.000000,
        trans = (0.000000, 0.000000, 0.000000),
        index = 0.000000,
        )
   SPHERE
```

```
    (loc = (0.387770, 0.730635, 0.729516),
     radius = 0.055556,
    diff = (0.00000, 0.450000, 0.0000),
    reflect = 0.500000,
    sreflect = 3.000000,
    trans = (0.000000, 0.000000, 0.000000),
    index = 0.000000,
    )
SPHERE
    (loc = (0.239622, 0.582487, 0.655442),
     radius = 0.055556,
    diff = (0.00000, 0.450000, 0.0000),
    reflect = 0.500000,
    sreflect = 3.000000,
    trans = (0.000000, 0.000000, 0.000000),
    index = 0.000000,
    )
SPHERE
    (loc = (0.429300, 0.615031, 0.544331),
     radius = 0.055556,
    diff = (0.00000, 0.450000, 0.0000),
    reflect = 0.500000,
    sreflect - 3.000000,
    trans = (0.000000, 0.000000, 0.000000),
    index = 0.000000,
    )
SPHERE
    (loc = (0.643951, 0.672546, 0.000000),
     radius = 0.166667,
    diff = (0.50000, 0.0000, 0.0000),
    reflect = 0.500000,
    sreflect = 3.000000,
    trans = (0.000000, 0.000000, 0.000000),
    index = 0.000000,
    )
SPHERE
    (loc = (0.802608, 0.881471, -0.111111),
     radius = 0.055556,
    diff = (0.00000, 0.450000, 0.0000),
    reflect = 0.500000,
    sreflect = 3.000000,
    trans = (0.000000, 0.000000, 0.000000),
```

```
            index = 0.000000,
            )
        SPHERE
            (loc = (0.643951, 0.672546, -0.222222),
             radius = 0.055556,
            diff = (0.00000, 0.450000, 0.0000),
            reflect = 0.500000,
            sreflect = 3.000000,
            trans = (0.000000, 0.000000, 0.000000),
            index = 0.000000,
            )
        SPHERE
            (loc = (0.594141, 0.858439, -0.111111),
             radius = 0.055556,
            diff = (0.00000, 0.450000, 0.0000),
            reflect = 0.500000,
            sreflect = 3.000000,
            trans = (0.000000, 0.000000, 0.000000),
            index = 0.000000,
            )
        SPHERE
            (loc = (0.802608, 0.781471, 0.111111),
             radius = 0.055556,
            diff = (0.00000, 0.450000, 0.350000),
            reflect = 0.500000,
            sreflect = 3.000000,
            trans = (0.000000, 0.000000, 0.000000),
            index = 0.000000,
            )
        SPHERE
            (loc = (0.594141, 0.858439, 0.111111),
             radius = 0.055556,
            diff = (0.00000, 0.450000, 0.350000),
            reflect = 0.500000,
            sreflect = 3.000000,
            trans = (0.000000, 0.000000, 0.000000),
            index = 0.000000,
            )
        SPHERE
            (loc = (0.643951, 0.672546, 0.222222),
             radius = 0.055556,
            diff = (0.00000, 0.450000, 0.350000),
```

```
    reflect = 0.500000,
    sreflect = 3.000000,
    trans = (0.000000, 0.000000, 0.000000),
    index = 0.000000,
    )
SPHERE
    (loc = (0.852418, 0.595579, 0.000000),
     radius = 0.055556,
    diff = (0.00000, 0.450000, 0.350000),
    reflect = 0.500000,
    sreflect = 3.000000,
    trans = (0.000000, 0.000000, 0.000000),
    index = 0.000000,
    )
SPHERE
    (loc = (0.693760, 0.486654, 0.111111),
     radius = 0.055556,
    diff = (0.00000, 0.450000, 0.350000),
    reflect = 0.500000,
    sreflect = 3.000000,
    trans = (0.000000, 0.000000, 0.000000),
    index = 0.000000,
    )
SPHERE
    (loc = (0.693760, 0.486654, -0.111111),
     radius = 0.055556,
    diff = (0.00000, 0.450000, 0.00000),
    reflect = 0.500000,
    sreflect = 3.000000,
    trans = (0.000000, 0.000000, 0.000000),
    index = 0.000000,
    )
SPHERE
    (loc = (0.172546, 1.143951, 0.000000),
     radius = 0.166667,
    diff = (0.800000, 0.0000, 0.00000),
    reflect = 0.500000,
    sreflect = 3.000000,
    trans = (0.000000, 0.000000, 0.000000),
    index = 0.000000,
    )
SPHERE
```

```
         (loc = (0.281471, 1.302608, -0.111111),
          radius = 0.055556,
         diff = (0.00000, 0.450000, 0.00000),
         reflect = 0.500000,
         sreflect = 3.000000,
         trans = (0.000000, 0.000000, 0.000000),
         index = 0.000000,
         )
    SPHERE
         (loc = (0.358439, 1.094141, -0.111111),
          radius = 0.055556,
         diff = (0.00000, 0.450000, 0.00000),
         reflect = 0.500000,
         sreflect = 3.000000,
         trans = (0.000000, 0.000000, 0.000000),
         index = 0.000000,
         )
    SPHERE
         (loc = (0.172546, 1.143951, -0.222222),
          radius = 0.055556,
         diff = (0.00000, 0.450000, 0.00000),
         reflect = 0.500000,
         sreflect = 3.000000,
         trans = (0.000000, 0.000000, 0.000000),
         index = 0.000000,
         )
    SPHERE
         (loc = (0.095579, 1.352418, -0.000000),
          radius = 0.055556,
         diff = (0.00000, 0.450000, 0.00000),
         reflect = 0.500000,
         sreflect = 3.000000,
         trans = (0.000000, 0.000000, 0.000000),
         index = 0.000000,
         )
    SPHERE
         (loc = (-0.013346, 1.193760, -0.111111),
          radius = 0.055556,
         diff = (0.00000, 0.450000, 0.00000),
         reflect = 0.500000,
         sreflect = 3.000000,
         trans = (0.000000, 0.000000, 0.000000),
```

```
    index = 0.000000,
  )
SPHERE
    (loc = (-0.013346, 1.193760, 0.111111),
     radius = 0.055556,
    diff = (0.00000, 0.450000, 0.00000),
    reflect = 0.500000,
    sreflect = 3.000000,
    trans = (0.000000, 0.000000, 0.000000),
    index = 0.000000,
  )
SPHERE
    (loc = (0.281471, 1.302608, 0.111111),
     radius = 0.055556,
    diff = (0.00000, 0.450000, 0.00000),
    reflect = 0.500000,
    sreflect = 3.000000,
    trans = (0.000000, 0.000000, 0.000000),
    index = 0.000000,
  )
SPHERE
    (loc = (0.172546, 1.143951, 0.222222),
     radius = 0.055556,
    diff = (0.00000, 0.450000, 0.00000),
    reflect = 0.500000,
    sreflect = 3.000000,
    trans = (0.000000, 0.000000, 0.000000),
    index = 0.000000,
  )
SPHERE
    (loc = (0.358439, 1.194141, 0.111111),
     radius = 0.055556,
    diff = (0.00000, 0.450000, 0.00000),
    reflect = 0.500000,
    sreflect = 3.000000,
    trans = (0.000000, 0.000000, 0.000000),
    index = 0.000000,
  )
SPHERE
    (loc = (-0.371785, 0.599619, 0.544331),
     radius = 0.166667,
    diff = (0.800000, 0.0000, 0.00000),
```

```
      reflect = 0.500000,
      sreflect = 3.000000,
      trans = (0.000000, 0.000000, 0.000000),
      index = 0.000000,
      )
  SPHERE
      (loc = (-0.393621, 0.720501, 0.729516),
       radius = 0.055556,
      diff = (0.00000, 0.450000, 0.00000),
      reflect = 0.500000,
      sreflect = 3.000000,
      trans = (0.000000, 0.000000, 0.000000),
      index = 0.000000,
      )
  SPHERE
      (loc = (-0.191247, 0.666275, 0.655442),
       radius = 0.055556,
      diff = (0.00000, 0.450000, 0.00000),
      reflect = 0.500000,
      sreflect = 3.000000,
      trans = (0.000000, 0.000000, 0.000000),
      index = 0.000000,
      )
  SPHERE
      (loc = (-0.314270, 0.814270, 0.544331),
       radius = 0.055556,
      diff = (0.00000, 0.450000, 0.00000),
      reflect = 0.500000,
      sreflect = 3.000000,
      trans = (0.000000, 0.000000, 0.000000),
      index = 0.000000,
      )
  SPHERE
      (loc = (-0.574159, 0.653845, 0.618405),
       radius = 0.055556,
      diff = (0.00000, 0.450000, 0.00000),
      reflect = 0.500000,
      sreflect = 3.000000,
      trans = (0.000000, 0.000000, 0.000000),
      index = 0.000000,
      )
  SPHERE
```

```
    (loc = (-0.494808, 0.747614, 0.433220),
     radius = 0.055556,
    diff = (0.00000, 0.450000, 0.00000),
    reflect = 0.500000,
    sreflect = 3.000000,
    trans = (0.000000, 0.000000, 0.000000),
    index = 0.000000,
    )
SPHERE
    (loc = (-0.552323, 0.532964, 0.433220),
     radius = 0.055556,
    diff = (0.00000, 0.450000, 0.00000),
    reflect = 0.500000,
    sreflect = 3.000000,
    trans = (0.000000, 0.000000, 0.000000),
    index = 0.000000,
    )
SPHERE
    (loc = (-0.451136, 0.505851, 0.729516),
     radius = 0.055556,
    diff = (0.00000, 0.450000, 0.00000),
    reflect = 0.500000,
    sreflect = 3.000000,
    trans = (0.000000, 0.000000, 0.000000),
    index = 0.000000,
    )
SPHERE
    (loc = (-0.429300, 0.384969, 0.544331),
     radius = 0.055556,
    diff = (0.00000, 0.450000, 0.00000),
    reflect = 0.500000,
    sreflect = 3.000000,
    trans = (0.000000, 0.000000, 0.000000),
    index = 0.000000,
    )
SPHERE
    (loc = (-0.248762, 0.451625, 0.655442),
     radius = 0.055556,
    diff = (0.00000, 0.450000, 0.00000),
    reflect = 0.500000,
    sreflect = 3.000000,
    trans = (0.000000, 0.000000, 0.000000),
```

```
        index = 0.000000,
        )
    SPHERE
        (loc = (-0.471405, 0.971405, 0.000000),
         radius = 0.166667,
        diff = (0.800000, 0.0000, 0.00000),
        reflect = 0.500000,
        sreflect = 3.000000,
        trans = (0.000000, 0.000000, 0.000000),
        index = 0.000000,
        )
    SPHERE
        (loc = (-0.508983, 1.190426, -0.000000),
         radius = 0.055556,
        diff = (0.00000, 0.450000, 0.00000),
        reflect = 0.500000,
        sreflect = 3.000000,
        trans = (0.000000, 0.000000, 0.000000),
        index = 0.000000,
         )
    SPHERE
        (loc = (-0.335322, 1.107487, 0.111111),
         radius = 0.055556,
        diff = (0.00000, 0.450000, 0.00000),
        reflect = 0.500000,
        sreflect = 3.000000,
        trans = (0.000000, 0.000000, 0.000000),
        index = 0.000000,
         )
    SPHERE
        (loc = (-0.335322, 1.107487, -0.111111),
         radius = 0.055556,
        diff = (0.00000, 0.450000, 0.00000),
        reflect = 0.500000,
        sreflect = 3.000000,
        trans = (0.000000, 0.000000, 0.000000),
        index = 0.000000,
         )
    SPHERE
        (loc = (-0.645066, 1.054344, -0.111111),
         radius = 0.055556,
        diff = (0.00000, 0.450000, 0.00000),
```

```
    reflect = 0.500000,
    sreflect = 3.000000,
    trans = (0.000000, 0.000000, 0.000000),
    index = 0.000000,
    )
SPHERE
    (loc = (-0.471405, 0.971405, -0.222222),
     radius = 0.055556,
    diff = (0.00000, 0.450000, 0.00000),
    reflect = 0.500000,
    sreflect = 3.000000,
    trans = (0.000000, 0.000000, 0.000000),
    index = 0.000000,
    )
SPHERE
    (loc = (-0.607487, 0.835322, -0.111111),
     radius = 0.055556,
    diff = (0.00000, 0.450000, 0.00000),
    reflect = 0.500000,
    sreflect = 3.000000,
    trans = (0.000000, 0.000000, 0.000000),
    index = 0.000000,
    )
SPHERE
    (loc = (-0.645066, 1.154344, 0.111111),
     radius = 0.055556,
    diff = (0.00000, 0.450000, 0.00000),
    reflect = 0.500000,
    sreflect = 3.000000,
    trans = (0.000000, 0.000000, 0.000000),
    index = 0.000000,
    )
SPHERE
    (loc = (-0.607487, 0.835322, 0.111111),
     radius = 0.055556,
    diff = (0.00000, 0.450000, 0.00000),
    reflect = 0.500000,
    sreflect = 3.000000,
    trans = (0.000000, 0.000000, 0.000000),
    index = 0.000000,
    )
SPHERE
```

```
        (loc = (-0.471405, 0.971405, 0.222222),
         radius = 0.055556,
        diff = (0.00000, 0.450000, 0.00000),
        reflect = 0.500000,
        sreflect = 3.000000,
        trans = (0.000000, 0.000000, 0.000000),
        index = 0.000000,
        )
    SPHERE
        (loc = (-0.643951, 0.327454, 0.000000),
         radius = 0.166667,
        diff = (0.500000, 0.0000, 0.00000),
        reflect = 0.500000,
        sreflect = 3.000000,
        trans = (0.000000, 0.000000, 0.000000),
        index = 0.000000,
        )
    SPHERE
        (loc = (-0.835815, 0.342357, 0.111111),
         radius = 0.055556,
        diff = (0.00000, 0.450000, 0.00000),
        reflect = 0.500000,
        sreflect = 3.000000,
        trans = (0.000000, 0.000000, 0.000000),
        index = 0.000000,
        )
    SPHERE
        (loc = (-0.643951, 0.327454, 0.222222),
         radius = 0.055556,
        diff = (0.00000, 0.450000, 0.00000),
        reflect = 0.500000,
        sreflect = 3.000000,
        trans = (0.000000, 0.000000, 0.000000),
        index = 0.000000,
        )
    SPHERE
        (loc = (-0.693760, 0.513346, 0.111111),
         radius = 0.055556,
        diff = (0.00000, 0.450000, 0.00000),
        reflect = 0.500000,
        sreflect = 3.000000,
        trans = (0.000000, 0.000000, 0.000000),
```

```
     index = 0.000000,
   )
SPHERE
   (loc = (-0.835815, 0.342457, -0.111111),
    radius = 0.055556,
   diff = (0.00000, 0.450000, 0.00000),
   reflect = 0.500000,
   sreflect = 3.000000,
   trans = (0.000000, 0.000000, 0.000000),
   index = 0.000000,
   )
SPHERE
   (loc = (-0.693760, 0.513346, -0.111111),
    radius = 0.055556,
   diff = (0.00000, 0.450000, 0.00000),
   reflect = 0.500000,
   sreflect = 3.000000,
   trans = (0.000000, 0.000000, 0.000000),
   index = 0.000000,
   )
SPHERE
   (loc = (-0.643951, 0.327454, -0.222222),
    radius - 0.055556,
   diff - (0.00000, 0.450000, 0.00000),
   reflect = 0.500000,
   sreflect = 3.000000,
   trans = (0.000000, 0.000000, 0.000000),
   index = 0.000000,
   )
SPHERE
   (loc = (-0.786005, 0.156565, -0.000000),
    radius = 0.055556,
   diff = (0.00000, 0.450000, 0.00000),
   reflect = 0.500000,
   sreflect = 3.000000,
   trans = (0.000000, 0.000000, 0.000000),
   index = 0.000000,
   )
SPHERE
   (loc = (-0.594141, 0.141561, -0.111111),
    radius = 0.055556,
   diff = (0.00000, 0.450000, 0.00000),
```

```
        reflect = 0.500000,
        sreflect = 3.000000,
        trans = (0.000000, 0.000000, 0.000000),
        index = 0.000000,
        )
   SPHERE
        (loc = (-0.594141, 0.151561, 0.111111),
         radius = 0.055556,
        diff = (0.00000, 0.450000, 0.00000),
        reflect = 0.500000,
        sreflect = 3.000000,
        trans = (0.000000, 0.000000, 0.000000),
        index = 0.000000,
        )
   SPHERE
        (loc = (0.099619, 0.128215, 0.544331),
         radius = 0.166667,
        diff = (0.800000, 0.0000, 0.00000),
        reflect = 0.500000,
        sreflect = 3.000000,
        trans = (0.000000, 0.000000, 0.000000),
        index = 0.000000,
        )
   SPHERE
        (loc = (0.220501, 0.106479, 0.729516),
         radius = 0.055556,
        diff = (0.00000, 0.450000, 0.00000),
        reflect = 0.500000,
        sreflect = 3.000000,
        trans = (0.000000, 0.000000, 0.000000),
        index = 0.000000,
        )
   SPHERE
        (loc = (0.314270, 0.185730, 0.544331),
         radius = 0.055556,
        diff = (0.00000, 0.450000, 0.00000),
        reflect = 0.500000,
        sreflect = 3.000000,
        trans = (0.000000, 0.000000, 0.000000),
        index = 0.000000,
        )
   SPHERE
```

```
    (loc = (0.166275, 0.308753, 0.655442),
     radius = 0.055556,
    diff = (0.00000, 0.450000, 0.00000),
    reflect = 0.500000,
    sreflect = 3.000000,
    trans = (0.000000, 0.000000, 0.000000),
    index = 0.000000,
    )
SPHERE
    (loc = (0.005851, 0.048861, 0.729516),
     radius = 0.055556,
    diff = (0.00000, 0.450000, 0.00000),
    reflect = 0.500000,
    sreflect = 3.000000,
    trans = (0.000000, 0.000000, 0.000000),
    index = 0.000000,
    )
SPHERE
    (loc = (-0.048375, 0.251238, 0.655442),
     radius = 0.055556,
    diff = (0.00000, 0.450000, 0.00000),
    reflect = 0.500000,
    sreflect = 3.000000,
    trans = (0.000000, 0.000000, 0.000000),
    index = 0.000000,
    )
SPHERE
    (loc = (-0.115031, 0.070700, 0.544331),
     radius = 0.055556,
    diff = (0.00000, 0.450000, 0.00000),
    reflect = 0.500000,
    sreflect = 3.000000,
    trans = (0.000000, 0.000000, 0.000000),
    index = 0.000000,
    )
SPHERE
    (loc = (0.153845, -0.074159, 0.618405),
     radius = 0.055556,
    diff = (0.00000, 0.450000, 0.00000),
    reflect = 0.500000,
    sreflect = 3.000000,
    trans = (0.000000, 0.000000, 0.000000),
```

```
        index = 0.000000,
        )
    SPHERE
        (loc = (0.032964, -0.052323, 0.433220),
         radius = 0.055556,
        diff = (0.00000, 0.450000, 0.00000),
        reflect = 0.500000,
        sreflect = 3.000000,
        trans = (0.000000, 0.000000, 0.000000),
        index = 0.000000,
        )
    SPHERE
        (loc = (0.247614, 0.005192, 0.433220),
         radius = 0.055556,
        diff = (0.00000, 0.450000, 0.00000),
        reflect = 0.500000,
        sreflect = 3.000000,
        trans = (0.000000, 0.000000, 0.000000),
        index = 0.000000,
        )
    SPHERE
        (loc = (-0.172546, -0.143951, 0.000000),
         radius = 0.166667,
        diff = (0.800000, 0.0000, 0.00000),
        reflect = 0.500000,
        sreflect = 3.000000,
        trans = (0.000000, 0.000000, 0.000000),
        index = 0.000000,
        )
    SPHERE
        (loc = (-0.157543, -0.335815, 0.111111),
         radius = 0.055556,
        diff = (0.00000, 0.450000, 0.00000),
        reflect = 0.500000,
        sreflect = 3.000000,
        trans = (0.000000, 0.000000, 0.000000),
        index = 0.000000,
        )
    SPHERE
        (loc = (0.013346, -0.193760, 0.111111),
         radius = 0.055556,
        diff = (0.00000, 0.450000, 0.00000),
```

```
    reflect = 0.500000,
    sreflect = 3.000000,
    trans = (0.000000, 0.000000, 0.000000),
    index = 0.000000,
    )
SPHERE
    (loc = (-0.172546, -0.143951, 0.222222),
     radius = 0.055556,
    diff = (0.00000, 0.450000, 0.00000),
    reflect = 0.500000,
    sreflect = 3.000000,
    trans = (0.000000, 0.000000, 0.000000),
    index = 0.000000,
    )
SPHERE
    (loc = (-0.343435, -0.286005, -0.000000),
     radius = 0.055556,
    diff = (0.00000, 0.450000, 0.00000),
    reflect = 0.500000,
    sreflect = 3.000000,
    trans = (0.000000, 0.000000, 0.000000),
    index = 0.000000,
    )
SPHERE
    (loc = (0.358439, -0.094141, 0.111111),
     radius = 0.055556,
    diff = (0.00000, 0.450000, 0.00000),
    reflect = 0.500000,
    sreflect = 3.000000,
    trans = (0.000000, 0.000000, 0.000000),
    index = 0.000000,
    )
SPHERE
    (loc = (-0.358439, -0.094141, -0.111111),
     radius = 0.055556,
    diff = (0.00000, 0.450000, 0.00000),
    reflect = 0.500000,
    sreflect = 3.000000,
    trans = (0.000000, 0.000000, 0.000000),
    index = 0.000000,
    )
SPHERE
```

```
        (loc = (-0.157543, -0.335815, -0.111111),
         radius = 0.055556,
        diff = (0.00000, 0.450000, 0.00000),
        reflect = 0.500000,
        sreflect = 3.000000,
        trans = (0.000000, 0.000000, 0.000000),
        index = 0.000000,
        )
    SPHERE
        (loc = (-0.172546, -0.143951, -0.222222),
         radius = 0.055556,
        diff = (0.00000, 0.450000, 0.00000),
        reflect = 0.500000,
        sreflect = 3.000000,
        trans = (0.000000, 0.000000, 0.000000),
        index = 0.000000,
        )
    SPHERE
        (loc = (0.013346, -0.193760, -0.111111),
         radius = 0.055556,
        diff = (0.00000, 0.450000, 0.00000),
        reflect = 0.500000,
        sreflect = 3.000000,
        trans = (0.000000, 0.000000, 0.000000),
        index = 0.000000,
        )
    SPHERE
        (loc = (0.471405, 0.028515, 0.000000),
         radius = 0.166667,
        diff = (0.800000, 0.0000, 0.00000),
        reflect = 0.500000,
        sreflect = 3.000000,
        trans = (0.000000, 0.000000, 0.000000),
        index = 0.000000,
        )
    SPHERE
        (loc = (0.690426, -0.008983, 0.000000),
         radius = 0.055556,
        diff = (0.00000, 0.450000, 0.00000),
        reflect = 0.500000,
        sreflect = 3.000000,
        trans = (0.000000, 0.000000, 0.000000),
```

```
    index = 0.000000,
  )
SPHERE
    (loc = (0.607487, 0.164678, -0.111111),
     radius = 0.055556,
    diff = (0.00000, 0.450000, 0.00000),
    reflect = 0.500000,
    sreflect = 3.000000,
    trans = (0.000000, 0.000000, 0.000000),
    index = 0.000000,
    )
SPHERE
    (loc = (0.607487, 0.164678, 0.111111),
     radius = 0.055556,
    diff = (0.00000, 0.450000, 0.00000),
    reflect = 0.500000,
    sreflect = 3.000000,
    trans = (0.000000, 0.000000, 0.000000),
    index = 0.000000,
    )
SPHERE
    (loc = (0.554344, -0.145066, 0.111111),
     radius = 0.055556,
    diff = (0.00000, 0.450000, 0.00000),
    reflect = 0.500000,
    sreflect = 3.000000,
    trans = (0.000000, 0.000000, 0.000000),
    index = 0.000000,
    )
SPHERE
    (loc = (0.471405, 0.028595, 0.222222),
     radius = 0.055556,
    diff = (0.00000, 0.450000, 0.00000),
    reflect = 0.500000,
    sreflect = 3.000000,
    trans = (0.000000, 0.000000, 0.000000),
    index = 0.000000,
    )
SPHERE
    (loc = (0.335322, -0.107487, 0.111111),
     radius = 0.055556,
    diff = (0.00000, 0.450000, 0.00000),
```

```
       reflect = 0.500000,
       sreflect = 3.000000,
       trans = (0.000000, 0.000000, 0.000000),
       index = 0.000000,              )
   SPHERE
       (loc = (0.554344, -0.145066, -0.111111),
        radius = 0.055556,
       diff = (0.00000, 0.450000, 0.00000),
       reflect = 0.500000,
       sreflect = 3.000000,
       trans = (0.000000, 0.000000, 0.000000),
       index = 0.000000,
       )
   SPHERE
       (loc = (0.335322, -0.107487, -0.111111),
        radius = 0.055556,
       diff = (0.00000, 0.450000, 0.00000),
       reflect = 0.500000,
       sreflect = 3.000000,
       trans = (0.000000, 0.000000, 0.000000),
       index = 0.000000,
       )
   SPHERE
       (loc = (0.471405, 0.028595, -0.222222),
        radius = 0.055556,
       diff = (0.00000, 0.450000, 0.00000),
       reflect = 0.500000,
       sreflect = 3.000000,
       trans = (0.000000, 0.000000, 0.000000),
       index = 0.000000,
       )
       END_BBOX

{
```

```
+--------------------------------------------+
|                                            |
|              Plate 09.ray                  |
|                                            |
|         Pictures of quadric shapes         |
|                                            |
|        By Roger T. Stevens - 6/17/90       |
|                                            |
+--------------------------------------------+
```

```
FILE_NAME = SHAPES2.RAW

{  PATTERNS USED}
PATTERN ( x_size = 80,                     { CHECKERED GROUND }
          y_size = 80,
          name   = CHECK,
          RECTANGLE (
            start_x = 0,
            start_y = 0,
            end_x   = 40,
            end_y   = 40,
            diff    = (.75, .25, .75),
            dither  = 0,
          )
          RECTANGLE (
            start_x = 40,
            start_y = 40,
            end_x   = 80,
            end_y   = 80,
            diff    = (.75, .25, .75),
            dither  = 0,
          )
        )
PARALLELOGRAM ( loc  = (  -10000, 0,  -10000),
                v1   = (20000, 0,     0),
                v2   = (  0, 0, 20000),
                diff = (  1, 1, .75),
                dither  = 0,
                pattern = CHECK
                xmult = 2
                ymult = 2
              )
BEGIN_BBOX
      QUADRATIC       (loc= (230, 60, -100)    {elliptic cone -
cyan}
                a       = 2500, b  = -625, c  = 2500,
                d       = 0,
                xmin    = -25, xmax = 25,
                ymin    = -50,   ymax = 50,
                zmin    = -25, zmax = 25,
                diff    = (0, 1.0, 1.0),
```

```
                )
END_BBOX

BEGIN_BBOX
     QUADRATIC          (loc= (300, 0, -55)    {cylinder - green}
                a      = 1, b  = 0, c  = 1,
                d      = 300,
                xmin   = -18, xmax = 18,
                ymin   = 0,   ymax = 60,
                zmin   = -18, zmax = 18,
                diff   = (0, 1.0, 0),
                )
END_BBOX

BEGIN_BBOX
     QUADRATIC          (loc= (220, 60, 25)    {elliptic
paraboloid -
purple}
                a      = 60, e  = -60, c  = 60,
                d      = 0,
                xmin   = -20, xmax = 20,
                ymin   = -40,   ymax = 60,
                zmin   = -20, zmax = 20,
                diff   = (1.0, 0, 1.0),
                )
END_BBOX

BEGIN_BBOX
     QUADRATIC          (loc= (160, 30, -35)    {hyperbolic
paraboloid -
blue}
                a      = 2, e  = -100, c  = -2,
                d      = 0
                xmin   = -15, xmax = 15,
                ymin   = -25,   ymax = 40,
                zmin   = -15, zmax = 15,
                diff   = (0, 0, 1.0),
                )
END_BBOX

BEGIN_BBOX
     QUADRATIC          (loc= (230, 60, 90)    {hyperboloid of
```

```
one sheet
- orange}
                a       = 1, b  = -1, c  = 1,
                d       = 300,
                xmin    = -25, xmax = 25,
                ymin    = -60,  ymax = 60,
                zmin    = -25, zmax = 25,
                diff    = (1.0, 0.5, 0),
                )
END_BBOX

BEGIN_BBOX
    QUADRATIC           (loc= (500, 60, 30)}   {hyperboloid of two
sheets - red}
                a       = -5, b  = -7, c  = 3,
                d       = 700,
                xmin    = -22, xmax = 22,
                ymin    = -60,  ymax = 60,
                zmin    = -22, zmax = 22,
                diff    = (1, 0, 0),
                )
END_BBOX

BEGIN_BBOX
    QUADRATIC           (loc= (130, 30, 35) {ellipsoid - white}
                a       = 8, b  = 4, c  = 1,
                d       = 500,
                xmin    = -25, xmax = 25,
                ymin    = -40,  ymax = 60,
                zmin    = -25, zmax = 25,
                diff    = (1.0, 1.0, 1.0),
                )
END_BBOX

OBSERVER ( loc     = (-20 , 70, -80)
           lookat = (200, 50, -15)
           )
LAMP ( loc = (120, 400, -50),
       radius = 5,
       dist = 250
    )
LAMP ( loc = (-200, 450, 140)
```

```
             radius = 5,
             dist = 220
           )
LAMP    ( loc = (-200, 200, 140)
             radius = 5,
             dist = 220
           )
SKY     ( horiz  = (0, .4, .8),
             zenith = (0, .4, .9),
             dither = 1
           )
XRES = 320
YRES = 200
FOC_LENGTH = 65


{
                      Plate 10.ray

                 Pictures of Trojan Horse

              By Roger T. Stevens - 6/24/90

                                                           }


FILE_NAME = Horse.RAW

PARALLELOGRAM ( loc  = (  -10000, 0,  -10000),
                 v1   = (20000, 0,     0),
                 v2   = (  0, 0, 20000),
                       amb = (.48, .32, .40)
                 diff = (  1.0, .8, .4),
                 dither  = 0,
                 )

BEGIN_BBOX

      QUADRATIC            (loc= (130, 60,-20) {ellipsoid}
                 a        = 8, b  = 4, c  = 1,
                 d        = 4000,
                 xmin     = -100, xmax = 100,
                 ymin     = -80,   ymax = 80,
```

```
          zmin    = -100, zmax = 100,
          diff    = (1.0, .6, .4),
    )
QUADRATIC         (loc= (130, 100, -60) {ellipsoid}
          a       = 4, b  = 8, c  = 1,
          d       = 1000,
          xmin    = -100, xmax = 100,
          ymin    = -150,   ymax = 100,
          zmin    = -100, zmax = 100,
          diff    = (1.0, .6, .4),
    )
QUADRATIC         (loc= (140, 0, -50)   {cylinder}
          a       = 1, b  = 0, c  = 1,
          d       = 50,
          xmin    = -18, xmax = 18,
          ymin    = 0,    ymax = 30,
          zmin    = -18, zmax = 18,
          diff    = (1.0, .6, .4),
    )
QUADRATIC         (loc= (120, 0, -50)   {cylinder}
          a       - 1, b  - 0, c  - 1,
          d       = 50,
          xmin    = -18, xmax - 18,
          ymin    = 0,    ymax = 30,
          zmin    = -18, zmax = 18,
          diff    = (1.0, .6, .4),
    )
QUADRATIC         (loc= (140, 0, 10)   {cylinder}
          a       = 1, b  = 0, c  = 1,
          d       = 50,
          xmin    = -18, xmax = 18,
          ymin    = 0,    ymax = 30,
          zmin    = -18, zmax = 18,
          diff    = (1.0, .6, .4),
    )
QUADRATIC         (loc= (120, 0, 10)   {cylinder}
          a       = 1, b  = 0, c  = 1,
          d       = 50,
          xmin    = -18, xmax = 18,
          ymin    = 0,    ymax = 30,
          zmin    = -18, zmax = 18,
          diff    = (1.0, .6, .4),
```

```
                )
END_BBOX

OBSERVER ( loc    = (-20 , 70, -80)
           lookat = (200, 50, -15)
)

LAMP ( loc = (120, 180,  80),
       radius = 5,
       dist = 70
     )
LAMP ( loc = (-20, 350, -400),
       radius = 5,
       dist = 1500
      )
SKY  ( horiz  = (0, .4, .7),
       zenith = (0, .4, .7),
       dither = 1
     )
XRES = 320
YRES = 200

FOC_LENGTH = 50

{
```

```
+---------------------------------------------------+
|                                                   |
|                  Plate 11.ray                     |
|                                                   |
|               The Reflecting Blimp                |
|                                                   |
|            By Roger T. Stevens - 6/24/90          |
|                                                   |
+---------------------------------------------------+
```

```
}




FILE_NAME = BLIMP.RAW
BEGIN_INSTANCES
          name = PYRAMID
BEGIN_BBOX
                 TRIANGLE (loc 0, 0, 0)
```

```
                              v1 = (52, 0, 30)
                              v2 = (34.3, 30, 0)
                              diff = (1, 0, 0)
                  )
                  TRIANGLE (loc 0, 0, 0)
                              v1 = (52, 0, -30)
                              v2 = (34.3, 30, 0)
                              diff = (1, 0, 0)
                  )
                  TRIANGLE (loc 52, 0, -30)
                              v1 = (0, 0, 60)
                              v2 = (-17.7, 30, 30)
                              diff = (1, 0, 0)
                  )
END_BBOX
END_INSTANCES

{  PATTERNS USED}

PATTERN ( x_size = 80,                      { CHECKERED GROUND }
              y_size — 80,
              name   = CHECK,
              RECTANGLE (
                  start_x = 0,
                  start_y = 0,
                  end_x   = 40,
                  end_y   = 40,
                  diff    = (.25, .85, .25),
                  dither  = 0,
              )

              RECTANGLE (
                  start_x = 40,
                  start_y = 40,
                  end_x   = 80,
                  end_y   = 80,
                  diff    = (.25, .85, .25),
                  dither  = 0,
              )
          )
PARALLELOGRAM ( loc  = (  -10000, 0,  -10000),
              v1   = (20000, 0,    0),
```

```
                v2   = (  0, 0, 20000),
                diff = (  1, 1, .75),
                dither  = 0,
                pattern = CHECK
                xmult = 2
                ymult = 2
              )
INSTANCE_OF name = PYRAMID
          loc = (150, 0, -60)
          scale = (2, 2, 2)
    )
    QUADRATIC            (loc= (250, 70, 20) {ellipsoid}
              a      = 12, b  = 4, c  = 1,
              d      = 4000,
              xmin   = -100, xmax = 100,
              ymin   = -80,  ymax = 80,
              zmin   = -100, zmax = 100,
              diff   = (.5, .3, .5),
                  mirror  = (.9, .9, .9);
                )

      TRIANGLE   loc = (250, 70, 80)
                   v1 = (0, 30, 25)
                   v2 = (0, -30, 25)
                   diff = (.5, .3, .5)
                   mirror = (.9, .9, .9)
                 )

OBSERVER ( loc      = (-20 , 70, -80)
          lookat = (200, 50, -15)
         )

LAMP ( loc = (-200, 200, 140)
      radius = 5,
      dist = 220
    )
SKY ( horiz = (0, .4, .8),
      zenith = (0, .4, .9),
      dither = 1
    )
XRES = 320
YRES = 200
```

```
FOC_LENGTH = 65
{
```

```
                    Plate 12.ray

               Picture of Fractal Mountain

               By Roger T. Stevens - 6/2/90
```

```
                                                              }
COLOR
          diff (.75, .43, .14)
          diff (.85, .43, .14)
          diff (.95, .65, .65)
          amb (.2, .3, .3);
)
BEGIN_BBOX
          SPHERE                                loc = 230, 50, -50
                                          radius 8
                                              diff 1, .35, .35
                              )
          RING                          loc - 230, 50, -50
                                          v1 = 1, 0, 0
                                          v2 = 0, 0, 1
                                          rad_2 = 20
                                          rad_1 = 8
                                          diff = .2, .8, .8
                              )
          SPHERE                        loc = 180, 50, 0
                          radius 8
                                  diff 1, .35, .35
                              )
          RING                          loc = 180, 50, 0
                                          v1 = 1, 0, 0
                                          v2 = 0, 0, 1
                                          rad_2 = 20
                                          rad_1 = 8
                                          diff = .2, .8, .8
                              )
          SPHERE                        loc = 230, 50, 50
                          radius 8
                                          diff 1, .35, .35
```

```
                                    v1 = 1, 0, 0
                                    v2 = 0, 0, 1
                                    rad_2 = 20
                                    rad_1 = 8
                                    diff = .2, .8, .8
                      )
END_BBOX

PARALLELOGRAM ( loc  = (  -10000, 0,  -10000),
                v1   = (20000, 0,     0),
                v2   = (  0, 0, 20000),
                      amb = (.48, .32, .40)
                diff = (  1.0, .8, .4),
                dither  = 0,
                    )

      FRACTAL (loc = (300, 0, 100)
            scalar = 0.01
            dimension = 0.8
            v1 = (502,0,-650)
            v2 = (502, 0, 750)
)
OBSERVER ( loc   = (-20 , 70, -40),
             lookat = (200, 50, 0)
           )
LAMP  (  loc = (120, 180,  80),
         radius = 5,
         dist = 270
      )
LAMP  (  loc = (-20, 350, -400),
         radius = 5,
         dist = 200
      )
SKY  (  horiz  = (0, .4, .7),
        zenith = (0, .4, .7),
        dither = 1
      )
XRES  = 320
YRES  = 200

FOC_LENGTH = 75
```

{

```
+-------------------------------------------------------+
|                                                       |
|                     Plate 13.qat                      |
|                                                       |
|                  Quaternion Julia Set                 |
|                                                       |
|              By Roger T. Stevens - 7/1/90             |
|                                                       |
+-------------------------------------------------------+
```

}

BACKGROUND
                    (1, 0, 1)
AMB
                    (0, .4, .4)
DIFF
                    (0, .8, .8)
SREFLECT
                4
REFLECT (0, .8, .8)

FILE_NAME
                    julia
FLIP

                45

LIGHT_PHI:
        -20
LIGHT_THETA:
        50
VIEW_PHI:
        45
XRES
        319
YRES
        199
XMAX
        1.8
XMIN

        -1.8

```
YMAX
      1.0
YMIN
     -1.0
ZMAX
      1.0
ZMIN
      0.0
MAX_SIZE
      256
MAX_ITERATIONS
      100
QUATERNION
      (-1, 0, 0, 0)
JULIA

{
```

```
                        Plate 14.qat

                    Quaternion Julia Set

                 By Roger T. Stevens - 7/1/90
```

```
                                                              }
```

```
BACKGROUND
                  (1, 1, 0)
AMB
                  (0.3, 0.3, 0.6)

DIFF
                  (0.5, 0.5 1.0)
SREFLECT
                  3
REFLECT (0.3, 0.3, .9)

FILE_NAME
                  plate14
FLIP
      1
LIGHT_PHI:
```

```
        -40
LIGHT_THETA:
        45
VIEW_PHI:
        75
XRES
        319
YRES
        199
XMAX
        2.0
XMIN
        -2.0
YMAX
        1.3
YMIN
        -1.3
ZMAX
        0.6
ZMIN
        0.0
MAX_SIZE
        128
MAX_ITERATIONS
        64
QUATERNION
        (-0.743036, 0.113467, 0, 0)
JULIA
{
```

```
                        Plate 15.qat

                    Quaternion Julia Set

                By Roger T. Stevens - 7/1/90
```

```
BACKGROUND
                (1, 1, 0)
```

```
AMB
                (0, 0, .4)
DIFF
                (0, 0, .8)
SREFLECT
                4
REFLECT (0, 0, .8)

FILE_NAME
                plate15
FLIP
                1
LIGHT_PHI:
     -32
LIGHT_THETA:
     70
VIEW_PHI:
     60
XRES
     319
YRES
     199
XMAX
     1.3
XMIN
     -1.3
YMAX
     1.3
YMIN
     -1.3
ZMAX
     2.0
ZMIN
     0.0
MAX_SIZE
     128
MAX_ITERATIONS
     64
QUATERNION
     (0.2809, 0.53, 0, 0)
DRAGON
```

{

```
+------------------------------------------------------+
|                    Plate 16.qat                      |
|                                                      |
|                Quaternion Dragon Curve               |
|                                                      |
|            By Roger T. Stevens - 7/1/90              |
+------------------------------------------------------+
```

}

BACKGROUND

(0, 0, 0)

AMB

(.9, 0, 0)

DIFF

(.9, .7, .4)

SREFLECT

2

REFLECT (.9, .7, 4)

FILE_NAME

goodrag

FLIP

0

LIGHT_PHI:

-32

LIGHT_THETA:

40

VIEW_PHI:

100

XRES

319

YRES

199

XMAX

1.2

XMIN

-0.2

YMAX

0.8

YMIN

```
       -0.8
ZMAX
       0.8
ZMIN
       0.0
MAX_SIZE
       128
MAX_ITERATIONS
       32
QUATERNION
       (1.646009, 0.967049, 0, 0)
DRAGON
```

Appendix B:
Format for .PCX Files

The ZSoft .PCX file format begins with a 128 byte header, the contents of which are shown below:

Header Data for .PCX Screen File

Byte	Size (Bytes)	Name	Description
0	1	Password	0AH designates ZSoft.PCX Files.
1	1	Version	Versions of PC Paintbrush are: 0 = vers. 2.5 2 = vers. 2.8 with palette information. 3 = vers. 2.8 without pallete information. 5 = vers. 3.0
2	1	Encoding	Encoding scheme used. 1 = .PCX run length encoding.
3	1	Bits per pixel	No. of bits required to store data for 1 pixel from 1 plane. 1 = EGA, VGA, or Hercules 2 = CGA

Byte	Size (Bytes)	Name	Description
4	8	Window Dimensions	4 integers (2 bytes each) giving top left and bottom right corners of display in order x1, y1, x2, y2.
12	2	Horizontal Resolution	Horizontal resolution of display device (columns) 640 = EGA, VGA 320 = CGA 720 = Hercules
14	2	Vertical Resolution	Vertical resolution of display Resolution divide (rows) 480 = VGA 350 = EGA 200 = CGA 348 = Hercules
16	48	Color Map	Information on color palette settings. See following figures for details.
64	1	Reserved	
65	1	Number of planes	Number of color planes in the original image 1 = CGA, Hercules 4 = EGA, VGA
66	2	Bytes per line	Number of bytes per scan line in the image

Byte	Size (Bytes)	Name	Description
68	2	Palette description information	How to interpret the palette
70	56	Not used	Fill to the end of the header block

Except for the color map, most of the header contents are self-evident. The part of the header that is not currently being used by ZSoft may be used to include some of your own variables to identify particular programs, but do so at your own risk, as ZSoft may make use of these spaces in a future version.

The contents of a palette register for the EGA color system is described as follows. Six bits are used, with two each for the primary colors red, green, and blue. The capital letters represent colors of 75% amplitude; the small letters colors of 25% amplitude. So for each of the primary colors, four levels are available: 0 (none of that color), 25% amplitude, 75% amplitude, and 100% amplitude (both capital and small letter bits are one). The color map in the file header contains 16 sets of triples, one for each EGA palette. For the first byte of a triple, the values of the capital and small letter position for red are extracted and combined to produce a number from one to three. This number is multiplied by 85 and stored in the header. The same procedure takes place for the second byte of the triple for green and the third byte for blue. The process is repeated sixteen times, once for each palette. Note that when you set the palette registers on the EGA you are setting a write-only register, this means that you will not be able to recover the contents at a later date if you need to know what the setting was. Consequently, our *setEGApalette* function saves the palette register information in a global array *PALETTE* [16]. Use this data to write the color map in the header when you are saving a screen.

The VGA is quite different in the way that it handles colors. With the VGA, each palette register contains the number of a color register. The color register contains six bits, permitting 64 shades of each color. With the VGA you can read the six bit value for each of the colors red, green, and blue, as well as information in the palette registers and in the color registers. To create the color map, read each palette register and then go and read the color register pointed to by that palette register. Then multiply the red, green, and blue values by four and store the results in the triple associated with that palette. Note that when you restore a screen, you may not assign a color value to the same color register that it was obtained from originally, and that the palette registers may not select the same color registers. The net result is the same, however, because each palette register points to a color register that contains the same color information that was contained in the original screen. The VGA also has a color mode in which 256 different colors may be displayed simultaneously. This is the mode that we use for reproducing the ray traced pictures. The format is the same as that used to display the 16 color palette, but due to the 256 colors, the palette information is much longer. It is appended at the end of the .PCX file. To access this information, you must first ascertain that the version number data in the header (byte 1) is 5 (version 3.0). Then read to the end of the file and count back 769 bytes. If the value in this byte position is '0CH' (12 decimal), the succeeding information is 256 color palette data.

Data is read from the screen, horizontally from left to right, starting at the pixel position for the upper left corner. For EGA and VGA, which have multiple memory planes, a line is read of the color red (to the end of the window boundary), then the green information for the same line is read, and finally the blue.

Data is run length encoded in the following manner. If the byte is unlike the ones on either side of it, and if its two most significant bits are not *11*, it is written to the file. Otherwise a count is made of the number of like bytes (up to

63) and this count is ANDed with *C0H* and the result written to the file, followed by the value of the byte. If there are more that 63 successive like bytes, the count for 63 and the byte are written, and then the count begins all over again. (Note that the case for a singular byte having the two most significant bits 1 is handled by writing a count of one followed by the byte value.)

Contents of EGA Palette Register

Byte 7	Byte 6	Byte 5	Byte 4	Byte 3	Byte 2	Byte 1	Byte 0
		red (25%)	green (25%)	blue (25%)	Red (75%)	Green (75%)	Blue (75%)

Contents of .PCX File Color Map

Byte	Palette	Color	Description
16 17 18	0 0 0	Red Green Blue	For the EGA, the values of color of each byte of each triple are: 00H to 54H = 0% 55H to A9H = 25% AAH to FEH = 75%
19 20 21	1 1 1	Red Green Blue	For the VGA, the value of each byte is the value of the six-bit color value from the color register pointed to by the appropriate palette register multiplied by four.
22 23 24	2 2 2	Red Green Blue	
25 26 27	3 3 3	Red Green Blue	
28 29 30	4 4 4	Red Green Blue	

Byte	Palette	Color
31 32 33	5 5 5	Red Green Blue
34 35 36	6 6 6	Red Green Blue
37 38 39	7 7 7	Red Green Blue
40 41 42	8 8 8	Red Green Blue
43 44 45	9 9 9	Red Green Blue
46 47 48	10 10 10	Red Green Blue
49 50 51	11 11 11	Red Green Blue
52 53 54	12 12 12	Red Green Blue
55 56 57	13 13 13	Red Green Blue
58 59 60	14 14 14	Red Green Blue
61 62 63	15 15 15	Red Green Blue

Appendix C:
Hardware Requirements

With the wide variety of PC clones that are now available, including some that use 80286 and 80386 microprocessors at speeds far higher than anything envisioned by IBM, there is no telling when some strange glitch is going to wreak havoc with your program. To attempt to minimize that kind of problem, I have attempted to run most of the programs described in this book on several different systems. The primary system consists of the following:

Motherboard: Bullet 386 from Wave Mate, Incorporated, 2341 205th Street, Torrance, CA 90501. The quality of this board is such that you drop it in and it works the first time around. Highly recommended. It is a 20 MHz machine, used with 4 megabytes of 1M by 1 memory chips. The board will use either an 80387, 80287, or Weitek 1167 math coprocessor. I used an 80287.

Disk Controller: Perstor PS180-16FN from Hard Drives International, 1912 West Fourth Street, Tempe, Arizona 85281. This controller not only controls two floppy disk drives of any type (5 1/4 inch or 3 1/2 inch), but also just about doubles the capacity of your hard drive. I have found it to be completely reliable with no signs of drop-outs or deterioration.

Floppy Disk Drives: 1 Fujitsu 1.2 Megabyte disk drive, from Gems Computer, 2115 Old Oakland Road, San Jose, CA 95131.

1 Mitsubishi 360Kbyte floppy disk drive.

I/O Board: AT Multi I/O #AI-2 from Gems Computer.

Hard Disk Drive: Seagate ST251-1 from Hard Drives International 1912 West Fourth Street, Tempe, AZ 85281. If you've had trouble with a recently purchased hard drive and the people you bought it from seemed to disappear, then you need to buy your next drive from Hard Drives International. They stand 100 percent behind their products and provide quick and efficient service when it is needed. This is a 28 msec., 40 megabyte drive, but with the Perstor controller, it stores 78 megabytes.

Keyboard: KeyCat Keyboard. (This is a 101 key keyboard with a built-in trackball) from Dexxa International, 189 Airport Boulevard, Burlingame, CA 94818.

VGA Card: Vega VGA from Headland Technology, 46221 Landing Parkway, Fremont, CA 94538.

VGA Monitor: Classic Professional Graphics Display, (no longer available for purchase). This is actually one of the original IBM VGA monitors. The most important point to remember is that whatever brand you use, it must be fully IBM compatible.

The Second System

Motherboard: MCT-386SX from JDR Microdevices, 2233 Branham Lane, San Jose, CA 95124. This is a 16 MHz machine which contains 4 megabyte of 1M by 1 memory chips. It uses the Chips and Technology Neat chip set, which gives a lot of flexibility in memory assignment, clock speeds, and shadow memory.

Disk Controller: Perstor PS180-16FN from Hard Drives International, 1912 West Fourth Street, Tempe, Arizona 85281. This controller not only controls two floppy disk drives of any type (5 1/4 inch or 3 1/2 inch), but also just about doubles the capacity of your hard drive. I have found it completely reliable with no signs of drop-outs or deterioration.

Floppy Disk Drives: 1 Fujitsu 1.2 Megabyte disk drive, from Gems Computer, 2115 Old Oakland Road., San Jose, CA 95131.

1 Mitsubishi 360Kbyte floppy disk drive.
1 Sony 1.44 M 3 1/2 inch Drive

I/O Board: AT Multi I/O #AI-2 from Gems Computer.

Hard Disk Drive: Miniscribe 3085, from Hard Drives International, 1912 West Fourth Street, Tempe, AZ 85281. This is a 72 megabyte drive that formats to 113 megabytes with the Perstor controller.

Keyboard: CAT105 Keyboard. (This is a 101 key keyboard with a built-in trackball) from CAD and Graphics, 1301 Evans Avenue, San Francisco, CA 94124.

VGA Card: Video Seven VGA 1024i from Headland Technology, Incorporated, 46221 Landing Parkway, Fremont, CA 94538. This card contains extensions of the standard VGA for higher resolution. However, you must buy another manual to learn how to use them. The one that comes with the product doesn't provide you with enough information.

VGA Monitor: NEC Multisync Plus from NEC Technologies Incorporated, 1255 Michael Drive, Wood Dale, IL 60191.

In addition, some programs were tested on a Dell 310 computer (a 386 machine with a VGA) and on a JDR 12 MHz 286 motherboard used in the second system described. Text was printed out on a Hewlett-Packard LaserJet IIP Printer, and color pictures were printed out on a Hewlett-Packard PaintJet Printer.

Programs that work satisfactorily on such a wide variety of systems as this should have a good chance of working on your system too. If you encounter problems, try to identify how your system differs from the two described above. In troubleshooting your system, try to pinpoint which card or peripheral may be the cause of the problem and then proceed from there. Once again, the most important thing is to make sure that your system is fully IBM compatible.

Display Considerations

In order to run the ray tracing programs described in this book, you must have a VGA display. The Newton's method and quaternion programs can also be run on an EGA display. If you have a Video Seven 1024i display, you will be able to create scenes that have much higher resolution than the ones in this book. If you have another enhanced VGA card, the techniques are similar, but you'll have to discover the right ones for your particular card.

Processor Speed

Some of the ray tracing displays can take hours or days to generate, even using a 386 machine with a math coprocessor. As you downgrade from this, things get slower and slower, but if you have enough patience, you can usually complete the program. One good thing; once you have the data file generated, it only takes a few seconds to recreate the picture on your screen, and if you have converted it to a .PCX file, you can reproduce it even faster.

Index

GetTriangle function 299
Get_Poly_Pattern function 135, 155
get_quaterion function, listing of 339
Get_Rect_Pattern function 133, 154
get_string function 106, 332
get_string function, listing of 337
Get_SubPattern function 136, 153, 154
get_vector function 146
GetAttrib 145
GetAttrib function 142
GetCone function 122, 152
GetFractal function 128
getting Vector data from input file 56
GetParallelogram function 120
GetPattern function 136, 153
GetQuadratic function 125
GetRing function 118
GetTriangle function 116
get_vector function, listing of 338
glassdist 245
graphics functions 22
Graphics Programming in C 22, 266
gu 225
gv 225

-H-

Haines, Eric 89, 90
Hamilton, Sir William 12, 306
hard disk drive 443, 444
hardware requirements 13, 442
HEIGHT 176
height, cone 152
high resolution VGA, plot function for 268, 275
high resolution VGA, setMode function for 268, 274
high resolution VGA, using 268
HORIZ 143, 177
hyperbolic paraboloid 219, 221
hyperboloid of one sheet 219, 221
hyperboloid of two sheets 219, 221

-I-

IBM PC 4
I/O board 442, 444
IEEE Computer Graphics and Applications 89
init_color function 82
init_world 79
init_world function 81
input.cpp file 100, 152, 299
input with C++ 36
instance 101
instance, transferring to object list 155
INSTANCE_OF 155
instances, processing 146
Intensity function 357
Intensity function, listing of 356
interface procedures, RenderMan 92
interface, RenderMan 90, 91, 92
interfaces, rendering, ray tracing 89
Intersect function 216, 217, 218, 231, 242, 244
intersection equations for quadric curves 222

A Library of Technical References from M&T Books

NetWare User's Guide
by Edward Liebing

Endorsed by Novell, this book informs NetWare users of the services and utilities available, and how to effectively put them to use. Contained is a complete task-oriented reference that introduces users to NetWare and guides them through the basics of NetWare menu-driven utilities and command line utilities. Each utility is illustrated, thus providing a visual frame of reference. You will find general information about the utilities, then specific procedures to perform the task in mind. Utilities discussed include NetWare v2.1 through v2.15. For advanced users, a workstation troubleshooting section is included, describing the errors that occur. Two appendixes, describing briefly the services available in each NetWare menu or command line utility are also included.

Book only	**Item #071-0**	**$24.95**

Blueprint of a LAN
by Craig Chaiken

Blueprint of a LAN provides a hands-on introduction to microcomputer networks. For programmers, numerous valuable programming techniques are detailed. Network administrators will learn how to build and install LAN communication cables, configure and troubleshoot network hardware and software, and provide continuing support to users. Included are a very inexpensive zero-slot, star topology network, remote printer and file sharing, remote command execution, electronic mail, parallel processing support, high-level language support, and more. Also contained is the complete Intel 8086 assembly language source code that will help you build an inexpensive to install, local area network. An optional disk containing all source code is available.

Book & Disk (MS-DOS)	**Item #066-4**	**$39.95**
Book only	**Item #052-4**	**$29.95**

C++ Techniques and Applications
by Scott Robert Ladd

This book guides the professional programmer into the practical use of the C++ programming language—an object-oriented enhancement of the popular C programming language. The book contains three major sections. Part One introduces programmers to the syntax and general usage of C++ features; Part Two covers object-oriented programming goals and techniques; and Part Three focuses on the creation of applications.

Book/Disk (MS-DOS)	**Item #076-1**	**$39.95**
Book only	**Item #075-3**	**$29.95**

Fractal Programming and Ray Tracing with C++
by Roger T. Stevens

Finally, a book for C and C++ programmers who want to create complex and intriguing graphic designs. By the author of three best-selling graphics books, this new title thoroughly explains ray tracing, discussing how rays are traced, how objects are used to create ray-traced images, and how to create ray tracing programs. A complete ray tracing program, along with all of the source code is included. Contains 16 pages of full-color graphics.

Book/Disk (MS-DOS)	**Item 118-0**	**$39.95**
Book only	**Item 134-2**	**$29.95**

Advanced
Fractal
Programming
in C

Roger T. Stevens

Advanced Fractal Programming in C
by Roger T. Stevens

Programmers who enjoyed our best-selling *Fractal Programming in C* can move on to the next level of fractal programming with this book. Included are how-to instructions for creating many different types of fractal curves, including source code. Contains 16 pages of full-color fractals. All the source code to generate the fractals is available on an optional disk in MS/PC-DOS format.

Book/Disk (MS-DOS)	**Item #097-4**	**$39.95**
Book only	**Item #096-6**	**$29.95**

1-800-533-4372 (in CA 1-800-356-2002)

Advanced Graphics Programming in Turbo Pascal

Roger T. Stevens and Christopher D. Watkins

Advanced Graphics Programming in Turbo Pascal
by Roger T. Stevens and Christopher D. Watkins

This new book is must reading for Turbo Pascal programmers who want to create impressive graphic designs on IBM PC's and compatibles. There's 16 pages of full color graphic displays along with the source code to create these dramatic pictures. Complete explanations are provided on how to tailor the graphics to suit the programmer's needs. Covered are algorithms for creating complex 2-D shapes including lines, circles and squares; how to create advanced 3-D shapes, wire-frame graphics, and solid images; numerous tips and techniques for varying pixel intensities to give the appearance or roundness to an object; and more.

Book/Disk (MS-DOS)	Item #132-6	$39.95
Book only	Item #131-8	$29.95

Advanced Graphics Programming in C and C++

Roger T. Stevens

Advanced Graphics Programming in C and C++
by Roger T. Stevens

This book is for all C and C++ programmers who want to create impressive graphic designs on thier IBM PC or compatible. Though in-depth discussions and numerous sample programs, readers will learn how to create advanced 3-D shapes, wire-frame graphics, solid images, and more. All source code is available on disk in MS/PC-DOS format. Contains 16 pages of full color graphics.

Book/Disk (MS-DOS)	Item #173-3	$39.95
Book only	Item #171-7	$29.95

Graphics Programming with Microsoft C 6.0

Mark Mallet

Graphics Programming with Microsoft C 6.0
by Mark Mallet

Written for all C programmrs, this book explores graphics programming with Microsoft C 6.0, including full coverage of Microsoft C's built-in graphics libraries. Sample programs will help readers learn the techniques needed to create spectacular graphic designs, including 3-D figures, solid images, and more. All source code in book is available on disk in MS/PC-DOS format. Includes 16 pages of full-color graphics.

Book/Disk (MS-DOS)	Item #167-9	$39.95
Book only	Item #165-2	$29.95

1-800-533-4372 (in CA 1-800-356-2002)

**The Verbum
Book of Digital
Typography**

Michael Gosney,
Linnea Dayton, and
Jason Levine

The Verbum Book of Digital Typography
by Michael Gosney, Linnea Dayton, and Jason Levine

The Verbum Book of Digital Typography combines information on good design principles with effective typography techniques, showing designers, illustrators, and desk-top publishers how to create attractive printed materials that communicate effectively. Each chapter highlights the talents of professional type designers as they step readers through interesting real-like projects. Readers will learn how to develop letterforms and typefaces, modify type outlines, and create special effects.

Book only   **Item #092-3**   **$29.95**

**The Verbum
Book of
Electronic
Design**

Michael Gosney and
Linnea Dayton

The Verbum Book of Electronic Design
by Michael Gosney and Linnea Dayton

This particular volume introduces designers, illustrators, and desktop publishers to the electronic page layout medium and various application programs, such as PageMaker, QuarkXPress, Design Studio, and Ventura Publishing. Each chapter highlights the talents of a top designer who guides readers through the thinking as well as the "mousing" that leads to the creation of various projects. These projects range in complexity from a trifold black and white brochure to a catalog produced with QuarkXPress. More than 100 illustrations, with 32 pages in full-color, are included.

Book only   **Item #088-5**   **$29.95**

**The Verbum
Book of Digital
Painting**

Michael Gosney,
Linnea Dayton, and
Paul Goethel

The Verbum Book of Digital Painting
by Michael Gosney, Linnea Dayton, and Paul Goethel

Contained herein are a series of entertaining projects that teach readers how to create compelling designs using the myriad of graphics tools available in commercial painting programs. Presented by professional designers, these projects range from a simple greeting card to a complex street scene. This book also includes portfolios of paintings created by the featured artists, plus an extensive gallery of works from other accomplished artists and 64 pages of full-color paintings.

Book only   **Item #090-7**   **$29.95**

1-800-533-4372 (in CA 1-800-356-2002)

ORDER FORM

To Order:

Return this form with your payment to M&T books, 501 Galveston Drive, Redwood City, CA 94063 or **call toll-free 1-800-533-4372 (in California, call 1-800-356-2002).**

ITEM #	DESCRIPTION	DISK	PRICE

Subtotal	
CA residents add sales tax ____%	
Add $3.50 per item for shipping and handling	
TOTAL	

Charge my:

☐ **Visa**

☐ **MasterCard**

☐ **AmExpress**

☐ **Check enclosed, payable to M&T Books.**

CARD NO. _____

SIGNATURE _____ EXP. DATE _____

NAME _____

ADDRESS _____

CITY _____

STATE _____ ZIP _____

M&T GUARANTEE: If your are not satisfied with your order for any reason, return it to us within 25 days of receipt for a full refund. Note: Refunds on disks apply only when returned with book within guarantee period. Disks damaged in transit or defective will be promptly replaced, but cannot be exchanged for a disk from a different title.

8002